PETO'S REGISTER OF
GREAT WESTERN RAILWAY LOCOMOTIVES

Edited by Martin Smith

Having worked a race day special, No.6010 KING CHARLES I turns at Newbury Racecourse on 5 March 1960. PHOTOGRAPH: R.C.RILEY

VOLUME ONE
King 4-6-0s

IRWELL PRESS

Acknowledgements

Sincere thanks are due to those who provided advice and assistance - often in exceedingly generous helpings - during the preparation of this book. They are: Eric Youldon, Bryan Wilson, Mr.K.J.Cook, Mr.A.S.Peck, Chris Hawkins, Philip Atkins, George Reeve and Michéle Smith.

Bill Peto, London
Martin Smith, Coleford, Somerset
August 1995

First Published in the United Kingdom by
IRWELL PRESS 1995
P.O.Box 1260, Caernarfon, Gwynedd, LL55 3ZD
Printed in Huddersfield by The Amadeus Press

Contents

Foreword

This book - the first of what is hoped to be a lengthy series - owes itself to Bill Peto's researches. Bill is one of the best respected authorities on the Great Western Railway, and combines his role as the Historical Research Officer of the Great Western Society with a genuine enthusiasm for all things GWR. Over many years he has amassed a vast amount of detailed information about GWR locomotives, most of it from Swindon records and other official sources, and has gradually collated the material in the form of the *Peto Registers*.

Deriving, as they do, from primary reference sources, the Peto Registers are, in effect, the 'final word' on the subject. Allocations, works visits, repairs, boiler and tender changes and so on - the details given here are those quoted in official Swindon records and, therefore, can be considered wholly reliable. That said, it must be explained that the original Swindon allocation register for 1933 is missing, and so details for that year have, of necessity, been deduced from works and repair records; although a perfectly sound method, it sometimes fails to provide the exact date on which a move was made.

In an attempt to provide an overall picture of the locomotives in question, this book extends beyond their day-to-day engine histories. We discuss details of the class's background, development and, importantly, their working lives. Where possible we have relied again on primary source reference material, although in the case of GWR locomotives such material is often sparse - frustratingly, GWR Locomotive and Traffic Committee minutes have nothing approaching the detail of similar records of other companies. We have, therefore, sometimes had to consult previously published works - particularly the well-respected series of GWR locomotive books published by the Railway Correspondence & Travel Society - but we have conducted additional research in order to provide the fullest possible picture.

As for the working lives of the engines, much of the information was gleaned from contemporary reports in magazines such as the *'Railway Observer'* and *'Trains Illustrated'*. Where appropriate, we have conducted extensive research to confirm or enlarge on certain events. We have also featured many extracts from other contemporary sources (appropriately acknowledged in the text, we trust), but we have fought shy of including performance reports, despite the apparent popularity of the 'racing pages' in the railway press.

Our aim - bold, conceited, or just plain idealistic - is that this and others in the series will be the most comprehensive works on their respective subjects. With that aim in mind, we would positively welcome any further information or, where appropriate, confirmation (or otherwise!) of matters raised in the text. On that score, we would particularly like to hear from anybody who has a photograph of two Kings working to Ebbw Vale in 1938........

The class leader, No.6000 KING GEORGE V, in a classic pose at Swindon in 1933. It had, by this time, lost the 'garter' coat of arms from the tender and had had the feed pipes modified, but the top lamp iron was still in the original position and it retained the step on the smokebox door. PHOTOGRAPH: NATIONAL RAILWAY MUSEUM

Chapter One

BACKGROUND

The Great Western Railway was relatively unaffected by the grouping in 1922/23, and was therefore able to perpetuate established policies and practices. One field in which continuity was clearly seen was that of locomotive development, the company being able to follow the leads which George Jackson Churchward had established to such good effect in the early 1900s.

The GWR's continuity of locomotive development is, perhaps, best illustrated by its four-cylinder 4-6-0s. The design of Churchward's Star class of 1907 was updated and enlarged by Charles Collett for the Castle class, which made their debut in 1923. Apart from the logical upgrading of certain components, that design was largely unaltered when the last Castle was completed twenty-seven years later. Furthermore, the basic Castle design was itself enlarged - albeit with important alterations to many of the principal dimensions - for what became the GWR's best-known and maybe most celebrated locomotive class ever. These were the Kings.

In order to understand why the Kings were developed, one needs to go back to the introduction of the Castles in 1923. As had been intended, the Castles took over many of the company's best express workings. Much was expected of them, but during the first two or three years of their existence performances sometimes disappointed. This caused no little concern in the GWR Traffic Department, as sights had already been set on train loadings and schedules which, to many observers, seemed rather adventurous. There are unconfirmed reports that the traffic officers genuinely considered trains of up to *thirty coaches* - presumably the problems of platform length were insurmountable, and although some stations were in fact rebuilt in the late 1920s and early 1930s, thirty-coach trains were *not* catered for. For example, the longest platforms at Paddington *after* its 1930 rebuilding were 1,150ft - hardly adequate for thirty 70ft coaches!

Nevertheless, in the mid-1920s a degree of increase in the weights of the trains was definitely on the cards, and something more powerful than the Castles was required. To many, it seemed as if a Pacific was the logical option, but the GWR's locomotive department had only recently dispensed with the less-than-successful No.111 THE GREAT BEAR. The locomotive department's opinion of its unlamented Pacific was, perhaps, best summed up by Churchward's reaction to Nigel Gresley's GREAT NORTHERN: 'There was no need for that young man to build a Pacific', observed G.J., 'we could have sold him ours'.

As for the problem of even heavier train weights, the need for quick action ruled out the development of a completely new type of locomotive and so the GWR's only sensible option was a more-powerful 4-6-0. That, however, presented one particularly thorny problem. Such a design would inevitably necessitate an increase in axle weight and, ominously, the axle weights of the Castles were already within a few hundredweight of the 20-ton limit permitted by the Civil Engineer. The fact that the Castles (and their proposed successors) were well-balanced four cylinder locomotives - i.e. with a proportionately low hammer-blow - seemed to count for little at first.

Investigations were made by the GWR General Manager, Sir Felix Pole, and they revealed that all new bridge work had,

No.6000 KING GEORGE V after the repositioning of its smokebox lamp iron. In this and other early pictures of No.6000, note the 'lever' on the left-hand side of the bell - it was dispensed with circa 1935. PHOTOGRAPH: R.M.CASSERLEY COLLECTION

for some time, actually provided for a maximum axle-weight of 22½ tons. Indeed, on the all-important Paddington-West of England main line, by the end of 1926 only four bridges were still subject to the old 20-ton limit. Sir Felix therefore ordered the upgrading of those four bridges and, simultaneously, he instructed his CME, Charles Collett, to design a new type of express engine which, if necessary, went to the absolute limit of permitted axle-weight.

The order for twenty 4-6-0s (albeit of an unspecified class) was ratified by the Locomotive Committee on 17 December 1925, at an estimated cost of £120,000. On the same day as the order for the new 4-6-0s was placed, authorisation was given to condemn ten Atbara and ten City class 4-4-0s, valued at a total of £92,300.

The new 4-6-0s were initially referred to as 'Supercastles'. The design incorporated the salient features of the Stars and Castles, albeit enlarged to the absolute limits and, therefore, departing from almost every standard Swindon dimension. The necessity to go to the limits with the dimensions was due partly to Sir Felix Pole's directive. The explanation lies, at least partly, in factors other than the strictly engineering or operational....

To a good part of the public, a locomotive's tractive effort was all-important. The railway companies were well aware of the public fascination with TE figures and there was much prestige to be gained

from a locomotive with a very high 'power' of this sort. Naturally, this was not ignored by the GWR - indeed, it was the GWR itself which, earlier, had put so much emphasis on tractive effort figures - and no little satisfaction was gained from the fact that the proposed 'Supercastle' would have the highest tractive effort of any British passenger locomotive. Since August 1926, the Southern Railway's Lord Nelson 4-6-0s had claimed the title of Britain's 'most powerful passenger engines' (on the contentious basis of tractive effort), but their figure of 33,510lb stood to be beaten hands down by the GWR's new engine.

However, even before construction of the first 'Supercastle' had begun, the all-round obsession with the tractive effort figure left a profound mark. By late 1926 it was known that Henry Fowler (or, rather, the North British Locomotive Co drawing office) had a powerful express passenger locomotive in the planning stage for the LMSR, and also that Gresley was planning experiments with higher boiler pressures for LNER locomotives. Rather than see the GWR lose out - or even be subjected to a close challenge - for the 'most powerful' title, Sir Felix Pole instructed Collett to ensure that the 'Supercastle' had a tractive effort of no less than 40,000lb.

Collett's preliminary design already incorporated the largest possible boiler and cylinders, and so, in order to break the

40,000lb barrier, the diameter of the driving wheels was reduced from the standard 6ft 8½in to 6ft 6in. In conjunction with the other principal dimensions, this resulted in a tractive effort of 40,300lb. It must be emphasised once again that the decision to use tractive effort figures to denote power was one chosen by the railway companies themselves. The use of these figures was at least questionable, but perhaps the companies felt that it would be unkind to confuse the general public with such mysteries as drawbar brake horsepower and the like. The 'tractive effort' debate has, over the years, filled countless column inches in the letters pages of railway magazines. It is not intended to further the debate here.

Returning to more pertinent matters, the design of the 'Supercastle' included, of course, four cylinders, but these were 16¼in x 28in instead of the 16in x 26in of the Castles. Cylinders with 30in stroke had previously been used on two-cylinder GWR locomotives such as the Saint class 4-6-0s and the 28XX and 47XX 2-8-0s, but Collett fought shy of using such a lengthy stroke where inside cylinders (and crank axles) were involved.

The boiler was specially designed and was designated Standard No.12 (coded 'WA'). Tapered and domeless, in true GWR fashion, it was 16ft long and its outside diameters tapered from 6ft to 5ft 6¼in (1ft 2in longer than a Castle boiler, and between 3in and 4¼in larger in diameter).

Four-month-old No.6003 KING GEORGE IV waits at Newton Abbot on 24 November 1927. The bogie springs represent the first modification (following the Midgham derailment in August - see text), a later modification incorporating larger section springs. Note the straight feed pipes and the position of the top lamp iron. PHOTOGRAPH: NATIONAL RAILWAY MUSEUM

No.6009 KING CHARLES II at Old Oak circa 1934. PHOTOGRAPH: R.K.BLENCOWE

Importantly, the boiler was intended to have a working pressure of 250lb per sq.in - the highest used on any conventional locomotive in Britain. The firebox was 11ft 6in long, but unlike the long grates used on some foreign engines it wasn't sloped; furthermore, the fire-hole was higher above the footplate than on other GWR classes. Those aspects almost seemed as if they were deliberately designed to make the fireman's task even more arduous.

The original intention was that the 'Supercastles' should be named after cathedrals. Indeed, it has been suggested that TRURO CATHEDRAL was earmarked for the first of the class (with subsequent names working up from the west, perhaps?) but there is no firm evidence to support that theory. Furthermore, there were only around fifteen cathedral cities in the area served by the GWR - not enough 'local' names for a class of thirty engines.

Whatever the case, the matter of a name theme for the 'Supercastles' was effectively settled in 1927 when the first engine under construction was booked for a visit, in August of that year, to the United States of America. It was considered that, as the engine would act as an ambassador for British engineering, nothing could be more patriotic than naming it after the reigning monarch.

The GWR had to obtain royal permission to use the name of the monarch, and the company's formal request was accompanied by an artist's impression of the engine. The drawing was, apparently, retained at Buckingham Palace, and it is alleged that a visiting representative from the Royal College of Heralds saw the picture and objected to the use of the garter emblem in the GWR's logo - in heraldry, the garter was reserved for those holding the Order of Chivalry 'Knight of the Garter'. That story is uncorroborated, but it is rather conspicuous that, at the time in question, the GWR hastily changed its livery, this time omitting the garter.

Livery problems aside, with the name KING GEORGE V agreed on for the class leader, the class as a whole became known as 'Kings'. The subsequent plan was that the other locomotives would carry the

Still only a few months old, No.6014 KING HENRY VII passes Taunton with the up 'Torbay Express' in 1928. Note the straight feed pipes and the absence of a whistle shield: PHOTOGRAPH: RAIL ARCHIVE STEPHENSON.

No.6026 KING JOHN, built in July 1930, under the Old Oak coaler in 1934. The last ten Kings, Nos.6020-6029, had modified covers for the inside valves and were fitted from new with curved feed pipes. PHOTOGRAPH: RAIL ARCHIVE STEPHENSON

names of English kings in reverse chronological order and so, in order to avoid confusion, ten of the Star class, Nos.4021-4030, had their 'king' names promptly changed to 'monarchs'. Furthermore, in deference to the new engines, Bulldog class 4-4-0 No.3361 lost its name of EDWARD VII and Duke 4-4-0 No.3257, quite unnecessarily, lost its name of KING ARTHUR.

The Kings were allotted numbers in the 6000 series, the first logically taking No.6000 to itself. As an aside, KING GEORGE V was not the first GWR engine to wear No.6000 - between September 1920 and August 1922 that number had been carried by a hired ROD 2-8-0. Indeed, four of the GWR's ROD engines had had numbers in the 6000 series (6000-6003), but all had been returned to the Government by October 1922. The GWR's ROD No.6000, incidentally, was subsequently purchased by the LNER in 1924, ultimately becoming BR No.63729. It was withdrawn in March 1959.

The first of the Kings, No.6000 KING GEORGE V, emerged from Swindon Works in June 1927 - it was fitted with its ATC equipment (at Swindon) on 29 June. The engine's completion date had originally been scheduled for September, but the promise of sending it to America had necessitated a swifter completion than had been envisaged. The new engine cost £6,383 to construct, of which £1,699 was accounted for by the boiler. The ATC

equipment is believed to have cost an additional £44. The 4,000-gallon Collett tender - No.2389 of Lot A113 - was priced at £1,163, although the new tenders for the next five Kings were priced a little lower at £1,036 apiece. The price difference was presumably accounted for by No.6000 being necessarily fitted with different braking and coupling equipment for its forthcoming American trip.

The principal dimensions of the new engine were (*see table opposite*).

The outside cylinders drove the middle coupled axle while the inside cylinders drove the leading axle; the inside connecting rods had forked big-ends fitted with gibs and cotters while the outside rods had solid bushed ends. In view of the locomotive's lengthy wheelbase, the rear axle was permitted a degree of side play.

Just another King? Well....most pictures of No.6028 show it carrying the name of KING GEORGE VI, but until January 1937 it was named KING HENRY II. The location is Old Oak Common, and the year is 1933. PHOTOGRAPH: R.K.BLENCOWE

CYLINDERS: (4) 16¼in x 28in
VALVE GEAR: Walschaert's (inside) with 9in piston valves; piston valves of outside cylinders driven by horizontal rocking arms.
HEATING SURFACES: Tubes - 2007½ sqft; firebox - 193½sqft; superheater (Standard 16-unit) - 313sqft; Total - 2,514sqft
FIREBOX: 11ft 6in long; fitted with direct steel stays to the outside casing
GRATE AREA: 34⅓sqft (firebox outside length 11ft 6in)
BOILER: Barrel - 16ft 0in; diameter - 5ft 6¼in to 6ft 0in; pitch - 8ft 11¼in
BOILER PRESSURE: 250lb
DRIVING WHEELS: 6ft 6in; hollow bored axles.
BOGIE WHEELS: 3ft 0in
WHEELBASE (loco): 29ft 5in (7ft 8in + 5ft 6in + 8ft 0in + 8ft 3in)

WEIGHT FULL:
Bogie - 21tons 10cwt
Leading coupled - 22tons 10cwt
Centre coupled - 22tons 10cwt
Trailing coupled - 22tons 10cwt
TOTAL (loco) - 89tons 0cwt

TENDER - 46tons 14cwt

TENDER: Self-trimming type; capacities - 4,000 gallons, 6 tons. With pick-up apparatus.
BRAKES: Equalised vacuum brakes operating on all the coupled wheels

The bogie was of the plate-frame type, the earlier Churchward-style bar-frame bogies having developed an occasional tendency to break rivets. On the Kings, the well-forward positioning of the inside cylinders left inadequate room for overhung springs between the leading bogie wheels, and so it was necessary to use outside springs, axleboxes and frame-plates for the bogie's leading axle. The rear bogie axle, however, incorporated inside springs and bearings, features dictated by the position of the outside cylinders. Another consequence of the restricted clearances was that the bogies were fitted with 3ft diameter wheels, the standard Swindon bogie wheel having previously been 3ft 2in.

The combination of outside and inside frames on the bogie was very unusual, and it became a boon to myopic schoolboys who, suffering the taunts of so-called 'chums' upon failing to differentiate between a Hall and a Grange at a distance, could readily distinguish a King from a Castle at a thousand paces.

In its issue for 15 July 1927, *'The Locomotive'* magazine commented that No.6000 had a '...new pattern cab with an extended roof' which was '...roomy and well protected while the various fittings are very well arranged'. It was also noted that 'A novelty is the arrangement for carrying the fire irons alongside the firebox...the damper gear, too, is of a somewhat refined type'.

Five more Kings, Nos.6001-6005, were completed in July 1927 and a further fourteen, Nos.6006-6019, between February and July 1928. All nineteen were built under Lot 243 (as was No.6000) at a cost of £6,383 each. Another ten Kings were constructed between May and August 1930. These were Nos.6020-6029, built under Lot 267 and costing £6,172 each (including £1,687 for the boiler). The tenders of Nos.6020 and 6021 were priced at £1,014 each, those of Nos.6022 and 6023 at £1,010, and the others at £1,003 each. Another King was nominally built in 1936, but all was not what it seemed. Following its serious accident, No.6007 was officially condemned and a replacement was built under Lot 309 at a cost of £4,393. The 'new' locomotive, which entered traffic on 24 March 1936, was, however, little more than the original one repaired.

Ignoring the 'new' No.6007, the total number of Kings remained at thirty. It might be asked why, as they were such powerful engines, the class wasn't expanded. The simple answer is the 22½ton axleweights - which restricted them to 'full strength' main lines, and thirty engines were sufficient for the heaviest trains on these routes.

Below:- The erectors cheer patriotically as No.6028 KING GEORGE VI leaves Swindon 'shops with its new nameplates in January 1937. The engine was formerly KING HENRY II. PHOTOGRAPH: BY ARRANGEMENT JOHN TATCHELL

No.6000 KING GEORGE V on 'Cambrian Coast'
duties on 6 August 1960. The location is
Westbourne Bridge. PHOTOGRAPH: R.C.RILEY

Chapter Two

OVER THERE

When in America, No.6000 KING GEORGE V was presented with a pair of medallions which were subsequently mounted above the cab-side numberplate. This fine view was taken at Brent (facing towards Plymouth) on 3 April 1931. PHOTOGRAPH: H.C.CASSERLEY

As mentioned earlier, even before No.6000 had been delivered it had been earmarked for a trip to the United States of America, where it was to participate in the Baltimore & Ohio Railroad's centenary celebrations. The arrangement for a GWR locomotive to attend the celebrations had been made as early as 1925; at the Stockton & Darlington centenary exhibition that year Sir Felix Pole had met a representative from the Baltimore & Ohio and, on learning about the American company's forthcoming centenary shindig, Pole had offered to send a GWR engine as an exhibit. At the time, Pole had naturally assumed that the locomotive would be a Castle; little did he realise that the engine would be the first of a much-heralded new class.

Prior to it's American trip (which was funded by the Baltimore & Ohio) No.6000 was fitted with Westinghouse brake apparatus so that it would be able to work main line trains - the pump was carried on the right-hand side of the smokebox.

The engine's trans-Atlantic trip started at Roath Dock in Cardiff on 3 August 1927, where it had been separated into two sections - boiler and chassis - on the quayside prior to being loaded aboard the Bristol City Line's SS CHICAGO CITY.

Separation into boiler and chassis was required firstly, as the biggest available crane - which was used in conjunction with No.9 lifting beam, sent down from Swindon for the loading - had a capacity of only 70 tons (the complete 6000 weighing 96 tons) and, secondly, for security of stowage during the voyage. The security aspect had to be given special attention as the vessel was a very modest 285ft long and 1,478grt - only slightly bigger than a wartime destroyer - and would have rolled violently in an Atlantic swell. No.6000 travelled as deck cargo and, by loading it in two sections (or three, counting the tender) the centre of gravity could be kept at a lower, i.e. safer, level. Furthermore, the vessel was thirty-five years old and, although undoubtedly of strong construc-

tion, the deck plates wouldn't have been wholly rust-free after that length of time - the load had to be secured to eye-bolts on deck, and in exceptionally heavy seas, an 89-ton load might conceivably have torn out the bolts, whereas two smaller loads were less likely to be wrenched free. The ship's master, Capt C.B.Short, later revealed that the locomotive had been a 'rather unwelcome guest' on board - a reference to the difficulty of carrying the load on a such small ship.

On arriving in America, No.6000 was reassembled at the Baltimore & Ohio's Mount Clare workshops. It was also necessary to make and fit new coil springs to its bogie, as had been done to the five other Kings following No.6003's partial derailment at Midgham on 10 August (see later). Matters in America were supervised by William Stanier who, since 1922, had been principal assistant to Charles Collett. When Stanier left the GWR for the LMSR in 1931, he took with him a sound Swindon upbringing. His first Pa-

Above and right:- No.6000 KING GEORGE V was shipped to and from the United States aboard the S.S.CHICAGO CITY. These pictures are believed to show its return in November 1927 - despite the vagaries of the British climate it is, perhaps, unlikely that there would have been such a display of overcoats and jackets when the locomotive departed in August. PHOTOGRAPHS: WELSH INDUSTRIAL & MARITIME MUSEUM

cific design for the LMSR - the 'Princess Royal' - was virtually an extended GWR King with a larger (albeit 250lb) boiler and wide firebox, but with exactly the same dimensions for its cylinders and driving wheels.

In America, the Baltimore & Ohio's centenary exhibition lasted from 24 September to 15 October 1927. No.6000 was not the only British representative, the GWR also having sent along a full-size 14-ton replica of Daniel Gooch's 2-2-2 NORTH STAR. To the American public, the two GWR engines represented not only the company, but *all* of Britain's railways. It was superb publicity for the GWR.

No.6000 was the star of the show, its subtle lines, impressive finish and relative compactness providing a marked contrast to the modern American locomotives which, on the whole, adhered to the 'big is beautiful' school of thought. An American journalist wrote that '...*the Great Western Railway of England had easily the most popular exhibit in that triumph of British locomotive design, the* King George V...*it took me a solid half-hour to get on to the footplate when the pageant was over*'. Among the British reports, '*The*

Locomotive' magazine opined that KING GEORGE V '....*did more than any press or eloquent speakers could accomplish in assuring our cousins that we are far from being down and out. A nation in the doldrums could hardly build and send out such a machine as this*' - a reference to the economic gloom of mid- and late-1920s Britain.

At the exhibition, all the locomotives paraded on a circular track at Halethorpe, Maryland, seven miles from Baltimore itself. It had been arranged for No.6000 to perform on the 'open road' after the exhibition was over, and on 17 October it made a 272-mile triangular trip from Baltimore to Washington, on to Philadelphia, and then back to Baltimore. The load was six carriages plus a dynamometer car but, due to the American penchant for substantial construction, that ensemble weighed some 450 Imperial tons.

Despite the crew's unfamiliarity with the route and the locomotive's lack of response to a diet of poor-quality coal, No.6000 performed superbly. American engineers who witnessed the trip were positively astounded by the engine's clear exhaust - to them, hard work was usu-

ally synonymous with a steady stream of dense black smoke.

No.6000's departure from America was slightly delayed. The problem, according to Capt Short of the SS CHICAGO CITY, was that the only suitable crane at Baltimore was owned and operated by a family concern - a father and his four sons - and all five were in gaol at the time. For the sake of good PR, the local judiciary released the family temporarily so that the locomotive could be loaded on board ship.

The SS CHICAGO CITY arrived back at Cardiff on 24 November 1927. Its important, if troublesome, cargo was reassembled on the quayside, and then ran under its own power to Swindon. The GWR's publicity machine was still revelling in the glory of the engine's exploits in America, and the return to Swindon, despite being undertaken in broad daylight in order to attract maximum attention, was hardly documented at all.

No.6000 had created a lasting impression in America. That was evidenced shortly after its visit when a number of the Baltimore & Ohio's locomotives were treated to copper-capped chimneys! In order to commemorate the visit No.6000 retained the regulation bell which had been attached to its buffer-beam during its test run, although in GWR service the bell was mounted directly on to the platform, instead of on a block, as had been the case in America. The bell was inscribed with the legend:

PRESENTED TO
LOCOMOTIVE KING GEORGE V
BY THE
BALTIMORE AND OHIO RAILROAD
COMPANY
IN COMMEMORATION OF ITS
CENTENARY CELEBRATION
SEPT.24th - OCT.15th 1927

The engine also wore two medals on its cab sides - another gift from the American hosts. That said, it appears that the medals were, in fact, replicas of those presented by the Baltimore & Ohio, the originals, which were affixed on the *inside* of the cab for special occasions, having been stolen in the early 1930s. The bell and the medals remained a distinctive feature of the locomotive, although the former didn't always find favour. It hindered maintenance work on the inside piston valves, and at Laira - where the shed fitters became acquainted (sometimes infuriatingly so) with the engine during the 1940s - the bell was sometimes removed and 'mislaid'. There were, of course, other occasions when it went missing, though these were usually pranks.

On the subject of pranks, the bell served another purpose. 'Initiation ceremonies' for new employees were as common on the railways as in any other industry, and a speciality at Old Oak shed was to tell a new fireman that, if he was strong enough to throw a shovelful of coal and hit the far end of the locomotive's lengthy firebox, the bell on the buffer-beam would ring automatically. But, of course, no matter how well the fireman did, the bell did not ring. A senior fireman would then step up to demonstrate what was expected of his colleagues, and each time *he* threw a shovelful of coal into the firebox, the bell would duly ring. The new fireman was given a second opportunity to prove that he was capable of doing the job for which he had been hired, but no matter how far he threw that coal the bell would not ring. How was it done? A long piece of string had been tied to the clapper of the bell and then run along the outside of the frames to the cab, where the other end was tied to the driver's leg. When a ring of the bell was required, the driver merely gave a little kick of the leg at the appropriate moment.

The American trip - on which No.6000 had received its bell - had, as already mentioned, been arranged by Sir Felix Pole. After his retirement in 1929 Sir Felix went to live at Calcot Grange, almost alongside the GWR main line just to the west of Reading, and until his sight failed completely he enjoyed watching the trains pass. As a sign of their respect for their former general manager, the crews in charge of the 'Riviera' or a directors' special (usually to Newbury races) would sound the engine's whistle as they passed Sir Felix's home. If the engine were No.6000, the bell would also be rung.

As a final word on the American expedition, the trip might have generated a vast amount of publicity for the GWR, but it has been suggested that there was a payback. Despite its public status, in ordinary service No.6000 was not the best of the Kings - far from it. Until being refurbished in the 1950s, it was considered by some railwaymen to be something of a dud - hot 'boxes were its speciality, and during the 1940s it seemed to spend a fair amount of its life under the hoist at Laira. There was a feeling that the engine's trans-Atlantic trip, which had necessitated a partial dismantling and reassembly on two occasions and a less-than-smooth on-deck sea voyage, had had a long-term effect on the frames. It was also considered that the speed with which the locomotive had been completed - due to its booking in America - hadn't helped.

Chapter Three

DETAILS and MODIFICATIONS

After the 'garter' livery had been dispensed with, the Kings wore standard GWR livery with the company's coat of arms between the two words on the tender. This fine picture appears to have been taken very early on in No.6017's life, as the engine still has its straight feed pipes and 'smokebox-top' position for the upper lamp iron. PHOTOGRAPH: RAIL ARCHIVE STEPHENSON.

Liveries

The Kings were originally painted in the standard GWR livery of the period. This was middle-chrome green, lined with black, green and orange chrome, with brass and copper fittings and embellishments. The handrails, incidentally, were of polished steel, whereas since 1916 other classes had normally had their handrails painted green or black.

The first six Kings, Nos.6000-6005, were the last *new* GWR locomotives to be turned out with the garter coat of arms on the tenders, allegedly dispensed with following an objection had been raised by a representative from the Royal College of Heralds. The RCoH could not actually insist on the removal of the coat of arms, but the GWR nevertheless dropped the symbol, presumably out of a sense of propriety. Also dispensed with around the same time (1927) was the ermine from the old badge, the RCoH no doubt having

pointed out to the GWR that ermine was reserved for royalty. Starting with No.6006, the revised version of the standard GWR lettering ('GREAT [badge] WESTERN', minus garter) was applied to the tenders. In 1934, this gave way to a circular totem formed by the letters 'GWR' - officially described as a roundel but popularly known as the 'shirt button' emblem.

Before World War II, the Kings' cylinder covers and driving wheel bosses were kept bright, but thereafter they were painted black. In terms of livery that was a relatively small war-time sacrifice, as the Kings retained green liveries throughout the hostilities. From spring 1942 until late 1945 all repaints were minus lining but, even so, the perpetuation of any sort of green livery, lined or unlined, during the war was exclusive to the GWR, the three other major companies painting even their top-link classes black. The war-time livery for the Kings' tenders included the com-

pany's coat of arms flanked by the letters 'G' and 'W', most other engines simply having 'GWR' on their tenders or tanks.

After Nationalisation on 1 January 1948, the first livery change on the Kings was the inscribing of the tender sides with BRITISH RAILWAYS, albeit in the traditional GWR style of lettering. The temporary 'W' suffix - quite superfluous, most GWR enthusiasts felt - was carried by Nos.6000, 6003, 6017 and 6020. The Kings were almost certainly the first complete WR class to be fitted with smokebox numberplates, the last being applied in February 1950; a few of the early smokebox plates had brass figures, but BR soon put a stop to that.

In an attempt to find a livery unlike anything used during the previous quarter-century, British Railways experimented with ultramarine with cream, red and grey lining (not dissimilar to the old Great Eastern livery) for its crack express

Several of the Kings were subjected to various experiments but, to our acute embarrassment, we cannot shed any light on the 'additions' to No.6009 KING CHARLES II. For what it's worth, the leading 'box' is stamped 'OOC LOCO SHEDS', and the locomotive's straight feed pipes and the style of springing on its bogie point to a date no later than the very early 1930s. Any suggestions welcome! PHOTOGRAPH: R.M.CASSERLEY COLLECTION

locomotives, and this was applied to Nos.6001 (June 1948), 6009 (May 1948), 6025 (June 1948) and 6026 (June 1948). The livery incorporated blue-backed name and cabside number-plates. The tenders of those four locomotives were lettered BRITISH RAILWAYS in full in unshaded cream characters.

However, the ultramarine livery did not give satisfaction, and it was subsequently decided to substitute a light blue livery with black and white lining (similar to the old Caledonian Railway livery). This was applied to a total of nine classes - five ex-LNER types, two LMSR, the SR Merchant Navy Pacifics, and the GWR Kings - and the first King to be so treated was No.6000, reliveried in June 1949. The blue was fairly short-lived, and the last King to have it renewed (and, ultimately, the last to retain it) was No.6014 in January 1952.

The blue gave way to lined Brunswick green, although the new version of the livery differed from the pre-1949 version in

that the firebox bands and the cab-side windows were not lined. Starting in March 1952 - after the Swindon supply of blue paint had been exhausted - the Kings were treated to green as they passed through the works, the last to receive the new green livery being No.6014 in February 1954. The dates on which each locomotive had its livery changed are given in a later table. In common with all other locomotives, the Kings were inscribed with the BR emblem of the day. From 1949, the 'lion and wheel' (subversively known as the 'ferret and dartboard') emblem replaced the 'BRITISH RAILWAYS' lettering on the tenders, and from March 1957 the second style of BR crest was applied.

Tenders

The Kings' tenders were the standard Collett 4,000-gallon type, of which a total of 481 were built between September 1926 and July 1946. The Kings' individual tender numbers and subsequent changes are noted in the lists. The Lot numbers of the original tenders were:

Locos.	Tender Lot Nos.	Costs (each)
6000-6014, 6016-6018	A113	£1,011 - £1,163
6015/6019	A117	£1,011
6020-6029	A121	£1,003 - £1,014
6007 (rebuild)	A144	

A few of the Kings were occasionally paired with one of the two 3,800-gallon coal-weighing tenders, Nos.4127 (lined green) and 4128 (lined black), which were built to a Hawksworth design in 1952. At least five of the Kings are known to have run with one or other of these tenders -

The 'shirt-button' GWR emblem appeared in 1934, and is carried here by No.6029 KING EDWARD VIII at Bath Road shed on 19 May 1936. The locomotive had previously been named KING STEPHEN, and had only recently been renamed when this picture was taken. It is being prepared for hauling the 'Bristolian' to Paddington. PHOTOGRAPH: BY ARRANGEMENT JOHN TATCHELL

A very good view of the seldom photographed GWR style of lettering used for the BRITISH RAILWAYS inscription on the tender. The engine is No.6000 KING GEORGE V, the location is Newton Abbot, and the date July 1948. PHOTGRAPH: P.W. GRAY.

only short-term and, presumably, for experimental purposes or, alternatively, as an emergency 'spare' at the discretion of the shed staff - but, unfortunately, the Swindon registers make no mention of this. We are, therefore, reliant on contemporary observation reports for even the sparsest details. Unconfirmed sightings noted in the *'Railway Observer'* and *'Trains Illustrated'* include 6000 with tender 4127 on Paddington-Bristol workings w/e 30.8.52; 6004 and tender 4127 at Wolverhampton on 15.2.53 (a blue-liveried engine with a green-liveried tender); 6003 with one of the two tenders at Paddington on 18.2.53;

6005 and one of the two tenders at Paddington, 4.3.53. At least three Stafford Road engines, including No.6020, were noted with one of the tenders 'early in 1953'.

As a general note on the subject of the coal-weighing tenders, former Swindon official A.S.Peck states that they were, in fact, in regular use as spares. Old Oak had one on its books semi-permanently but, perversely, in between outings it was normally to be found at Swindon. Both tenders were observed at Swindon Stock shed on 1 January 1956, but subsequent stock shed listings appear to make no mention of either of them. No.4128 was

condemned in August 1958 and No.4127 in August 1962 - a popular move among fireman, no doubt, as the tenders were, apparently, very hard to work.

Bogies - 1927
When only a little over a month old, No.6003 KING GEORGE IV was involved in a potentially disastrous incident at Midgham, near Newbury. On 10 August, it was hauling the down 'Riviera' at 60mph when the bogie left the track; fortunately - miraculously, perhaps - the train remained on the track and there were no casualties. In later years, it was also suggested that, during its initial trials, No.6000's bogie had left the track. Prior to the incident involving No.6003, crews had filed reports that the Kings had been prone to 'rolling' at high speeds - something not hitherto associated with GWR four-cylinder 4-6-0s. Armed with this information, it seemed that the cause of No.6003's partial derailment might have something to do with the bogie, and a prompt but thorough investigation revealed that the springing provided the axleboxes with only a limited margin for drop - if the axlebox dropped more than about three quarters of an inch (which, as had been seen, was far from impossible on anything other than perfectly-laid track) the wheel 'floated'.

The Midgham derailment could easily have been a major incident, but luck was on the side of the GWR. The derailment, moreover, largely stayed out of the public eye, and so the fast-growing reputation of the Kings was not impaired. The cause of the derailment having been identified, the problem was solved by the addition of coil

The other style of early BR lettering - and also the short-lived first style of BR blue livery, albeit at a fairly oblique angle, on No.6025 KING HENRY III. The date is 10 June 1949, and the train is the up 'Riviera' which comprises the newly-painted crimson lake and cream coaching stock. The location, needless to say, is near Teignmouth. PHOTOGRAPH: E.D.BRUTON

Sporting a blue livery but an unlettered tender, No.6016 KING EDWARD V hauls the 4.10pm Paddington-Birkenhead near Seer Green on 5 July 1952. Note the new-style square tops to the inside valve covers. PHOTOGRAPH: BRIAN MORRISON

springs between the bogie frame and the hangers of the laminated springs. This was a relatively simple procedure in the case of five of the six Kings, but No.6000 was, at the time, halfway across the Atlantic. The only solution was to make and fit the new springs in America, and this was done under the supervision of William Stanier, as mentioned earlier. The later Kings, Nos.6006-6029, had the new style bogie coil springs from the outset.

One King bogie had a slotted front cross-stay. Despite extensive enquiries it has not proved possible to determine the purpose of this feature - it could hardly have been intended as a weight saving measure for it would have had a negligible effect, and it is unlikely that it was done to aid the flow of air around the inside cylinders as cooling would not have been desirable. A stab in the dark is that, as the bogie was, apparently, first fitted to No.6004 - the first new King to be completed *after* the Midgham incident - it might have had something to do with the balance of the bogie. This, it must be re-

peated, is only a guess - informed enlightenment would be positively welcome. It is, unfortunately, impossible at this stage to provide a definitive list of which Kings used the slotted bogie and when. Combining reports in the RCTS *'Locomotives of the GWR'* and photographic evidence, it is possible to offer only the following scant details:

No.6004 seems to have had the bogie in 1927
No.6000 in July 1931
No.6023 in 1935 and maybe through to 1938 or later
No.6018 either to or from September 1948
No.6028 (unconfirmed) possibly *circa* 1950
No.6014 in 1954/55
No.6024 in 1957, possibly also No.6000 in 1957
No.6005 seemingly from 1958 to 1961
No.6021 in 1962

The King bogies gave considerable trouble in the early 1950s, but this will be discussed later on.

Springing
The first twenty Kings, Nos.6000-6019, were fitted from new with equalising beams between the coupled wheel spring hangers. The beams were intended to help distribute the axle loading, but in practice they had negligible effect and, as from 1931, were removed so that each wheel was independently sprung. Nos. 6000-6029 were built *without* equalising beams.

Inside valve casing
The 1930 engines, Nos.6020-6029, had modified covers for the inside valves, most

With its BR blue livery - complete with 'ferret and dartboard' emblem - applied only the previous week, immaculate No.6023 KING EDWARD II stands in the centre road at Bath station while on a running-in trip. Smashing picture! PHOTOGRAPH: IVO PETERS

Standard pre-1957 BR livery - No.6011 KING JAMES I at Paddington in 1955.
PHOTOGRAPH: NATIONAL RAILWAY MUSEUM

The later style of BR emblem has been applied to the tender of No.6012 KING EDWARD VI. The train is a regular Sunday excursion from London to Birmingham and Wolverhampton, passing Widney Manor station on 8 November 1959. PHOTOGRAPH: MICHAEL MENSING

The slotted bogie was attached to various Kings at various times (see text); this is No.6023 KING EDWARD II, photographed at Snow Hill in 1962. PHOTOGRAPH: MICHAEL MENSING

if not all the first twenty engines (Nos.6000-6019) being similarly modified in due course. The original style of casing (in front of the smokebox saddle) on all engines had a curved top but from 1948, that gradually gave way to square tops with tread plates. A further change came when the exhaust passages were later altered, the centre portion of the tread plate (above the valve covers) being raised to provide the necessary clearance.

Feed pipes

Nos.6000-6019 were built with straight feed pipes, but Nos.6020-6029 had feed pipes which curved back behind the nameplates. Eventually, the feed pipes of Nos.6000-6019 were altered accordingly, the programme being virtually complete by the end of 1934.

Whistle shields

Nos.6020-6029 had whistle shields from new. The shields were small trough-shaped fitments which, being placed behind the whistles, prevented steam from obscuring the view from the footplate. The first twenty engines, Nos.6000-6019, were soon brought into line.

Cabs

No.6000 was the first GWR locomotive to have a motor car-style windscreen wiper; it was fitted to the driver's lookout and when still fairly new - probably in December 1927 - the same locomotive was also fitted with a small brass-rimmed hinged 'windscreen', on the driver's side. Such 'screens' were widely favoured as they helped to shield the driver's eyes when it was necessary to lean out of the cab, but the GWR did not favour the general use of such fitments, the corporate philosophy being that 'in normal circumstances in is not necessary for a driver to lean out of his cab when running forward'. During World War II the Kings had the side windows removed from the cabs, the resultant gaps being plated over; the windows were restored after the war. From March 1954 cab-roof ventilators were added.

Cylinders

A relatively unpublicised detail difference was that No.6002 was built with cylinders of 16 inches diameter, a quarter of an inch less than the others. This was disclosed only when the engine was tested against No.6005 in November 1927. The tests had been instigated following reports that No.6005 wasn't as powerful as the other Kings but, somewhat unsurprisingly, under test conditions no evidence was found to substantiate the claims.

No.6005 was subjected to further tests in 1930 and 1931. Those conducted between 9 January and 30 March 1931 at Swindon were listed as 'Drawing Office Tests', and a similar title was applied to

The last ten Kings, Nos.6000-6029, had different style inside valve covers, as evidenced here by No.6027 KING RICHARD I, working hard with a heavy express. Note also the original style of inside cylinder casing (rounded top), the 'shirt button' emblem on the tender, and the lamp iron on the smokebox door. PHOTOGRAPH: NATIONAL RAILWAY MUSEUM

The repair sheets record yet another variation in cylinder sizes, in August 1947, when new inside cylinders of 18½in diameter are noted for No.6028. Despite the unmistakable statement on the relevant repair sheet, the fitting of these has been questioned, the argument being that, if it were possible to fit such large diameter cylinders, it would surely have been done from day one. Research continues...

Speedometers

In 1932/33, at least four of the class were fitted with experimental type speedometers. The first was No.6001, which had a device fitted on 10/11 March 1932, removed on 1 April, refitted in mid-April, and readjusted on 18-21 May. The speedometer required an instrument box to be fitted between the cutaway and the window on the outside of the driver's side of the cab, requiring in turn a cab window that was narrower than usual - a feature retained by No.6001 for the rest of its days.

The fitting of speedometers to Nos.6010 (2 September 1933), 6017 (18 September 1933) and 6023 (25 August 1933) is noted in the Swindon registers, but although other sources state that experimental devices were also fitted to Nos.6007, 6025 and 6028, the registers do not confirm this. It is believed that, by 1937, the entire class had been fitted with standard speedometers.

tests in September of that year. In December, field trials were conducted between Swindon and Frome, but although they were carried out with great care, Collett was unconvinced of the accuracy of the results, declining to release them for publication. In February 1934 it was the turn of No.6006 to undergo 'experiments' at Swindon Works.

As mentioned above, the fact that No.6002 was built with 16in diameter cylinders attracted little attention. A similar lack of publicity later prevailed with No.6024 which, in March 1938, had its original right-hand outside cylinder replaced by one of 16in diameter. Furthermore, little was said about the fact that, in March 1945, No.6023 was fitted with a second-hand left outer cylinder which was 16.32in in diameter. That situation prevailed until December 1949 when new 16in-diameter outer cylinders were fitted.

The date of this picutre might possibly be the mid-1950s for, during repairs to the frames, additional lifting holes had been provided; the engine has, however, not yet been fittted with larger-diameter steam pipes or, seemingly, a mechanical lubricator. The absence of a shed-plate would, it seem, be nothing more than a red herring. There appears to be few clues as to the identity of the locomotive. PHOTOGRAPH: NATIONAL RAILWAY MUSEUM

Tread plates were later added above the inside cylinder covers, as demonstrated by No.6003 KING GEORGE IV, which has just arrived at Wolverhampton (Low Level) on 21 July 1954, having brought in the 'Inter-City' from Paddington. PHOTOGRAPH: BRIAN MORRISON

Lamp irons

Starting in 1932, the engines had their upper lamp irons removed from the top of the smokeboxes and resited on the smokebox doors. The reasons for this were twofold: firstly, in the new positions they were far easier to reach and, secondly, the currents of air around the smokebox door were far less than those above the smokebox and, consequently, the flame in the lamp would be less likely to be blown out. A side-effect of the resiting of the irons was that the smokebox door footsteps (added to each engine soon after building principally to improve access to the upper iron) were rendered largely superfluous, and were eventually removed.

Blow-down apparatus

Between January 1935 and May 1936, No.6021 was fitted with non-automatic continuous blowdown apparatus. Exter-nally, this was identifiable by a pipe leading from the nearside of the cab, along the side of the firebox, to the top side of the boiler. Blow-down was a method of discharging a quantity of water steadily en route, and was used to help prevent a build-up of soluble salts in the boiler water. It was not, however, ideal; if the discharged water included water-softening chemicals, the permanent way could be adversely affected. Indeed, an accident on

The tread plates above the inside cylinders were later modified, usually in conjunction with the fitting of new front ends, and the valve covers on Nos.6000-6019 were modified along the lines of those fitted from new to Nos.6020-6029. This is No.6009 KING CHARLES II at Paddington on 7 June 1960. PHOTOGRAPH: NATIONAL RAILWAY MUSEUM

No.6006 KING GEORGE I at Torquay in 1928. Note the original style of straight feed pipes. PHOTOGRAPH: NATIONAL RAILWAY MUSEUM

the LMSR at Watford in the 1930s was blamed largely on a rail breakage, ascribed to blow-down of 'treated' water. Blow-down was, therefore, subsequently regarded with some caution.

'Streamlining'

The biggest and easily the saddest, cosmetic change ever imposed on a King - or any GW loco for that matter - was the partial (the official description, not ours!) streamlining applied to No.6014 KING HENRY VII in 1935. The contemporary vogue for streamlining had been triggered in 1934 by the LNER's impressive P2 2-8-2s, while the streamlined A4 Pacifics were in the development stage at that time. It was believed that the LMSR also had plans for streamlined locomotives, and in Britain's railway boardrooms the

conviction of the day was that streamlining brought publicity.

The GWR's directors didn't want the company to be denied its share of the limelight, and so they instructed Charles Collett to prepare drawings for the streamlining of one Castle and one King. The story runs that Collett was not amused by the prospect of desecrating such classic designs but, mindful maybe of the

From 1932, the upper lamp irons were repositioned on the smokebox door. This is evident on No.6018 KING HENRY VI, hauling a two-coach Swindon-Bristol local as part of its running in duties after a visit to Swindon Works. PHOTOGRAPH: NATIONAL RAILWAY MUSEUM

Although the GWR did most things in a rather stylish manner, the same could not be said about the so-called 'streamlining' of No.6014 KING HENRY VII. Here, the locomotive displays its full set of streamlining; the fairings over and around the cylinders and the tender cowling lasted for only five months (from March to August 1935) and so that narrows down the date of this picture. The engine is running through Temple Meads station and will reverse on to the the London train in Platform Nine. One point of interest - the old signalbox at the west end of Platform Nine is awaiting demolition after its supercession during a huge modernisation programme, which had included the resignalling of the station. PHOTOGRAPH: G.SOOLE

politics of 'something being seen to be done', he dutifully obeyed. The locomotives selected were No.5005 MANORBIER CASTLE and No.6014 KING HENRY VII.

Unfortunately, official documents fail to shed any light on how the method of streamlining was decided, but it is abundantly clear that Collett wanted as little to do with the matter as possible. One popular suggestion is that he simply smeared Plasticine over a model locomotive in his office, and subsequently informed the hierarchy that the necessary modifications had been designed. Whatever the behind-the-scenes stories, the aesthetic outcome was disastrous - a bulbous hinged cover (officially described - with some optimism - as a 'bullet nose') over the smokebox door, coverings over the front steam chests and in front of the outside cylinders and steam pipes, fairings behind the chimney and safety valves, a continuous splasher with a straight nameplate, a wedge-fronted cab, and cowling on the tender. It has often been suggested that Collett made the streamlining as ugly as possible so that it would be taken off before very

A different view of the partially denuded No.6014 - the date is 24 July 1936 and the place is Torquay. PHOTOGRAPH: E.R.MORTEN

Late afternoon sunshine at the Pylle Hill end of Bristol Temple Meads, and No.6014 KING HENRY VII brings in a London-bound train. The date is probably no later than 1935 or 1936, as Bristol West signalbox still looks quite new. **PHOTOGRAPH: G.SOOLE**

long. If that is true, he wholly succeeded on one of those counts and partly succeeded on the other.

The streamlining was applied to No.6014 during a works visit which lasted from 19 January to 11 March 1935, although the official photographs of the new creation are dated 6 March. It appears that the engine was already in the works for a 'general' when the decision to streamline was taken;

the repair sheet noted a cost of £691 for boiler repairs, £814 for the engine and £99 for the tender, but it is impossible to determine what proportions of those costs were incurred by the streamlining. For the record the tender involved was No.2612.

The streamlining was wholly for the sake of publicity and, to be fair, in that respect it certainly worked. Mechanically, though, it was a different matter. If an engine is

going to derive any benefit at all from streamlining, that benefit can be gained only when running into a headwind - as soon as the locomotive alters direction, the streamlining ceases to be any use whatsoever. Furthermore, the effect of a side wind on a lengthy train is likely to be several times that of a headwind.

Having had its so-called streamlining applied, the wretched 6014 was dis-

Another different angle on No.6014 KING HENRY VII after the removal of parts of its 'streamlining' - the year is 1939, the location is near Denham, and the train is the 9.10am Paddington-Birkenhead express. **PHOTOGRAPH: C.R.L.COLES**

During the transition period, the Kings fitted with the new WB boilers could be readily distinguished by the size of the superheater. No.6002 KING WILLIAM IV is seen (in the *upper* picture) has an original WA boiler at Old Oak Common on 7 August 1955 while, in the *lower* picture, No.6024 - in charge of the down 'Riviera' on 18 July 1956 - sports a new WB boiler. **PHOTOGRAPHS:** *top* ERIC SAWFORD; *bottom* R.C.RILEY

patched to Old Oak Common instead of its former home, Stafford Road. To make good the deficit at Stafford Road, No.6026 KING JOHN was transferred there from Old Oak. The corporate logic behind the exchange was that the London shed was a more suitable home for such a high-profile engine, but there were those at Old Oak who, considering the extra work required to service the engine, would have preferred it to be at Penzance or Fishguard, were that physically possible.

Mercifully, 6014's full set of streamlining lasted for only five months. The coverings over and around the cylinders were

In the *top* picture, No.6020 KING HENRY IV, photographed at Paddington station in 1956, sports its mechanical lubricator in the original position, i.e. behind the steam pipe, while No.6029 KING EDWARD VIII (in the *lower* picture - at Old Oak circa 1956) has its lubricator in front of the steam pipe. PHOTOGRAPHS: *top* T.MIDDLEMASS/PAUL CHANCELLOR COLLECTION; *bottom* NATIONAL RAILWAY MUSEUM.

regarded as a major hindrance to routine lubrication and were soon removed - along with the tender cowling - in August. The hideous bullet nose and the chimney and safety valve fairings were taken off in December 1942/January 1943, and during a works visit in August-October 1944 conventional splashers and nameplates were refitted. All that subsequently remained of the streamlining was the wedge-fronted cab (it was thought to reduce glare in certain lighting conditions) and the special snifting valves. These were retained until the engine's withdrawal.

Draughting - 1939
In May 1939, the Swindon Drawing Office issued a report comparing the steaming of its Kings - notably No.6005 - and French compound locomotives. The report opened by explaining that, in the previous twenty years, the horse power per ton weight of French compound locomotives had increased from 23 to 37, whereas the best figure ever recorded by a King was a relatively modest 20.4. It was explained that the huge improvement with the French locomotives had been achieved by three relatively slight modifications: (1) fitting Kylchap double blastpipes, (2) increasing

Swindon's test plant - known as the 'home trainer' - hosts No.6001 KING EDWARD VII in 1953.

the degree of superheat, and (3) increasing the size of all steam passages.

The report - and let it not be forgotten that it was prepared at Swindon - admitted that the Kylchap blastpipes were far superior to the GWR pattern blastpipes. The former enabled an equilibrium to be maintained between the supply and the demand of the steam whereas, during con-trolled tests in 1931, No.6005 had shown that an equilibrium could be maintained only by the use of a blower. As for the su-perheat temperature, the Houlet super-heater produced a temperature of around 350 degrees (Fahrenheit), while 100 was the norm for Swindon superheaters. Vari-ous figures were quoted for the steam pas-sages on both types of locomotives, but it was emphasised that direct comparisons were unfair due to the different nature of the two types.

It was stated that, in the case of a King, at 60mph its tractive effort fell to 28% of the theoretical maximum, whereas the cor-responding figure for the French compound was a remarkable 70%. This manifested itself in the French engine having greatly

The test train worked by No.6001 KING EDWARD VII on 2 July 1953 comprised a massive loading of 25 coaches. The dynamometer car and indicator shields were *de rigeur* for this trial. The location is Stoke Gifford - very close to where Bristol Parkway station now stands. PHOTOGRAPH: IVO PETERS

From 1953, the Kings were fitted with larger diameter outside steam pipes. The 'before' is modelled here by No.6000 KING GEORGE V, resplendent in newly-applied blue livery at Bath in June 1949, the 'after' being demonstrated by No.6008 KING JAMES II at Paddington on 6 September 1959. PHOTOGRAPHS: *top* IVO PETERS: *bottom* ERIC SAWFORD

superior acceleration and hill climbing - it could maintain 60mph on a 1 in 120 gradient with a 500-ton load, while a King could manage only 200 tons under the same conditions. The report suggested that, if a King were able to maintain its tractive effort at speed to the same degree as that of the French engine, it '...would revolutionise train working over the undulating routes from Paddington to Plymouth and Birmingham... the existing maximum loads on main lines could be drawn at a practi-

cally constant speed (of the order of 75mph) regardless of gradient - a far more effective method of cutting down point-to-point times than by raising downhill speeds to the 100mph mark'.

The report concluded by recommending that extensive experiments with blastpipes be instigated, and that attention should be paid to increasing the superheater units by at least 50%. The potential problem of increased wear and tear - as had been encountered in France,

where steel fireboxes had been found essential - was considered unlikely as the train loads in England were lighter. With the benefit of hindsight, it can be appreciated that, although Churchward had learned much from the French in the early 1900s, by the late 1930s there was more to be learned.

The report was far-reaching in its content, but it appeared at a bad time. With the outbreak of war later in 1939, experimentation had to be shelved - energies

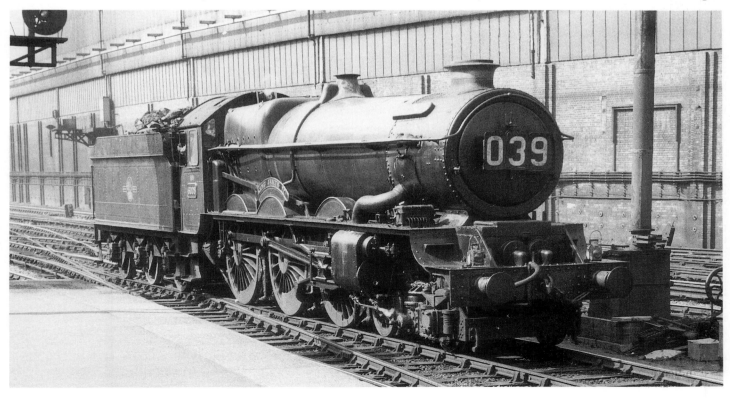

The fitting of double chimneys transformed the performances of the Kings, several of the class subsequently being recorded at some very high speeds. The first King to be fitted with a double chimney was No.6015 in September 1955, and it is seen here on 19 September reversing on to Bath Road shed. Note the original narrow fabricated double chimney. PHOTOGRAPH: R.C.RILEY

had to be devoted to keeping the existing locomotives working, and unnecessary expenditure was out of the question. If it hadn't been for the war, might we have seen high-degree superheat or double-blastpipe Kings in the early 1940s? We will never know. Nevertheless, the matter of superheating was addressed soon after the war and draughting was tackled in the 1950s, as we shall see.

New boilers
Earlier revelations concerning the benefits of high-temperature superheating had not been forgotten on the GWR, and in March 1948 No.6022 was fitted with a rebuilt boiler (No.4670 - subsequently designated WB) which had a four-row high-degree superheater. This had a heating surface of 489sq ft (later reduced to 473.2sq ft) instead of the 313sq ft of the original - conspicuously, the increase in the superheating surface was 56%, the 1939 report having asked for 'at least 50%'. A total of thirty-four new WB boilers (Nos.4695-4699, 8600-8628) was built between 1951 and 1955, and the reboilering programme was completed in October 1956 when Nos.6014 and 6026 received their WB boilers. While the reboilering of the class was in progress, the remaining WA boilers had the superheater heating surfaces reduced to 289sq ft. As will be seen from the registers, six Kings - Nos.6007, 6008, 6012, 6014, 6019 and 6021 - never actually had brand-new WB boilers, only 'secondhand' ones, while some of the class received brand-new WB boilers on more than one occasion.

Mechanical lubricators
From late 1949, all engines of the class were fitted with mechanical lubricators for cylinders, valves and regulators. Initially, twenty-three had lubricators placed on the running plate immediately to the rear of the right-hand outside steam pipe, but this was found to hinder access to the inside cylinder motion and so the lubricators were resited ahead of the right-hand outside steampipe. The original fitting of the lubricators was usually undertaken during reboilering; the subsequent repositioning was, in some cases, not carried out until the engines were fitted with double chimneys.

Mechanical lubrication was a controversial innovation. Previously, GWR men had been happy with the sight-feed lubricators, and considered that only the most inexperienced drivers could fail to realise when their engine needed a faster rate of lubrication. Almost inevitably, the pros and cons of mechanical lubrication occupied several column inches in the letters pages of contemporary railway magazines.

General observations
Initially, BR placed the Kings in the '7P' power classification, but they were reclassified '8P' as from 1 January 1951 although (disconcertingly) early in 1952, doubts about the longevity of the Kings were being voiced. It was noted that they required reboilering, and that heavy repairs to the frames were frequently necessary. A visitor to Swindon on 10 February 1952 reported that no less than eight

Kings were 'in or about' the works: Nos.6003 (light casual), 6004 (heavy intermediate), 6009 (light casual), 6019 (light casual), 6023 (heavy general), 6024 (light casual), 6025 (awaiting heavy general), and 6028 (heavy general).

Later that year, another report added fuel to the fire by noting that, in the last week of September, four of the class were in the works, nine were at sheds under or awaiting repair, one was stopped pending the delivery of material for repair, and another was fresh from the 'shops. In other words, half of the class was out of action at that particular time.

Draughting - the 1950s
Draughting experiments were carried out with No.6017 in the autumn of 1952 and with No.6001 early in 1953. These were conducted to see how revised draughting could facilitate an improved steaming capacity, albeit with the retention of the self-cleaning plates in the smokebox. This was achieved by the fitting of a longer but narrower chimney liner and a smaller diameter blastpipe.

No.6001 was subsequently put to extensive tests on the road and at the test plant, the latter taking place in April and July. It was revealed that the locomotive's steaming ability had been increased by some 30 per cent and that, in many aspects, the performances were comparable with more recent designs such as LNER V2s, LMSR Coronations and even the new BR Britannias. With a test load of twenty-five bogies (almost 800 tons) from Reading to Stoke Gifford and back (on 23 July), No.6001 covered the return leg at an average of 60mph. It was found that even with more conventional loads, the engine nevertheless had a rather hearty appetite for coal; while BR Standard designs in particular could cope well with most varieties, the King worked best on South Wales coal. The draughting experiments with No.6001 being deemed satisfactory, most of the class were similarly modified. A slight variation was applied to Nos.6000, 6003 and 6020, which were fitted with longer chimney casings and had their capuchons removed.

Steam pipes
Following experiments with No.6016 in 1953, the entire class was fitted with new outside steam pipes. These had a larger radius at the cylinder end, thereby increasing their flexibility and reducing the tendency to fracture at that point. It was later realised that the most common cause of fractures had been movement of the cylinders due to the flexing of the frames.

Water testing and treatment
During its Heavy General in January/ February 1954, No.6014 was fitted with a new type of blow-down apparatus. It was also fitted with a device in the cab which enabled samples of boiler water to be taken, to check the formation of deposit in the boiler. The equipment was developed in conjunction with ICI, and after re-entering traffic No.6014 was transferred to Stafford Road (being replaced at Laira by No.6017) so that it could be nearer to the ICI technicians. They travelled with the engine in the course of their observations and for their comfort a temporary seat was provided, on the fireman's side of the cab.

In an attempt to find a long-term solution to the hardness of the water supply at Stafford Road, from 1954 its Kings and Castles were fitted with 'Alfloc' water treatment equipment which enabled them to run for thirty days between boiler washouts. Eventually, 'Alfloc' equipment was fitted to seventeen Kings: 6000-6002, 6005-6009, 6011-6017, 6020 and 6022.

Double chimneys
As related earlier, the Kings benefited enormously from the improved draughting arrangements, albeit at the indirect cost of other problems. However, despite the initial satisfaction with the modified draughting it was soon considered that, to maximise the benefits, a reduction in exhaust pressure was required. The obvious way of achieving this was to use a double blastpipe and chimney - this was not uncharted waters for the technical staff at Swindon as they had been involved in the design of the front end for Standard '8P' No.71000.

During a lengthy works visit in 1955, No.6015 was experimentally fitted with a double chimney which had been fabri-

cated from sheet steel. It returned to traffic on 8 September, and performances were closely monitored. It had to wait until 26 September for the first official test run with the 'Cornish Riviera', and it comfortably achieved a speed of 103mph on a section where 85mph had been the norm for single chimney Kings. Three days later, during another trip on the 'Riviera' with an inspector on the footplate, No.6015 was timed at over 107mph. Those speeds became the subject of considerable debate - GWR partisans weren't averse to 'inflating' the figure each time the tale was repeated - but it is now generally accepted that 107mph was indeed exceeded - the highest authenticated speed achieved by any GWR locomotive.

Returning to the subject in hand, it was, perhaps, a little ironic that on 8-11 March 1955 - a few months *before* No.6015 had been fitted with its highly effective double chimney - No.6013 had, with its single chimney, been tested on the 'Riviera'

prior to the reintroduction of the four-hour schedule. No.6013 had met all targets concerning the margins of reserve. To further the case for the single chimney engines, on 9 September No.6019 gained no less than nineteen minutes on the four-hour schedule with the down 'Riviera'. But, when it came to high speeds, it was conceded that a single chimney King would have to be steamed very hard indeed to reach 100mph.

Although the single chimney Kings were clearly no slouches, the double chimney adaptation of No.6015 was such a success that, by March 1958, the entire class had been similarly treated. Initially, there were two types of double chimneys. Twelve of the class originally received narrow fabricated chimneys similar to that of No.6015, but from November 1956 a more pleasing cast iron chimney of elliptical cross-section was used, those engines with fabricated chimneys being later refitted with cast iron chimneys. A

The Kings' later double chimneys were of a far more pleasing elliptical type. Here, the engine is No.6016 KING EDWARD V, the train is the 2.40pm Birkenhead-Paddington leaving Wellington, and the date is 27 August 1962. PHOTOGRAPH: MICHAEL MENSING

Elliptical double-chimney and modified valve covers and treadplate - the date is stated to be 3 February 1957, but the modifications were carried out to No.6004 KING GEORGE III in November 1956. A brief return visit to Swindon, perhaps? PHOTOGRAPH: IVO PETERS

list of dates is given later in the main 'summary table'.

Frames

In November 1954 a worried magazine correspondent reported that: 'At Swindon, three Kings, Nos.6013, 6016 and 6022, have recently undergone drastic repairs. The entire front halves of their frames have been cut away and replaced by new or spare parts'. But things weren't quite as drastic as they sounded....at least, not at that time. The Kings' improved draughting (but not double chimneys as yet) and their new boilers with larger superheaters resulted in increased power and, in order to withstand the increase, from 1954 engines undergoing a 'heavy' were routinely fitted with new front half-frames, new cylinders, new valve gear and motion castings. They also had their bogie frames strengthened. Although the repairs were considered worthwhile at the time, a little over a year later serious flaws were revealed.

Frames and bogies - 1956

In January 1956, there were two serious failures of King bogies in quick succession. The WR was extremely concerned, and on 23 January the twenty-seven Kings which had had bogie frames welded during repairs were promptly taken out of service. Only Nos.6000, 6006 and 6022 were considered immune. To help offset the WR's sudden and severe loss of motive

power, two Stanier Pacifics, Nos.46254 and 46257, were imported from the LMR. The two Pacifics took up residency at Old Oak and were used on Paddington-Wolverhampton and Paddington-Bristol runs. Elsewhere, Castles deputised for Kings. The King bogies were repaired by welding additional strengthening strips to the frames; in the case of at least eleven engines the bogies were removed at running sheds and sent to Swindon for the necessary work to be done. Contemporary reports noted that, on 27 January, Nos.6007 and 6029 were at Bath Road minus bogies, on 28 January Nos.6003, 6013, 6019, 6024, 6025 and 6028 were all bogie-less at Old Oak, while on 12 February Nos.6014, 6015 and 6016 were in a similar state at Stafford Road.

January 1956 was not a good time for the Kings. On the last day of the month - just when it seemed that the bogie problem had been rectified - a new cause for alarm was discovered. This concerned the mainframes, which appeared to be feeling the strain of the recent front-end modifications. That shouldn't have caused as much surprise as it actually did, since for the best part of twenty-five years the Kings had been used almost day in and day out on long-distance runs with the heaviest expresses. To emphasise the point, a couple of years earlier it had been revealed that the Kings were notching up an average of 259 miles every day - the highest figure of any ex-GWR locomotive. It had been a hard life.

In the light of the mainframe problems, the entire class was taken out of service. As substitutes, Pacifics Nos. 46207 and 46210 arrived from the LMR to help out the two Duchesses, and in addition eight Standard 5MT 4-6-0s - three from the LMR and five from the SR - were acquired on loan. On Wolverhampton duties the Pacifics were turned on the Oxley triangle. The 5MTs released a number of Castles, which were more suitable substitutes for the Kings, albeit with a frequent need for double-heading. Four of Neasden's V2s had originally been offered, but the WR's civil engineer had prohibited them from working from Stafford Road shed. Fortunately, the 'King Crisis' - as it was dubbed in the contemporary railway press - was soon resolved, and six of the class were back in action by 18 February. By the end of the month, enough were in service to permit the LMR Pacifics to be sent home.

Roller bearings

In 1956 it was proposed to fit the Kings' axles with roller bearings. The engines' plain Swindon bearings were perfectly sound in design, but almost thirty years of handling the heaviest expresses had, inevitably, increased the instances of overheating. An order for eight complete sets of roller bearings was subsequently placed with Messrs Timken, and the materials delivered to Swindon in 1957/58. It was, however, a case of bad timing. Further modifications to the Kings were suspended when construction of diesel-hy-

This was a common sight at Old Oak, Laira and Stafford Road during the 'bogie crisis' in 1956. Nos.6013 KING HENRY VII and 6028 KING GEORGE VI wait solemnly at Old Oak Common on 4 February. PHOTOGRAPH: R.C.RILEY

about 1930 heavier section wheel centres were fitted; later, their bogie frames were stiffened; then, the replacement boilers incorporated heavier superheaters; later still double chimneys were fitted. Each stage might have added only a relatively small amount to the total weight, but the cumulative effect was far from insignificant.

The unreliability of published locomotive weights was emphasised by a magazine correspondent ('*Trains Illustrated*', April 1963) who explained that he had personally observed No.6023 being weighed in 1952. The real weights and their 'official' versions were:

	1952 weight	'official' weight
Bogie	21tons 4cwt	21tons 10cwt
Leading coupled axle		
	24tons 17cwt	22tons 10cwt
Centre coupled axle		
	24tons 17cwt	22tons 10cwt
Trailing coupled axle		
	25tons 0cwt	22tons 10cwt
TOTAL:	95tons 18cwt	89tons 0cwt
Available for adhesion		
	74tons 14cwt	67tons 10cwt

The correspondent was, however, at pains to point out that that was the most striking example he had encountered and, of course, that the situation was not unique to the Western Region.

draulic locomotives commenced, and the bearings were never fitted. It is interesting to speculate how the Kings would have fared with roller bearings - in the late 1950s the fitting of roller bearings to ER/NER A1 Pacifics increased the average mileages between shoppings from 80,000 to no less than 120,000.

General

As we have seen, until the mid-1950s the Kings were showing increasing signs of the hard work which they had undertaken, almost incessantly, for the previous twenty-five years or so. We have, however, also seen how the fitting of double chimneys and the front-end refurbishments were positively revitalising. This made for the irony that when the Kings were withdrawn in 1962 they were, in many respects, fairly new engines. To offset this, the declining standards of maintenance in the early 1960s brought a resurgence of failures, the Birmingham line, in particular, being badly affected. When a King failed on a passenger working, the first suitable engine - often from a freight - was commandeered as a replacement, and such was the frequency of King failures on the Birmingham line that the freight services became notoriously unreliable. In the eyes of officialdom, the Kings had actually become a liability. However, their abrupt withdrawal - all thirty were retired by BR in 1962 - was effectively due to their size. They had been displaced from their traditional duties by diesels but, unlike most other displaced engines, the Kings couldn't be found suitable alternative work. They were simply too big or too heavy to be used on all but a handful of routes.

As for their weights, things were, in fact, even more problematical than they appeared. It is seldom realised that, although the official engine weight was 89 tons, by the 1960s the engines actually weighed anything from 93 to 95 tons. A consequence of this was that the Kings' adhesive weight was at least 72 tons instead of the publicised 67½tons - no wonder they were widely regarded as being extremely 'sure-footed'. The explanation lies in the sort of 'accumulative process' undergone during series production - published weights of any locomotive class related, on the whole, to the first engine which, in many cases, would have been treated to a little more care and attention than the 'production line' models which followed. Furthermore, the continuing process of modification and improvement usually added to the weight. In the case of the Kings, from

It was not particularly unusual to see a King under the Laira hoist, although for many years No.6000 seemed to be the most regular one treated. Here, it's No.6002 KING WILLIAM IV. Please note, however, that this picture was taken after the 'bogie crisis' of early 1956. PHOTOGRAPH: TERRY NICHOLLS

Chapter Four

AT WORK

From the outset, the Kings were used on the best West of England services. No.6007 KING WILLIAM III is seen at Torquay in 1928 - note the first modification to the style of the bogie springing. PHOTOGRAPH: NATIONAL RAILWAY MUSEUM

The GWR period

Given the publicity surrounding the debut of No.6000, it was somewhat inevitable that the locomotive would undertake a round of special appearances. It spent the first few days of July on show at Paddington as part of a fund-raising exercise for the Social and Educational Union - the 'Helping Hands' fund - and then went 'on tour', being exhibited - to great acclaim, of course - at Reading, Taunton, Exeter, Newton Abbot, Plymouth and Swindon stations.

Turning to everyday events, the initial distribution of the first six Kings - four to Old Oak and two to Laira - emphasised the intention to use the class on the high-profile Paddington-Plymouth route, a line which had, over the years, usually been worked by the newest and/or best engines, not least because of the difficult gradients west of Newton Abbot. The Plymouth expresses included the boat trains from Millbay Docks, but the Kings were officially prohibited from the quayside lines. That said, a King was used for a Coronation Day special from the quayside in

1953, albeit with a modest load of just five or six coaches. The Kings' prohibition from the quayside lines at Millbay Docks was just one of many restrictions imposed on the class. Due to their axleweights, for many years they were allowed on only four routes: Paddington-Westbury-Plymouth, Paddington-Bristol-Plymouth, the Newton Abbot-Kingswear section (which included six miles of *single*-track line), and Paddington-Wolverhampton.

The Kings' sphere of activity expanded slightly in later years but, along with the hefty 47XX 2-8-0s, they were the most restricted of all GWR engines. On official GWR maps, the routes on which the Kings could work were indicated by 'hatched red' lines over the existing 'red' routes. The restriction was shown on the engines by twin red discs - usually referred to as 'Double Red' - on the cab sides. On No.6000, the discs had to be painted below the numberplate, the usual position above the numberplate being occupied by the two medals brought back from America. On the West of England main line, the best-known express was, of

course, the 'Cornish Riviera' (also referred to as the '10.30 Limited' on account of its departure time from Paddington), which nominally ran non-stop between Paddington and Plymouth - a distance of 225½ miles via Westbury. That said, it should be explained that, in normal service with a train over the prescribed weight, the usual practice was for the 'Riviera' to stop at Newton Abbot to attach (or detach) a pilot engine. For several years a stop at Exeter St.David's was also scheduled, but from the early 1950s it was omitted all year round.

The first King-hauled 'Riviera' was on 20 July 1927, with No.6000 in charge as far as Plymouth. The crew were Driver Young and Fireman Pearce of Old Oak - the very men who were to accompany No.6000 to America. The train left Paddington loaded to some 425 tons - nine 70ft coaches, a set of articulated dining cars, and two coaches which were slipped at Westbury for Weymouth. Slough to Exeter was covered at an average speed of 61.3mph, but the biggest test was on the gradients west of Newton Abbot. Having lost the slip coaches at Westbury the train weight was some 350 tons, but No.6000 hauled it with relative ease - and, significantly, without assistance - over the South Devon banks into Plymouth, where it arrived five minutes early. The Castles, incidentally, were then allowed 288 tons unaided south of Newton Abbot. The loading for an unpiloted King on the South Devon banks was officially set at 360 tons (390 tons on the Kingswear line) but on 22 July - just two days after No.6000's well-publicised trip with the 350-ton 'Riviera' - No.6001 hauled a 400-ton train up Rattery, Hemerdon and Dainton unaided. This paved the way for the schedule of the 'Riviera' to be formally accelerated, as from 26 September, to four hours.

As related earlier, the partial derailment of No.6003 at Midgham on 10 August 1927 somehow stayed out of the limelight and so, for all the right reasons (for the GWR, at least) the Kings quickly became one of the best-known locomotive classes in Britain - helped enormously by the American trip. The GWR wasn't exactly shy when it came to milking the publicity, and on 3 November 1927 the company arranged a special excursion from Paddington to Swindon, which included a conducted tour of the works where the already famous KING GEORGE V had been built. No less than 700 passengers bought tickets for the excursion, which was guaranteed to be hauled 'at high speed' in both directions by one of the Kings. The fare was 5/- (25p), which included the tour of the works. The demand for tickets had, in fact, out-

stripped supply, and so another excursion was arranged for the following Thursday, 10 November. This time, *two* trains - both King-hauled - were laid on.

British railway enthusiasts were eager to hear more about the Kings, and it was somewhat inevitable that they would be featured in that time-honoured tradition of railway journalism, *'Locomotive Practice and Performance'* (cynically referred to as the 'racing pages') in the *Railway Magazine*. The December 1927 issue told of a trip with No.6005 on the down 'Riviera' in mid-October, and compared the King's performance with those of a Star and a Castle in mid-October 1921 and 1924 respectively. The 'Riviera' was at its heaviest in mid-October, the Taunton and Exeter slip portions having been restored after the summer, and the trip with No.6005 started with a load of fourteen coaches - 491 tons tare and some 525 tons gross.

It seems that the GWR - or, at least, the shed staff at Old Oak - had been unusually lax in preparing No.6005 for its trip, especially as the RM's correspondent, Cecil J.Allen, and Chief Locomotive Inspector Robinson were to be on the footplate. The tender contained a considerable quantity of slack ('little better than dust', commented CJA), and despite strenuous efforts by the fireman, by the time Taunton was reached the boiler pressure had dropped from 240lb to 220lb. From then on, the engine was driven with less cut-off than would normally have been applied - indeed, the cut-offs subse-

quently used were fairly similar to those noted during the trip with a Castle in 1924. Nevertheless, the South Devon banks were climbed with comparative ease (CJA likening the passing of Rattery signalbox to 'running over the gable end of a house'), and the train was brought into North Road station at Plymouth nearly two minutes early. CJA remarked that, on inspection at Laira, the engine proved to be perfectly cool in every bearing and was apparently quite fit for an immediate return to London. However, he added that his clothing 'bore no uncertain evidences of the character of the coal which had been burned'.

Another report of a run on the 'Riviera' appeared in *'The Locomotive'* magazine on 14 January 1928. This report was of a trip on 21 November 1927, but with No.6005 in charge once again. Poor quality coal was not a problem this time, and a pressure of 250lb was maintained all the way save for a short stretch near Starcross when it fell to 240lb. The load at the start of the trip was 489 tons tare but, after losing the slip coaches, a less daunting 256 tons remained for the Exeter-Plymouth leg. Plymouth was reached one minute inside the four-hour schedule - *'...226 miles over a difficult road with a heavy train in under four hours; and this is to the Great Western Railway an ordinary everyday performance'*, wrote Douglas Seaton. During the journey 8,300 gallons of water had been used, 6,500 gallons from the four troughs *en route*. Some four and a half tons of coal - a fairly ac-

No.6013 KING HENRY VIII hauls the 1.30pm Paddington-Plymouth through Norton Fitzwarren. The empty stock train on the right is headed by No.4080 POWDERHAM CASTLE. The year is 1928. PHOTOGRAPH: RAIL ARCHIVE STEPHENSON

A Plymouth express leaves Reading with No.6029 KING EDWARD VIII in charge. It's 1948, and the tender is incribed with the legend BRITISH RAILWAYS, albeit in the GWR style of lettering (see text). PHOTOGRAPH: NATIONAL RAILWAY MUSEUM

ceptable 44lb per mile - had been consumed.

The latter report on the 'Riviera' trip was far more favourable than the one filed earlier by C.J.Allen. CJA's account generated a fair old debate in the letters pages of contemporary magazines, and there were several suggestions that the effects of inferior coal were worsened by the Kings' boiler design. There was a consensus of opinion that the wider fireboxes used on LNER designs were better suited to varying qualities of coal but Swindon seems to have been unimpressed.

Apart from assuming a monopoly of the 'Riviera', the Kings soon dominated on several other workings. These included the 1.30pm Paddington-Plymouth, the 3.15pm Paddington-Cheltenham (as far as Swindon), the 5.37pm Paddington-Didcot semi-fast, the 6.35pm Paddington-Cheltenham (again, only as far as Swindon) plus the relevant balancing workings. From July 1929, the Kings were also used on the newly inaugurated (but short-lived) 'Torquay Pullman', No.6018 of Newton Abbot being noted as the regular engine early in August that year.

The West of England route was the 'glamour' role for the Kings, typified by a contemporary magazine report of arrivals at Paddington on 19 July 1930: No.6007 with the Kingswear train at 3.50pm, No.6010 with the second part of the Penzance train at 4.30pm, No.6011 with the 'Riviera' at 4.45pm, No.6003 with the Penzance train at 7.0pm, and No.6013 with the Newquay train at 7.10pm. The correspondent enthused that those five

arrivals were all on or before time. For the winter of 1930, the Kings' West of England diagrams were as table below.

As already related, the original intention had been to use the Kings not only on the West of England route, but also on the Paddington-Wolverhampton line. This was certainly not forgotten, although the Kings didn't make their debut on the Wolverhampton route until 1928. On 16 July of that year, No.6000 took over the working of the 6.50am Wolverhampton-Paddington, returning with the 11.10am from Paddington, and No.6017 took over the 11.37am Wolverhampton-Paddington, returning with the 6.10pm from Paddington. Despite starting and finishing its day at Wolverhampton, No.6000 retained its status as an Old Oak engine, but No.6017 was actually transferred to Stafford Road shed, where it was soon joined by No.6019.

The use of Kings on the 'two-hour' Birmingham expresses actually preceded the use of Castles on those duties, the regular

engines previously having been the Stars. Those expresses were entertainingly described by W.A.Tuplin as 'hell for leather, hammer and tongs' jobs - the heaviest trains usually departed from Paddington with loadings close to 500 tons, and although coaches were slipped at Banbury and Leamington, that still left a not immodest 400 tons or so for the remainder of the journey. The schedule for the 110.5-mile Paddington-Birmingham trip was actually a fraction under two hours which, after a period of familiarisation on the part

1) DOWN: 10.30am Paddington-Plymouth (Old Oak engine Mondays, Wednesdays, Fridays; Laira engine Tuesdays, Thursdays, Saturdays).
UP: 8.35am Plymouth-Exeter and 11.0am Exeter-Paddington (Laira engine Mondays, Wednesdays, Fridays; Old Oak engine Tuesdays, Thursdays, Saturdays).
2) DOWN: 12 noon Paddington-Kingswear (Old Oak engine Mondays, Wednesdays, Fridays; Newton Abbot engine Tuesdays, Thursdays, Saturdays).
UP: 11.25am Kingswear-Paddington (Newton Abbot engine Mondays, Wednesdays, Fridays; Old Oak engine Tuesdays, Thursdays, Saturdays).
3) DOWN: 1.30pm Paddington-Plymouth (Old Oak engine Mondays, Wednesdays, Fridays; Laira engine Tuesdays, Thursdays, Saturdays).
UP: 12.30pm Plymouth-Paddington (Laira engine Mondays, Wednesdays, Fridays; Old Oak engine Tuesdays, Thursdays, Saturdays).
4) DOWN: 3.30pm Paddington-Plymouth (Old Oak engine Mondays, Wednesdays, Fridays; Laira engine Tuesdays, Thursdays, Saturdays).
UP: 3.55pm Plymouth-Bristol and the 7.32pm Bristol-Paddington (Laira engine Mondays, Wednesdays, Fridays; Old Oak engine Tuesdays, Thursdays, Saturdays).
5A) DOWN: 4.30pm Paddington-Plymouth (Laira engine)
UP: 4.10pm Plymouth-Paddington (Laira engines)
5B) same as above; second Laira engine
6A) DOWN: 6.30pm Paddington-Plymouth (Old Oak engine)
UP: 2.0pm Plymouth-Paddington (Old Oak engine)
6B) same as above; second Old Oak engine
7) DOWN: 11.15am Paddington-Bristol, 1.45pm Bristol-Kingswear, 5.40pm Kingswear-Newton Abbot (Old Oak engine Mondays, Wednesdays, Fridays; Newton Abbot engine Tuesdays, Thursdays, Saturdays).
UP: 6.20am Newton Abbot-Plymouth and then the 8.10am Plymouth-Paddington (Newton Abbot engine Mondays, Wednesdays, Fridays; Old Oak engine Tuesdays, Thursdays, Saturdays).

of the crews, rarely presented the Kings with any real problems.

By 1931 - when Stafford Road had five Kings on its books - the expresses were worked as follows:

> **Stafford Road:**
> 6.50am Wolverhampton-Paddington; 11.10am Paddington-Wolverhampton
> 8.35am Wolverhampton-Paddington; 2.10pm Paddington-Wolverhampton
> 9.33am Wolverhampton-Paddington; 4.10pm Paddington-Wolverhampton
> 11.37am Wolverhampton-Paddington; 6.10pm Paddington-Wolverhampton
> 3.14pm Wolverhampton-Paddington; 7.10pm Paddington-Wolverhampton
> **Old Oak Common:**
> 9.10am Paddington-Wolverhampton; 2.30pm Wolverhampton-Paddington

While the class was settling down to the routine of everyday service, special occasions had not been overlooked. Going back to 1930, a significant event in the railway calendar was the centenary of the Liverpool & Manchester Railway, and the GWR's representative at the celebrations was No.6029 which, between 10 September and 7 October, was looked after at Agecroft shed in Manchester. Earlier that year, the GWR's metaphorical flagship, No.6000, had undertaken special workings for the Crusaders Union (from Paddington to Swindon and back, 3rd, 8th and 10th January) and an educational excursion from Paddington to Swindon on 24 April. In 1931, No.6000 undertook another round of PR duties when it was used to promote the Empire Marketing Board's "Buy British Week", the second week of the campaign being launched on 23 November at Paddington station with No.6000 as the main attraction. The smokebox door was adorned with a circular 'EMB' hoarding. Between 30 September and 17 December of the same year, No.6005 was exhibited at Swindon.

The Kings gained a new duty in March 1934 when they started working the newly introduced 12.50am Paddington-West of England newspapers, the first such train being hauled by No.6027 which gained seven minutes on the schedule to Plymouth. That same month - on 26 March - alternative duties with a difference came the way of four Kings. Three Stafford Road engines, Nos.6005, 6014 and 6017, and Old Oak's No.6001 were used to test the new steel bridges on the recently quadrupled Olton-Lapworth section of the Birmingham line. The presence of No.6001 was required as it was fitted with the latest type of speedometer, some of the test runs having to be made at a fairly precise speed. During the tests the engines worked in pairs (coupled together, one pair without a train, the other pair with two carriages), and they made several runs side by side on adjacent tracks, thereby subjecting the bridges to the maximum possible stress. The spectacle was undoubtedly very impressive; one observer called it 'the sight of a lifetime'.

As had been anticipated, though, in everyday service, the Kings' revenue-earning activities were initially confined to the West of England and Wolverhampton routes, the engines consequently being divided among Old Oak, Laira, Newton Abbot and Stafford Road sheds. Those at Newton Abbot were used principally on trains to and from Kingswear. In later years, the only other sheds to have a permanent allocation of Kings were Exeter, Bath Road and, in the early 1960s, Canton.

Until the BR era, alternatives for the class were very few and far between, the use of No.6014 on a Paddington-West Wales special as far as Cardiff in 1935 being one of the very rare exceptions. Also in 1935, a King was officially rostered for the first time to one of the GWR's best-known trains, the 'Cheltenham Flyer'. It was customarily Castle-hauled - the loading of the train was rarely enough to warrant the muscle power of a King and, besides, Kings were not permitted on the Swindon-Gloucester section. However, on 18 May 1935 the newly-streamlined No.6014 KING HENRY VII broke with tradition and became the first of its class to be officially rostered to the 'Flyer', albeit only on the Swindon-Paddington leg. The train was driven by Jim 'Quality' Street, and took a mere 60 minutes - that was fast, but by no means a record. The GWR's

Where else but Teignmouth? No.6025 KING HENRY III heads an up express in 1955. PHOTOGRAPH: NATIONAL RAILWAY MUSEUM

The 6.25am ex-Penzance passes - nay, charges - through Hele & Bradninch on 5 August 1957 behind No.6021 KING RICHARD. PHOTOGRAPH: PETER GRAY

A Birmingham express is brought into Paddington on 17 July 1947 by No.6006 KING GEORGE I. PHOTOGRAPH: RAIL ARCHIVE STEPHENSON

Centenary fell in 1935, and on 31 August a celebration was held in the Great Hall of Bristol University. There was the obligatory round of speeches, and the address given by the GWR's chairman, Sir Robert Horne, included an important announcement: *'Up to now the best trains between Bristol and London have taken two hours. We propose - starting on September 9 - a new service in which a train from London to Bristol will take only one and three-quarter hours.*

'The train will be called "The Bristolian", and will be scheduled to do the 118¼ miles on the down journey, via Bath, and the 117 and a half miles, on the up journey via Badminton, in each direction, at an average speed of 67.6 miles per hour and 67.1 miles per hour respectively.

'The new train will leave Paddington at 10am and Bristol at 4.30pm on Mondays to Fridays inclusive, and will be the fastest in the country for a run of over 100 miles. The train will travel, for the greater part of its journey, at a speed of 80 miles per hour'.

The party attending the centenary luncheon was taken home to London in a special train - hauled by No.6000 - which was timed to run to the proposed 'Bristolian' schedule. The 'GWR Magazine' - that proud in-house organ - subsequently reported that: *'The run was so smooth that tea could be taken in comfort without being spilt'.*

A little over a week later, on Monday 9 September, the 'Bristolian' was formally inaugurated. The train comprised seven coaches - 230 tons gross - and was hauled in both directions by No.6000 with Driver Field at the helm. Although the 'Bristolian' was a very prestigious service, the Kings did not maintain a permanent hegemony on the duty. Similarly to the 'Cheltenham Flyer', the normal train loadings on the 'Bristolian' were compara-

tively light and, with speed more important than muscle-power, a Castle was perfectly adequate. Due largely to the higher maintenance costs of the Kings, Castles were usually preferred where jobs were within their capabilities.

On 15 January 1936 a King was again in the limelight - but this time for the wrong reason. No.6007 had taken charge of the 9.0pm Penzance-Paddington express passenger train at Newton Abbot, the train, which included sleeping cars, being routed via Bristol. From Wootton Bassett, it was following in the wake of an Aberdare-Old Oak coal train, hauled by 28XX No.2802 and comprising fifty-three loaded wagons plus a six-wheeled brake - a train weight of 1,108 tons. Unknown to all concerned the coal train had suffered a breakaway near Shrivenham, and the last five wagons and the brake van (some 122 tons in all) were completely stationary on the line in the path of the express.

The express was travelling at between 50 and 60mph when, at 5.24am, it hit the wagons. Much of the force of the collision was taken by the frame of the goods brake van, but the engine of the express derailed and turned over on its right-hand side, its train inevitably coming to a violent standstill. The steel frame of the leading carriage - corridor third No.4000, built in 1921 - was thrown out sideways, clear of the train and across the down line, but the body was projected beyond the frame and rolled down the bank, coming to rest almost upside down. Its five rear compartments were completely destroyed, as was the whole of the second coach (a twelve-wheeled newspaper and guard's van). The third and fourth carriages were modern steel-built sleepers, but although both were derailed neither overturned.

The express was carrying about 100 passengers. Miraculously, there were just two fatalities, a lady who was believed to have been in the leading coach, and Driver Starr. Ten passengers, most of whom had been in the leading carriage, were seriously injured, while seventeen others and Fireman Cozens suffered minor injuries or shock.

The obligatory Ministry of Transport report into the accident revealed that, although the prime cause was the failure of a drawhook coupling on the coal train (which resulted in the breakaway) human failings contributed to the ensuing collision. The guard of the coal train was heavily criticised for not having reacted promptly to the obvious deceleration of the stray wagons, but the greatest proportion of the blame was apportioned to the signalman at Shrivenham for his failure to notice that the coal train had been incomplete when it had passed the signalbox. As for engine No.6007, the official report listed the damage as: *'Frames: R.H. main frame, front end, bent (not cracked), standing off inside cylinders three eighths inch, wants rebolting. R.H.*

Footplate wants renewing, front and back. R.H. front corner brackets bent. R.H. hanging bar, bent front and back. R.H. motion plate bent. L.H. main frame, front end, bent and broken. L.H. corner bracket missing. L.H. hanging bar, front end, bent. L.H. motion plate, outside, bent. Buffer bar, box angle iron, angle irons and screw connection, broken.

Cylinders: *All cylinders good. R.H. back cover broken.*

Valve gear: *R.H. valve spindle bent.*

Reversing gear: *Reversing screw and box bent; will not reverse.*

Cab: *Weather board, cab sides, leg plates, windows, cab handrails, pillars and T-irons, smashed. 4 cone, handrails, top feed pipes R.H. side, all smashed.*

Boiler mountings: *Good.*

Sand gear: *R. trailing sandbox, smashed.*

Brake gear: *Brake hangers, cross stays and rods, smashed.*

Bogie: *Both frames bent. Leading cross stay and life guard missing. R.H. bogie centre controlling spring and case smashed. L.H. inside T-springs and hangers all bent. Bogie centre pin casting broken in two webs only.*

Springs: *Engine springs good. Spring hanger brackets and spring hangers on L.M.D. bent.*

Miscellaneous: *Damper gear and cylinder cock gear on footplate damaged. Cylinder cock gear and cocks on R.H. outside cylinder broken off.*

Tender No.2572: *All axleboxes broken. Brake rods, stays and hangers bent. Brake column broken and shaft bent. One brake hanger bracket missing. Draw gear side and centre links bent. Four handrails and two lamp irons back of tender bent. Tank water indicator gear column broken. Water pick-up scoop broken. Leading and trailing dragboxes damaged. Number plate broken. Intermediate buffers bent. Vacuum pipes damaged trailing end. Vacuum drip tap plate bent. Toolboxes badly damaged. Draghook bent. Middle wheels slightly out of gauge. Back and front footplates broken and buckled. Right hand side footplate broken and buckled, back end. Two toolbox angle irons broken, right side. Coal door broken, right side. Coal door wing broken, right side. Coal plate bent front end, right side. Shovel plate broken. Footboard supports broken. Tank, back end, badly bent and broken. Tank, back end, inside plates and top angle irons broken'.*

For accounting purposes the much damaged engine was condemned on 5 March 1936, and a replacement was ordered under Lot 309 at a cost of £4,393. Despite the seemingly damning report on the state of the original locomotive, the replacement - also numbered 6007 - incorporated a not insignificant proportion of the old one; indeed, it was not even necessary to lift the boiler of the damaged engine from the frames. The 'new' No.6007 entered traffic on 24 March 1936. It was paired with tender No.2572 - this too had its accident damage repaired, and, for bookkeeping purposes, had been written off and replaced by a 'new' tender, constructed under Lot A144. A far less hefty accident - little more than a minor bump, in fact - occurred at Newton Abbot on 21 August 1936, when No.6028 was run into by Castle No.5051, the driver of the latter having misread a signal. No.6028's bogie was forced off the track at catch points, but there was no damage.

A King broke new ground on 9 June 1937, but in a fairly modest manner. With the turntable at Reading out of action, No.6018 was turned on the Reading triangle - the first recorded occasion of a King on the West Loop. A somewhat more intriguing foray was made in 1938. Between the end of January (possibly the 29th) and late February (possibly the 28th), No.6004 of Laira and No.6015 of Old Oak were temporarily attached to Bath Road shed in Bristol, and on Sundays during that period they undertook clearance tests through the Severn Tunnel and on to Newport. The tests involved one of the engines running chimney first and the other ten-

The Birmingham line - and No.6019 KING HENRY V reaches the summit of Hatton bank on 6 November 1956 with a down express. PHOTOGRAPH: MICHAEL MENSING

No.6024 KING EDWARD I at Stafford Road shed on 19 August 1956. PHOTOGRAPH: RAIL ARCHIVE STEPHENSON

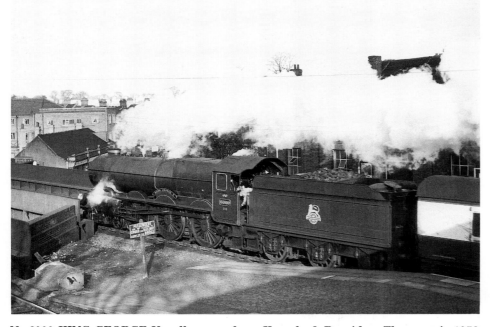

No.6000 KING GEORGE V pulls away from Knowle & Dorridge. The year is 1958. PHOTOGRAPH: MICHAEL MENSING

as the usual bankers. That situation prevailed until February 1954 when, after satisfactory clearance tests, Standard '9F' 2-10-0s arrived at Ebbw Junction shed for use on the ore trains.

Another interesting, albeit conspicuously uncorroborated, foray in 1938 involved No.6000 and what was said to be No.6025. Contemporary reports tell of the two engines being tested between Bristol and Shrewsbury via the Severn Tunnel in the February. Quite feasible, perhaps, but could these reports possibly represent incorrect assumptions based on the trips of two Kings through the tunnel at the period in question? There, knowledge ends. Still on Monmouthshire mysteries, according to the official Swindon registers, on 12 November 1937 No.6002 had its tender changed at Ebbw Junction shed. However, as that the engine is recorded as having entered Swindon Works for repairs the previous day, it is assumed that the tender change entry was purely for book-keeping purposes.

Ebbw Vale wasn't the only place to get its first glimpse of a King in 1938. It is known that, in the late spring or early summer of that same year, at least one representative of the class underwent trials across the Royal Albert Bridge to Cornwall - territory which, according to the rule book, was out of bounds. The engine was No.6028 which, on a Sunday morning, was observed a little beyond Saltash station with a one-coach train, presumably for test purposes. It has been suggested that there were, in fact, two separate test runs, roughly in the period in question - one as far as St.Germans and the other just beyond Doublebois. Frustratingly, no official documentation relating to such trials seems to be available, and details of proceedings appear to have eluded the contemporary railway press. Considering that the Kings were among the highest-profile engines of the day it is somewhat remarkable that their trials in Cornwall were kept out of public view. On that score, the oft-repeated tale of No.6000 working through to Penzance in 1934/35 with a special centenary train can surely be discounted - the GWR would surely have sought maximum publicity from such a trip, and said publicity is conspicuous by its absence.

Among the reports of 1939 was one in April, which stated that the Kings then had a monopoly of the four up expresses passing through Exeter on Sunday afternoons, although the trains rarely comprised more than six carriages. A rare treat for Birmingham enthusiasts on 28 December of that year was the sight of Newton Abbot's No.6024 on a Paddington-Wolverhampton working, and Stafford Road seemed intent on returning the compliment, for its own 6005 was observed in Plymouth.

On 20 August 1940 No.6010 was slightly damaged during an air raid at Newton

der-first, with four vacuum-fitted wagons between them to help spread the weight, but despite the unorthodox formation, local speculation was that the tests were conducted with a view to Kings being used on South Wales expresses. Such speculation was, however, some twenty years premature.

It later became known that, during the tests, the two Kings had ventured beyond Newport. The principal purpose was, in fact, to see how large four-cylinder engines coped on the heavy ore trains to Ebbw Vale. One of the Kings was tried with a 950-ton train (32 loaded wagons) from Newport to Aberbeeg, stopping and start-

ing on some of the steepest gradients. At Aberbeeg, twelve more wagons were added, bringing the load to some 1,350 tons, and the second King was attached to the rear of the train. The awesome pairing apparently coped well, despite gradients which peaked at 1 in 56.

No official account of the tests seems to have survived but whatever information the GWR gleaned from all this activity, previously-held ideas of a purpose-built locomotive (a 2-10-2T had been proposed) were discarded. Instead, the heavy ore trains from Newport to Ebbw Vale continued to be hauled by 2-8-0Ts, albeit with similar engines taking over from 0-6-0PTs

No.6027 KING RICHARD I, with BRITISH RAILWAYS on its tender, at Saltford on 22 January 1949. PHOTOGRAPH: IVO PETERS

Abbot, the cab roof and sides, the left-hand side of the tender and the water tank being holed. Just over two months later, on 4 November, No.6028 was involved in a far more serious accident, at Norton Fitzwarren near Taunton, resulting in a considerable loss of life.

On the fateful night No.6028 was in charge of the 9.50pm Paddington-Penzance passenger train, which comprised thirteen bogie coaches carrying some nine hundred passengers, many of them service personnel. The train was travelling at an estimated speed of 40-45mph on the down relief line, and passed two successive stop signals at danger before becoming derailed, at 3.47am, at the catch points protecting the down main line, where the two lines converge at the west end of Norton Fitzwarren station. The engine and the first six coaches were derailed, five of the coaches being wrecked. Twenty-six people were killed - thirteen Naval personnel, twelve civilians and Fireman Seabridge. Fifty-six passengers sustained injuries serious enough to warrant hospitalisation, and eighteen complained of minor injuries or shock. Sixteen of the injured were members of the Services.

It could have been even worse. The 12.50am Paddington-Penzance newspaper train, also hauled by a King, was travelling on the down main line at 55-60mph

and overtook the passenger train as the derailment actually occurred. Somehow, the newspaper train got clear momentarily before No.6028 derailed across its path. An inspection of the newspaper vans revealed just how close things had been - a rivet head from the bogie of the derailed engine had broken a window of the fourth van, and the panelling of the fifth van had been marked by flying ballast, caused by No.6028 having derailed virtually alongside it.

Initially, there was speculation that the accident had been caused by enemy action or sabotage, but it quickly became clear that human error was to blame. The driver of the passenger train had assumed that he was on the main line (as was usually the case) and not the relief line, and he mistook the main line signals (which were set clear for the newspaper train) for his own. Lt-Col Mount, who chaired the Ministry of Transport enquiry, was sympathetic towards the driver: '...he frankly admitted his responsibility, but his account of what happened, given in good faith, appears to have been affected by his experiences'. Lt-Col Mount declared that the driver's error '...must have been the outcome of failure to concentrate...', and that '...his breakdown may be partly attributed to operating conditions in the black-out, and to the general strain (for example, his house at Acton had been recently damaged) which Railway Serv-

ants, in common with other members of the community, are undergoing at the present time'. In the official report, it was emphasised that the driver was an experienced and capable man in the top link at Old Oak, who had forty years' service and an excellent record.

Many years later, the signalman on duty at the time of the accident privately admitted that, at the enquiry, he had been 'economical with the truth'. He had been less than diligent in his observance of the rule book, and his word had been taken in preference to that of the driver's. It did not, however, detract from the fact that the driver had made a simple - but disastrous - error in his reading of the signals. (For a fuller account of the signalman's story, see From Cleaner to Controller by W.J.Gardner.) Following the accident, No.6028 had been taken to Taunton shed for inspection, and had then spent the following ten weeks being repaired at Swindon. That was the second - and last - fatal accident involving a King, although some of them were not immune to the occasional minor scrape. For example, on 6 March 1941 No.6012 - running light near Ladbroke Grove - passed an automatic signal at danger and collided with the tail of a train 250yds beyond. There were no casualties.

In March and April 1941, the city of Plymouth was subjected to ferocious air

Another running-in turn in the early BR period - No.6011 KING JAMES I heads through Keynsham with the 10am local ex-Bristol in July 1949. PHOTOGRAPH: IVO PETERS

raids. Locally, it is often told how, during the raids, some of Laira's Kings were routinely driven over the Royal Albert Bridge at night so that they could be sheltered inside a tunnel - it has been suggested that the 'safe house' was, in fact, Shillingham Tunnel. That story is, however, widely disputed.

In 1943, a King once again made a tentative - and low profile - test run to South Wales. On 16 April, No.6007 of Old Oak was trialled on all the lines at Cardiff Canton shed, particular attention being paid to clearances at the coal stage and on the turntable. This, presumably, was a preliminary move in the working of Kings to Cardiff on a regular basis but, as has already been remarked, such events didn't come about for several years.

During the war, train loads of fifteen bogies or more - sometimes much more - were far from uncommon, and the haulage capabilities of the Kings proved extremely useful. One particular occasion was on 25 October 1941, when an unidentified King brought the fifteen-coach down 'Riviera' into Exeter fifteen minutes early - an average of 53.4mph despite the customary deceleration of the period! The availability of the Kings was, however, rather poor during the war years, and on more than one occasion at least eight of

the class were under the jurisdiction of Swindon Works simultaneously. Indeed, there were weeks when up to half of the Paddington-Plymouth expresses had to be hauled by Castles, simply through a lack of serviceable Kings.

The wartime disruption to conventional working patterns threw up various oddities. For example, Nos.6000, 6010 and 6019 of Laira and No.6017 of Bath Road were all observed on Paddington-Wolverhampton expresses during February 1943, while in July and August of that same year Nos.6006 and 6005 visited Plymouth for the first time since the 1930s. During 1944, all thirty Kings were seen in Plymouth at one time or another.

According to the Swindon registers, No.6015 moved to an untypical home in 1947. The records show that, between May and mid-June of that year, the engine was allocated to *Aylesbury*, but although this mysterious move has been recorded elsewhere, it must be seriously doubted. It is, really, more or less inconceivable, and the likeliest explanation is that a clerk mistakenly transposed engine numbers - the Aylesbury resident should have been No.6105.

The 1948 Exchanges

Much has been written elsewhere about

the various interchange trials, especially those which British Railways instigated in 1948. As there is little, if anything, new to say about them, it might be somewhat superfluous to go over familiar - even tired - ground yet again. A brief summary should suffice.

BR hoped that, during the trials, the selected locomotives would perform well on 'foreign' metals, thereby dispelling the widely-held notion that each region required locomotives specially designed for its own needs. For the express passenger locomotive trials, the ER supplied an A4 Pacific, the LMR a Duchess and a rebuilt Scot, the SR a Merchant Navy, and the WR a King. The plan was for each of the test locomotives to perform on each of the regions.

The Western Region representative was No.6018 KING HENRY VI but, due to loading gauge restrictions, it could be tried only on home territory (Paddington-Plymouth) and on the ex-LNER Kings Cross-Leeds route. Between 20 and 23 April 1948 it ran between Paddington and Plymouth, working the 1.30pm down train and returning on alternate days with the 8.30am from Plymouth (8.15am ex-Millbay). The runs between Kings Cross and Leeds were conducted between 18 and 21 May (preliminary tests having been undertaken on 10 May) with the 1.10pm from Kings Cross and the 7.50am from Leeds worked on alternate days. During the tests the performances of No.6018 gave general satisfaction, no special effort being required for the prescribed schedules, but to the disappointment of many enthusiasts there was a distinct lack of the spectacular. It has often been suggested that, in marked contrast to their counterparts in 1925, the WR crews were somewhat disinterested in competition. But despite the general satisfaction given by No.6018 during the tests, especially when it came to clean starts, there was one particularly conspicuous blot on the report. That concerned coal consumption, the King accounting for an average of 48.8lb per mile on its WR tests and 47.2lb on the ER tests - some 15% more than the LNER A4 and LMSR Duchess.

Almost inevitably, it was promptly claimed that the higher coal consumption of the King was due to the unfamiliar test diet of South Kirby hards. That, however, was not actually the case, an official report noting that '...the engine steamed freely...'. Furthermore, it had not been forgotten that, in the exchanges of 1925, the GWR Castle, fired with unfamiliar coal and running on LNER metals, had knocked the proverbial spots off a Gresley A1. The high coal consumption of the King in 1948 was, in fact, due largely to the slower than normal schedules and the numerous checks, which drastically hindered the continuity of steaming, but that was little consolation to GWR devotees who, perhaps naively, had anticipated a repeat of the 1925 exchanges.

The WR subsequently instigated a repeat of the Paddington-Plymouth tests, but this time with Welsh coal. In the course of four

During the locomotive exchanges of 1948, No.6018 KING HENRY VI performed between Kings Cross and Leeds. Here, it emerges from Wood Green Tunnel with the 1.10pm for Leeds, on 20 May. PHOTOGRAPH: RAIL ARCHIVE STEPHENSON

monitored runs (two up, two down) on 23-26 November 1948, No.6001 returned a more-respectable average of 42.28lb per mile - in terms of drawbar horse-power, the figure of 3.33lb/dhp hour could be compared with the 3.74lb which had been recorded with South Kirby coal. It was a significant improvement, but was still slightly inferior to the figures returned by the LNER A4 and the LMSR Duchess in April. The Paddington-Plymouth tests were repeated on 14-17 December 1948 with No.6022 which, in February of that year, had been fitted with a modified boiler having a four-row high-degree superheater (see earlier). Using familiar Welsh coal, No.6022 returned an average consumption of 41.7lb per mile, or 3.10lb/dhp hour. The

tests of Nos.6001 and 6022 in November and December 1948 were conducted with the WR's dynamometer car, but it was generally accepted that, if absolutely precise results were required, the stationary test plant at Swindon was the only place where all variables could be quantified. Indeed, after No.6022 had received its high-degree superheater boiler, it had spent over a month at the test plant. Due to its similarity to some contemporary exercise machines, the test plant was irreverently referred to as the 'home trainer'.

Below:- A King at Wakefield - No.6018 KING HENRY VI at work during the locomotive exchanges of 1948. Note the post-war style of lettering on the tender.

British Railways

As already emphasised, the Kings' heavy axleweights meant that they were effectively restricted to a small handful of main lines, and although their sphere of activity expanded slightly during the BR era, changes were gradual. For the sake of simplicity, the following details of the Kings' post-1948 activities have been divided roughly into routes.

West to North

Apart from the brief trials of Kings in South Wales and west of Plymouth, and the various 'guest appearances' and exchange workings, the class was restricted to familiar territory until 1948. Late that year, following track improvements, permission was given for them to be used between Bristol and Shrewsbury - the first time route availability had been officially extended. Also, in December 1949 a King was tried between Shrewsbury and Chester, but although the class was granted formal permission the following month there seems to be no known instances of one working that far in normal service.

Bath Road shed received Nos.6000 and 6018 in December 1948 and No.6019 the following month, a side effect of this and other transfers of the period being that Newton Abbot was deprived of an allocation of Kings for the first time since 1928. However, Nos.6018 and 6019 were transferred away from Bath Road in July 1950, leaving No.6000 to inaugurate the workings on the Shrewsbury route on 1 February 1951 - the first official revenue-earning King workings through the Severn Tunnel. The diagram took in the 4.30pm Bristol to Liverpool (9.55am ex-Penzance) as far as Shrewsbury, returning with the 8.20pm ex-Crewe which was scheduled to arrive at Bristol at 12.46am. The diagram was changed as from 20 October 1952, and No.6000 was transferred away from Bath Road - the last of its class to be allocated there.

Castles subsequently regained a domination of the 'west to north' trains, but on 20 May 1954 No.6009 of Old Oak worked the Bristol-Shrewsbury leg of the 10.5am ex-Penzance. This unusual course for an Old Oak engine was due to the failure of the designated Castle, No.5037 of Bath Road. The Kings had a reprise in the autumn of 1959, when one was rostered for the Shrewsbury-Newton Abbot leg of the 9.5am Liverpool-Plymouth on Mondays, Wednesdays and Fridays, returning on the remaining weekdays with the 8am Plymouth-Liverpool and Glasgow. During October, Stafford Road's No.6011 was such a regular performer on that diagram that a *Railway Magazine* correspondent excitedly, if mistakenly, reported that it had actually been transferred to Shrewsbury.

As evidenced by No.6009 in 1954, it was not unknown for 'foreign' Kings to appear on the 'west and north' route. Another instance occurred on 22 October 1960 when, as an indirect result of a roster change No.6021 of Old Oak had been noted working to Shrewsbury and back - on a Bristol diagram covering the 1.15pm Plymouth-Liverpool and the 7.0pm Liverpool-Bristol.

On 11 October 1961, due to a DMU having caught fire in the Severn Tunnel, 'west and north' trains were among those re-routed via Gloucester. One of the diverted trains was the 12 noon Penzance-Crewe, which was hauled by an unidentified King, and this brought about what is believed to be the first instance of a King in Gloucester. The engine was apparently taken off there and returned light to Bristol. Around that time, a regular King duty involved taking the 12.35am ex-Manchester-Penzance on from Shrewsbury, the engines usually being from Old Oak, taken off at Bristol. As late as 1962, Kings were still occasionally seen on 'north to west' duties and No.6014, for example, was noted hauling the 10.45pm ex-Manchester-West of England on from Shrewsbury in June.

Paddington-Wolverhampton

Kings had been employed on the Wolverhampton expresses since 1928, and from

Shrewsbury, 4 June 1960. This is *not* a 'west-to-north' working, as No.6003 KING GEORGE IV is backing on to the 2.35pm Birkenhead-Paddington at Platform Seven on the second half of a round trip from London. PHOTOGRAPH: S.D.WAINWRIGHT

No.6010 KING CHARLES I has just arrived at Shrewsbury with the down 'Cambrian Coast Express' on 19 May 1959. PHOTOGRAPH: P.W. GRAY.

1951 had started to appear in Shrewsbury regularly, but although Wolverhampton and Shrewsbury were less than twenty rail miles apart, the Kings were prohibited from working between those two points. The major stumbling block had been Shifnal Viaduct, but in 1953 it was reconstructed, the work requiring the complete closure of the Wolverhampton-Shrewsbury line on two Sundays - 18 October and 29 November.

The reconstruction of the viaduct enabled Kings to work northwards from Wolverhampton, although such instances remained sporadic for some time. Prior to the upgrading of the viaduct, as a form of preliminary foray, a King had - in the autumn of 1952 - tentatively undertaken clearance tests between Wolverhampton and Shrewsbury. At Codsall, the cylinders had been found to be uncomfortably close to the platform edge and the tests had been halted. One must assume that action was later taken to improve the clearances, but we have failed to find details of how this was achieved. It is, however, conspicuous that Kings were not used regularly north of Wolverhampton until 1959.

In 1952, the general condition of Stafford Road Kings (and, for that matter, many other locomotives at the shed) drew adverse comments from many quarters. The situation was partly excused by spare link men - i.e. the less experienced drivers - working the Kings; one irate passenger commented on the occasion when a spare link crew took over a down express at Leamington '...twelve bogies on a falling gradient and straight road, and the driver slipped the King so violently that the vibration could be felt in the second coach. This also occurred at the Knowle and Birmingham restarts'. Leaving driving techniques to one side, the best Paddington-Wolverhampton expresses were invariably hauled by Stafford Road or Old Oak Kings. One service on which they retained a monopoly until 1955 was the 6.10pm from Paddington but, subsequently, the 5.10pm took priority if there were a shortage of Kings. During the early 1950s, at least, a popular running-in turn for Stafford Road's Kings was the 8.28am Leamington-Wolverhampton semi-fast.

According to contemporary magazine reports, on 9 June 1956 No.6009 set a precedent by working through to Ruabon. It was stated that the engine had worked from Paddington with the 9am summer Saturday train for Pwllheli and was due to be replaced, as was customary, at Wolverhampton. However, Stafford Road shed was short of a suitable replacement and, to compound matters, nothing was available at Shrewsbury either. Consequently, there was little option but to retain the engine through to Ruabon - or so the story went. There is photographic evidence to confirm that Kings worked to Ruabon on a couple of occasions in 1961 and 1962, but doubts have been raised about the 1956 report as, although Shifnal Viaduct could accept the Kings, the clearance problem at Codsall had, seemingly, not yet been solved. Dare we solicit further corroborated information?

Moving ahead to 1958, on 25 February No.6005 was observed running light through Oakengates in the direction of Wellington, although the reason is unknown. Later that same year, on November 6, No.6000 worked the 'Cambrian Coast Express' through from Paddington to Shrewsbury - only the second King, it seems, to penetrate beyond Wolverhampton in everyday service. The up working that day was given to No.6028. At the time, those sightings of a King north of Wolverhampton were certainly considered newsworthy, as was the sight of No.6022 heading the 'Cambrian Coast' through to Shrewsbury and returning with the balancing working on 1 January 1959. Before very long, however, Kings ceased to have any significant rarity value on the Wolverhampton-Shrewsbury line, for the class was given the official all-clear after satisfactory clearance trials with No.6011 on 13 April (1959). As from 20 April, Kings formally took over the Paddington-Shrewsbury 'Cambrian Coast' diagram. For the first week No.6024 officiated, giving way to No.6000 on 25 April. This came to an end in late August when Castles regained a dominance, albeit interspersed with sporadic appearances by Nos.6010 and 6019.

The working pattern on the Paddington-Wolverhampton route was explained in the February 1960 issue of 'Trains Illustrated'. Leaning on that article, it is evident that the Monday-Friday diagrams for the winter of 1959/60 employed seven of Stafford Road's ten Kings each day, and eight on Fridays. The diagrams and the usual loading (total number of carriages in brackets) were:

6.45am	ex-Wolverhampton (11);
11.10am	ex-Paddington (11)
7.25am	ex-Wolverhampton (12);
6.10pm	ex-Paddington (11)
8.33am	ex-Wolverhampton (12);
6.23pm	ex-Paddington (11)
9.35am	ex-Wolverhampton (11);
2.10pm	ex-Paddington (12)
10.30am	ex-Wolverhampton (12);
4.10pm	ex-Paddington (12)
11.36am	ex-Wolverhampton (11);
5.10pm	ex-Paddington (13)
2.20pm (FO)	ex-Wolverhampton (10);
10.10am (SO)	ex-Paddington (9)
4.20pm	ex-Wolverhampton (9);
8.10pm	ex-Paddington (11)

The Old Oak engines engaged on the Wolverhampton route at that time had six diagrams on Monday-Thursday, and an additional one on Fridays:

8.30am	ex-Paddington (9);
1.34pm	ex-Wolverhampton (9)
9.00am	ex-Paddington (11);
4.35pm	ex-Wolverhampton (11)
9.10am	ex-Paddington (11);
2.35pm	ex-Wolverhampton (11)
10.10am	ex-Paddington (9);
3.33pm	ex-Wolverhampton (9)
1.10pm	ex-Paddington (12);
5.33pm	ex-Wolverhampton (11)
3.10pm	ex-Paddington (9);
7.29pm	ex-Wolverhampton (12)
6.08pm (FO)	ex-Paddington (10);
7.25am (SO)	ex-Wolverhampton (11)

The allocation of ten Kings to Stafford Road by the start of 1960 was the depot's biggest representation to date, the stud having been boosted - directly and indirectly - by engines displaced from the West of England route by diesels.

Due to a diagram revision, as from 16 May 1960 the down 'Cambrian Coast' became an almost everyday duty for the Kings, the engine returning home with the 2.35pm ex-Birkenhead. There was a hiatus to that pattern between January and June 1961, but the Kings resumed the duty for the summer 1961 timetable.

On 22 April 1961, No.6002 ventured through to Ruabon, this time with a well-corroborated working, the 'Festiniog Railway Special' from Paddington. Special permission was apparently required for No.6002 to work to Ruabon, similar permission presumably being required for No.6000 which, on 29 Sept. 1962, arrived at Ruabon with a Talyllyn special.

Early in 1962, the Kings took over the 8.25pm Shrewsbury (Abbey Foregate) - Wood Lane milk train, the working having recently been diverted at its southern end from Marylebone. In June of that same year, several of the new 'Western' diesels took up residency at Oxley for use on the best Paddington expresses, and this was at last the beginning of the end for the Stafford Road Kings. Nevertheless, the requirements of the summer timetable meant that the Kings remained surprisingly active on the Paddington-Birmingham-Wolverhampton route for a little while longer, albeit in what was described as a 'rapidly deteriorating mechanical condition'. On a less auspicious note, on 12 May 1962 No.6011 failed at Leamington with the 4.10pm from Paddington. A sign of much-changed times, it was replaced by Royal Scot No.46160, which had been appropriated (in turn a sign of much-changed times) from a Saltley freight.

In the northbound direction on the Birmingham line, during the summer of 1962 Old Oak Kings retained a dominance of the down 'Cambrian Coast' through to Shrewsbury while, due to a motive power shortage on 6 August (1962), Stafford Road's No.6016 was given the *up* 'Cambrian Coast'. That was stated to be the first occasion since September 1959 that the train had been King-hauled between Shrewsbury and Wolverhampton.

The rostering of Kings to Birmingham expresses came to an end with the introduction of the winter 1962 timetable but, inevitably, that didn't bring about an immediate cessation of such outings. One revival was undoubtedly rather pleasurable to steam enthusiasts. It concerned No.6002 which, in early September 1962, was exhibited at Snow Hill station (to mark the end of Kings on the Birmingham expresses) and when, on 4 September, the diesel on a Wolverhampton express failed, No.6002 stepped into the breach at a moment's notice. No.6000 also came to the rescue of a failed diesel that same month, taking over the 6.40pm Shrewsbury-Paddington from 'Western' No.D1008 on 29 September; the King had worked north that day with the Talyllyn Special, and its return trip to London with the 6.40pm was officially booked as a light engine working!

There were, of course, several other King workings on the Birmingham line during and after September 1962. For example, on 18 October No.6005 hauled the 8.20am Paddington-Shrewsbury (the 'Inter City') and returned with the 12.58pm up 'Cambrian Coast' from Shrewsbury, relieved at Birmingham by No.6011. On 30 October No.6011 worked the two-hour (10am) Birmingham-Paddington, and on 3 November No.6000 worked the up 'Inter City'; on 17 November No.6018 worked a special excursion to Wolverhampton while, on 21 December, the 10.50am Paddington-Shrewsbury was worked by

No.6011. By now, the Kings were close to extinction. The first to have been withdrawn was Stafford Road's No.6006, which had been retired on 15 February 1962. Just seven months later - on 20 September - it was reported that Nos.6012, 6014, 6015, 6017 and 6022 were stored in the open at Stafford Road (of those, Nos.6012 and 6017 had been withdrawn) while Nos.6009, 6010, 6019, 6020, 6021, 6026 and 6029 (all withdrawn) were stored outside Old Oak 'with name and number plates removed'. A word of caution about that report - although No.6020 was stated to have been at Old Oak, it had, in fact, been withdrawn from Stafford Road and was later sold to a scrap dealer in the Birmingham area. Its alleged presence at Old Oak so late in the day might, therefore, have been a case of mistaken identity.

West of England
The West of England route was the one most closely associated with the Kings. At the start of the BR era, the celebrated 'Cornish Riviera' - one of the Kings' long-standing regular duties on the West of England route - was scheduled at 4hr 30min for the down run to Plymouth and 4hr 40min up. That timing was retained until the summer of 1952, when a 4hr 15min timing was reintroduced. A good start was made to the summer schedules when, on 30 June, No.6008 brought the down 'Riviera' into Plymouth four minutes early, having made up almost ten minutes of lost time since Westbury.

For the summer of 1955, the 'Riviera' had, at long last, its four-hour schedule restored. Prior to the official reintroduction of the faster schedule, No.6013 was tested on a four-hour timing on 8-11 March, working down and up trains on alternate days. Apart from a few relatively minor gremlins on the first down run, No.6013 met all targets concerning the margins of reserve. More spectacularly, on 9 September of that same year No.6019 gained no less than nineteen minutes with the down 'Riviera'. It should be noted that, at the time, Nos.6013 and 6019 were still single-chimney engines.

Commencing on 28 January 1956, two other established West of England services - the 1.30pm Paddington-Penzance and the 11am Penzance-Paddington - were jointly christened the 'Royal Duchy' but, despite the use of chocolate and cream carriages, the 'Duchy' wasn't anywhere near as distinguished as the 'Riviera'. The inaugural down 'Duchy' was hauled as far as Plymouth by No.6000.

On summer Saturdays during much of the 1950s, two Kings could often be observed working double-headed between Newton Abbot and Plymouth - the only section of the Western Region where such a practice was officially permitted, authorisation having been given in January 1949. The regal double-heading resulted

No.6029 KING EDWARD VII emerges from Parsons Rock Tunnel with a Paddington-Plymouth express at some time in the mid-1950's PHOTOGRAPH: RAIL ARCHIVE STEPHENSON

from the down 'Riviera's' routine engine change at Newton Abbot, the Saturday train usually swopping its King for two smaller engines for the slog over the South Devon banks. Having been taken off the 'Riviera', the King then continued to Plymouth by piloting the next down train - the 10.35am ex-Paddington which, itself, was often King-hauled. That practice, which continued (nominally at least) until the start of the summer 1960 WTT - could cause much confusion to onlookers, as the King which had been taken off the 'Riviera' sometimes retained the train headboard while piloting the 10.35am.

In the up direction, the use of double-headed Kings had been routine during part of 1949. On Sunday nights, the 8.40pm Penzance-Paddington sleeper (which ran via Bristol) was sometimes hauled from Plymouth (dep. 11.55pm) by two Kings, although one was acting as pilot only as far as Newton Abbot. The sleeper was, in effect, the return working for the two Kings - one had worked into Plymouth with the 4.15pm local from Bristol, the other with the 5.45pm from Bristol (10.40am ex-Liverpool/10.45am ex-Manchester). A specific observation on 16 January 1949 was of No.6000 of Bath Road and No.6020 of Stafford Road. During 1956 the programme of fitting double

chimneys to the Kings was continued and, as noted elsewhere in this book, the results were excellent. The class was transformed, not only in terms of performance, but also reliability, a subtle indication being given, perhaps, by the report that, during December of that year, all but three of the Kings appeared at Paddington. A few years earlier, given the poor availability of the class due to mechanical problems, such a report would have been highly unlikely.

For the winter of 1956, three new 'out and back' West of England diagrams were established for Old Oak's double-chimney Kings:

> 9.30am Paddington-Plymouth;
> 3.45pm Penzance-Paddington perishables.
> 10.30am Paddington-Plymouth ('Riviera');
> 6.20pm Penzance-Southall milk
> 1.30pm Paddington-Plymouth;
> 8.45pm Penzance-Paddington
> There were also three new winter diagrams for
> Laira's double-chimney Kings:
> 7.15am Plymouth-Paddington;
> 6.30pm Paddington-Plymouth
> 12.30pm Plymouth-Paddington;
> 9.50pm Paddington-Plymouth
> 2.00pm Plymouth-Paddington;
> 12.30am Paddington-Plymouth newspapers

Matters are a little uncertain, but it seems that the above diagrams might have been changed before too long. The uncertainty stems from a contemporary report which refers to an Old Oak engine working the 12.30am newspaper train to Plymouth and returning with the perishables ex-Penzance. Unfortunately, it has not been possible to unearth further information.

On the West of England line, the first day of the 1957 summer service saw the newly-named 'Mayflower' (8.30am Plymouth-Paddington and 5.30pm return) get off to a dubious start, due largely to three special Ocean Liner trains having to be run from Plymouth. A potential embarrassment for the WR was that HRH Princess Margaret was due to travel on the named train and so, rather than incur Royal (and media) wrath, it was decided to run the train in two parts, the first part (with HRH on board) being hauled by No.6028. Although a huge embarrassment had been narrowly avoided, there were red faces the following day when No.6007 failed at Taunton on the up 'Mayflower'.

In January 1958 the WR's first Warship diesel-hydraulics (the D600 series) went into service. They proved very unsatisfactory, but the second breed of Warship diesels (the D800 series), which made their debut in August 1958, were altogether

The larger steam pipes are modelled here - in a most eye-catching manner - by No.6018 KING HENRY VI, approaching Reading General with the down 'Riviera' on 8 October 1955. PHOTOGRAPH: RAIL ARCHIVE STEPHENSON

better machines. Virtually from the off, they were drafted to the West of England route and, as their numbers increased (albeit slowly, due to financial problems at the North British Locomotive Co) the scope for steam locomotives diminished. In 1959 and 1960, Laira's Kings were all transferred away, the last to leave being Nos.6002 and 6016, which departed in September 1960. Perhaps ironically, they had been at Laira for just fifteen and eighteen months respectively, the shed's longer-term residents having already departed.

Early on during the diesel insurgence in the West of England (in late 1958 or possibly 1959) No.6026 was reported to have worked an express over the Royal Albert Bridge as far as Truro, returning to Plymouth (*sans* train) after dark. A late blow for steam? Perhaps - but considerable doubts have been voiced as to whether the event actually happened.

As for the diesel takeover, further emphasis - as if it were required - was supplied by local observers; during the summer of 1960 there were days when not one single King was spotted at work in Devon. Considering that Nos.6002 and 6016 were actually *based* at Laira at the time in ques-

tion, that shows just how thorough a takeover it was.

But all was not doom and gloom for the West Country steam enthusiast - at least, not quite yet. During the Easter period of 1961, No.6000 was noted at the head of the 10.10am Plymouth-Paddington (Easter Sunday), No.6010 was observed with the Kingswear portion of the up 'Royal Duchy' on the Tuesday, and on 17 April No.6026 worked the 4.10pm Plymouth-Paddington. Unfortunately, the manner in which those engines arrived in Devon seems not to have been observed. To the pleasant surprise of many, the start of the 1961 summer schedules saw the restoration of a fairly regular King working to Plymouth. It was on the 11.30am Paddington-Plymouth, the engine returning on the following day's 12.5pm from Plymouth. That, however, was short lived and, by July (1961), sightings of Kings in Devon were once again few and far between. Among the infrequent appearances were those of No.6018 with a fourteen-coach Colchester-Plymouth troop train on 13 July, and No.6016 on the 12 noon Penzance-Crewe on 22 July.

For the winter 1961 timetable, so far as express operations were concerned steam

traction was effectively eliminated west of Taunton. Nevertheless, No.6000 was noted at the head of the 'Riviera' on 22 December while, on 27 January 1962, Nos.6009, 6015 and 6027 worked football specials to Plymouth, where the Argyle were playing Tottenham Hotspur in the F.A. Cup. Other sightings of the period included those of No.6025, in charge of the 3.25pm Bristol-West of England parcels on 16 February, and No.6016 (at least as far as Exeter) on the second part of the 10.30am Paddington-Penzance on 26 May 1962.

During the summer of 1962, King-hauled relief workings on the West of England route included three on 2 June - No.6018 on the 9am Paddington-Plymouth, No.6015 on the 10.10am, and No.6019 on the 10.35am. On 9 June, No.6025 worked the 12.15pm Plymouth-Paddington. A regular relief working during that summer - the 10.40am Paddington-Penzance - was rostered for an Old Oak King, and was said at the time to be probably the last working to take a King to South Devon with any consistency. 'One-off' workings included those of No.6029 on the northbound 'Devonian' on 19 June, No.6009 on a Paddington-

Minehead train (but, of course, only as far as Taunton) and No.6018 on a Paddington-Penzance train on 30 June, No.6019 on the down 'Torbay Express' on 26 July, and No.6026 on the first part of the down 'Riviera' on 4 August. However, following the use of No.6000 on the 2.45pm Plymouth-Old Oak parcels on 10 August, no more Kings were observed in the West Country for the rest of the summer.

The class had a final, if sporadic, flourish in Devon towards the end of 1962. On 4 October No.6000 worked the 5.30pm Paddington-Plymouth (at least as far as Exeter) while on 14 December No.6011 worked the 10.40pm Paddington-Plymouth parcels, and on 17 December No.6025 was seen on the up 'Royal Duchy', although the manner of No.6025's arrival in the West Country appears to be unrecorded. What is believed to be the last BR King working in Devon was that of No.6018 which, on 21 December 1962 worked the 12.5pm Paddington - Penzance.

Paddington-Bristol

As already related, the fastest trains on the Paddington-Bristol route were not usually heavily loaded and, with speed more important than muscle power, Castles were normally considered more than adequate. However, Kings regained a brief monopoly of the highly-prestigious 'Bristolian' in 1954. For that year's summer timetable, the train was accelerated to a time of just 105 minutes. A preliminary trial was undertaken on 30 April 1954 by No.6003 which, with an eight-coach loading (254 tons tare), easily kept ahead of the schedule. On the outward trip, No.6003 was unofficially timed at 98mph on the descent of Dauntsey Bank while, on the return trip, Swindon to Paddington was covered in 60 minutes exactly.

The first public working of the 'Bristolian' to the new schedule was on 14 June. It was in the charge of No.6000, with Driver Potter and Fireman Kebble, and the seven-coach train was brought into Temple Meads three and a half minutes early. The return journey was via the Badminton line, No.6000 bringing its six-coach train into Paddington four minutes early. Between Badminton and Old Oak the train had averaged 80mph. The usual 'Bristolian' loading was relatively light, and the Kings had no trouble with the new schedule - indeed, on 17 June No.6015 brought the up train into Paddington no less than ten minutes early. It was, however, inevitable that the Kings would not be allocated indefinitely to such a lightly-loaded duty, and Castles gradually took over from early September. The first recorded instance was on 6 September, when No.7030 took charge. On 15 September the up 'Bristolian' arrived at Paddington behind Hall No.7904, but that was due to the failure of Castle No.5073, itself a late substitute for No.6009, which had failed at Bath Road.

During the first week of October 1954 Kings were given the 7.30am and 9.5am Paddington-Bristol trains, which had usually been Castle-hauled; as if to redress the balance, during much of that month several Paddington-Plymouth trains were worked by Counties instead of the customary Kings. Earlier in 1954 - on Sundays 9th and 16th May - an unusual sighting in Bristol had been that of the King-hauled 'Riviera', the train having been diverted from its normal route due to bridge renewal work at Newbury.

A slight mishap befell No.6016 at Bristol on 22 February 1955. It was bringing the empty stock of the up 'Bristolian' into Platform Nine of Temple Meads station when it struck the rear of the 4.15pm Paddington train, slightly injuring three passengers. The official report blamed 'poor lookout'. Also at Bristol in 1955, between 28 April and 20 May (at least), No.6024 was noted at Barrow Road - the former LMS shed in the city. The King's leading coupled wheelset had to be removed for some unspecified repair which could not be effected at Bath Road, with its traditional GW lifting shop. It was not the first time a King had been dealt with at Barrow Road, No.6017 having been noted on the wheel drop there on 10 August 1950.

By 1956 the usual 'Bristolian' engines were still Castles, but late that year Kings reappeared on Mondays following an increase in the loading of that day's trains to eight carriages. Normally, anything over seven coaches on the 'Bristolian' resulted in an extra time allowance, but on 8 August 1957 No.6019 illustrated the inappropriateness of that practice by hauling

On 30 April 1954 - as a prelude to the reintroduction of the 'Bristolian' schedule - No.6003 KING GEORGE IV undertook a trial run. This is the train at West Ealing. PHOTOGRAPH: NATIONAL RAILWAY MUSEUM

Sporting the later style of train headboard in this undated picture, No.6019 KING HENRY V approaches Bath with the down 'Bristolian'. PHOTOGRAPH: K. LEECH

a ten-coach special (some 350 tons) from Paddington to Bristol for a ship launching ceremony, in just 99 minutes - an average of 72.7mph. Nevertheless, the practice of relaxing the schedule for a heavier than normal 'Bristolian' continued.

During 1956 and 1957, regular King duties on the Bristol line included the 2.25am Paddington-Bristol newspaper train, returning with the 7.45am Bristol-Paddington, and occasionally the TPO via Bristol. Another regular duty was the 6.35pm Paddington-Cheltenham as far as Swindon (due at Swindon at 8.10pm - not exactly 'Cheltenham Flyer' scheduling!), returning with the milk train (3.50pm ex-Whitland) for Wood Lane.

Early in March 1958, gas turbine loco No.18100 failed on the 7.45am Bristol-Paddington on two consecutive days. On the second occasion - 4 March - it was hauled dead from Bathampton to Swindon by No.6021, which was running in on a local working after overhaul. By that time, the WR's first main line diesel-hydraulic locomotives had emerged but, despite the publicity given to BR's plan to eliminate steam traction, how many of us really believed that, within a decade or so, the steam locomotive would be completely eradicated from BR's stock lists? At the time, it seemed positively unthinkable.

In 1958 the WR conducted trials with a view to introducing a 100-minute schedule for the 'Bristolian'. One of the test runs was undertaken by No.6018 which, on 22

May, failed to achieve the target with a 247-ton train. The late arrivals (nearly four minutes with the down train and more than six minutes with the up) were, however, not the engine's fault as crippling permanent way checks were in force in both directions. Despite top speeds of 91mph on the down run and 86mph on the up, the lost time couldn't be regained. The 100-minute timing was introduced in 1959, but with Warship diesels in charge. The last scheduled steam-hauled weekday 'Bristolian' ran on 12 June 1959, with Castles in both directions.

Despite the gradual diesel take-over, the Kings maintained a presence on the Bristol line until 1962 - the last year of the class. During the summer of 1962 they were often used on the down 'Bristolian' on Saturdays, which was usually loaded to 14 bogies. The return working was the 2.35pm ex-Weston-super-Mare. Among those noted were No.6000 on 28 July and 4 August and No.6026 on 11 August. In August, No.6018 worked an excursion train through to Weston-super-Mare (Locking Road).

South Wales

On 6 April 1952 No.6009 undertook clearance tests at Newport and Cardiff, despite the fact that Kings had previously ventured through to Cardiff (albeit not on regular workings) seemingly without any mishaps. It is believed that, during the new tests, particular attention was paid to the Rumney River bridge, just to the east of

Cardiff, which had recently been strengthened. At Newport, Kings had, of course, been seen regularly on Bristol-Shrewsbury workings since early 1951, but those trains had turned off at Maindee East Curve and had not penetrated the centre of Newport itself. It was suggested that the testing of Kings at Newport and Cardiff in 1952 was with a view to their use on the 'Red Dragon', but that didn't happen until 1959.

The Kings finally made it beyond Newport in a revenue-earning capacity in 1955. On 19 February, No.6015 worked the 12.45am Paddington-Carmarthen newspaper train as far as Cardiff, returning with the up Irish boat train at 8.15am - the first appearance of a King, it is believed, on a regular working in the Welsh capital. Kings were suequently used with modest regularity on a similar out-and-back working (with Swindon crews), but for only a short period before Castles regained their domination. Another South Wales incursion was observed on the morning of 24 August that same year, when No.6022 of Old Oak was noted at Newport, heading in the direction of Cardiff with an unidentified fourteen-coach train.

The class made another of its rare appearances in South Wales on 30 September 1957 when No.6000 headed the down 'Capitals United Express' into Cardiff. An even more unusual South Wales working involved No.6008 of Laira which, on 10 May 1958, was turned out for the 9.5am Bristol-Cardiff. It returned from Cardiff with the 11.10am ex-Swansea, which it worked right through to Plymouth.

It was, however, late in 1959 before Cardiff started to see Kings on a regular basis. As from 23 November of that year, the diagram involving the 12.45am Paddington-Cardiff newspapers was revised so that the return trip was with the 8.0am ex-Cardiff - the 'Capitals United Express'. The round trip was given to an Old Oak King. Things got off to an uninspiring start, the engine on the first day being No.6024 which, at the time, was due for a works visit. It lost 25 minutes with the newspaper working, and steamed so badly on the return trip that the 'Capitals' was brought into Paddington 43 minutes late.

Time-keeping on the new diagram continued to be poor. During the first fortnight the only day the up 'Capitals' arrived at Paddington on time was 30 November - and that was when Castle No.7029 had been turned out for the duty. It was not exactly the Kings' finest hour - on 5 December No.6015 failed, on 7 December No.6024 brought the 'Capitals' into Paddington 60 minutes late, and on 8 December No.6015 had to stop for a 'blow up' and arrived at Paddington 65 minutes late.

With no small amount of egg on face, the WR abandoned the 'Capitals' experiment. An Old Oak King continued to be rostered to the down newspaper train, but the diagrams were revised so that it returned with

the 8.15am from Cardiff instead of the 'Capitals'. An unusual participant in that diagram on 14 December was No.6020 of Stafford Road. The Kings were, however, not excluded from another Cardiff named train, the 'Red Dragon'. On 16 February 1960, for example, No.6028 of Old Oak took the down 'Dragon' from Paddington, having worked up from Cardiff with the 8am ex-Neyland.

Despite the Kings' often unhappy experiences with South Wales workings, six of the class, Nos.6003, 6004, 6018, 6019, 6023 and 6028, were transferred from Old Oak to Canton shed in September 1960. One year later, No.6024 was similarly transferred. The influx was simply a reflection of the spread of diesel traction elsewhere - options for alternative work were severely restricted because of the weight of the Kings, and Canton offered what were the only real opportunities for alternative work.

The engines transferred to Canton were used principally on the regular Paddington turns - the 8.0am up and 1.55pm back, the 10am up and 3.55pm back, and the 12 noon up and 5.55pm back. The Kings were allowed 500 tons on the Severn Tunnel line, compared to the 455 tons allowed for Castles, Counties and Britannias. Other duties in which the Canton Kings regularly participated were the Fridays Only 7.5am to Paddington and 5.35pm return (an Old Oak job for the rest of the

week) the Sundays Only 7.10pm to Paddington and 1.20am (Monday) return, and two former Britannia workings as far as Shrewsbury and back - the 8.55am Cardiff-Manchester returning with the 12.15pm ex-Manchester-Plymouth, and the 11.50am ex-Swansea-Manchester, returning with the 3.5pm ex-Manchester-Cardiff. The Kings were barred west of Cardiff.

By the summer of 1961, a variation had crept into the Canton diagram involving the 8.55am Cardiff-Manchester. The new pattern was for the engine to leave from Shrewsbury with the 2.25pm to Bristol, work the 7.15pm Bristol-Pontypool Road, and return home with the Cardiff portion of the 8.30pm ex-Crewe. Another diagram revision took a King from Cardiff to Pontypool Road with the 7.20pm, from Pontypool Road to Shrewsbury with the 12 noon ex-Penzance, and back with the following day's 2.25pm Shrewsbury-Cardiff.

The last outings of Kings on the Cardiff routes seem to have attracted little attention, but their tenure suffered a sharp knock in March 1962 when Beyer Peacock Type 3s ('Hymeks') took over much of the main line work to and from Cardiff. Indeed, the following month it was reported that two Canton Kings (No.6024 plus one other) were unserviceable and in store 'unlikely to work again'. The last two Kings left Canton in July 1962, when

The up 'Red Dragon', hauled by No.6019 KING HENRY V, passes Badminton on 13 May 1961. PHOTOGRAPH: IVO PETERS

Nos.6004 and 6024 (already withdrawn) were dispatched to Swindon.

Off limits

In 1952, there was a case of an incorrect 'new' location for the Kings, and an instance of an 'almost'. The former involved No.6020 which, for a few days in April, was observed carrying an 84F (Stourbridge) shedplate! The latter involved No.6019 which, on 30 August 1952, was mistakenly assigned to the 10am Torquay-Oxford-Wolverhampton train. The problem was that the Kings were prohibited from the Didcot-Banbury line, and so No.6019 had to be replaced by a Hall (No.5934) at Swindon. In 1962, the prohibition north of Didcot was relaxed for a Wolverhampton-Swindon special which, on 9 September, travelled - with the necessary authority - via Didcot West Curve.

A King ventured on to forbidden territory on 18 July 1954, but by only a few yards. Returning to Paddington with a West of England semi-fast, No.6018's last stop had been at Reading, where a local crew had taken over. Whether or not the driver was preoccupied with his unfamiliar engine, he mis-read a signal at Subway Junction (about one mile short of Paddington) and passed through Old Oak station and into Paddington Suburban station (formerly Bishop's Road). Kings were barred from the suburban platforms at Paddington (the 61XX 2-6-2Ts were the largest engines permitted) but, fortu-

nately, the train had been routed into one of the outside platforms and no damage resulted. Embarrassingly for all concerned, the error wasn't easily concealed as two-thirds of the train was left out on the running lines.

As emphasised elsewhere in this book, the Kings' tightly restricted route availability meant that when they were superseded by diesels, it was virtually impossible to find suitable alternative duties for them. That said, two displaced at Stafford Road, Nos.6005 and 6011, were transferred to Old Oak in September 1962 and, from the 10th of that month, were used on the new (and rather modest) diagram which involved the 6.35pm Paddington-Didcot, returning the following morning with the 7.10am ex-Didcot. The engine working the down train on Fridays and spent the weekend at Didcot. Perhaps as a test for that new diagram, during August Nos.6000 and 6019 had both been observed on the 8.5am Didcot-Paddington semi-fast.

Throughout 1962 withdrawals made steady inroads into the class, but the remaining engines were not denied the occasional late flourish. For the opening of the huge new RTB Steelworks at Llanwern (near Newport) on 26 October 1962, Nos.6000 and 6018 hauled special VIP trains from Paddington. The event also warranted a Royal train, but that was diesel-hauled. The two Kings were serviced at Ebbw Junction shed in Newport in

readiness for the return trip - reckoned to be the first time two of the class had been at Ebbw Junction simultaneously since the Ebbw Vale trials of 1938.

On 27 October - the day after the Llanwern trip - Nos.6000, 6005 and 6011 all worked Paddington-Newbury race specials, the last steam-hauled trains to arrive at the racecourse station. Rather late in the day - in November 1962 - Nos.6011 and 6018 broke new ground when they spent several days at Chepstow acting as test loads for the rebuilding work in progress on the Wye Bridge.

By the beginning of December 1962, only four Kings remained active. They were No.6000 (wdn 4/12), Nos.6011 and 6025 (both quoted as being withdrawn on either 18 or 21 December) and No.6018 (which survived until the end of the month). Despite the official demise of all four during December, in the following spring it was rumoured that Nos.6000, 6011, 6025 and 6026 - all in store at Old Oak - might be held in reserve in case they were needed to help out on the forthcoming summer schedules. That, however, didn't come to pass. Another incorrect rumour of the period was that, due to a cracked frame, No.6000 was to be broken up and No.6018 would be preserved instead, the name- and numberplates and the bell being transferred accordingly. As if to emphasise No.6018's reasonable health, it was indeed steamed again. It was sent to Tyseley and employed between 22 and 25 April 1963 on local

Having stormed up the 1 in 100 bank from the Severn Tunnel, No.6019 KING HENRY V passes through Pilning with the 8am ex-Neyland on 10 February 1962. PHOTOGRAPH: HUGH BALLANTYNE

The practice of double-heading the 10.35am ex-Paddington between Newton Abbot and Plymouth on summer Saturdays often resulted in two Kings working together, but on 23 August 1958 a glimpse of the new order was evident. No.6000 KING GEORGE V pilots the train engine, D601 ARK ROYAL - something which wasn't often seen as, usually, a steam locomotive was coupled inside the diesel so as to prevent smoke from entering the exhaust intakes. PHOTOGRAPH: PETER GRAY

passenger duties, working the 6.5pm Birmingham-Leamington local and return. Those workings were a prelude to its run on 28 April, when it hauled an SLS special on a circular Birmingham-Southall-Swindon-Birmingham trip (fare 30s/6d!), notching up a speed of 90mph *en route*.

As will be seen from the registers, the highest mileage achieved by a King was the 1,950,462 miles credited to No.6013. The lowest was the 1,511,174 miles of No.6006. Another point which will become evident in the registers is that, in common with various engines of other classes, a few of the Kings had their tenders changed after withdrawal, usable tenders being taken off and defective ones substituted. The exchange of tenders resulted in some angry letters from scrap dealers who had purchased an engine and tender from BR, the dealers complaining that they had not received the actual tender which they had bought. Peace was restored when BR pointed out that there was as much metal in a poor tender as there was in a good one.

Preservation

Three Kings escaped cutting up, and despite the early doubts the first to be saved was, appropriately enough, No.6000 KING GEORGE V. After it had been rejected by the GWR Museum at Swindon

for reasons of space, No.6000 and a rake of five Pullman coaches were purchased in 1968 by Messrs H.P.Bulmer of Hereford with the intention of using the ensemble as a mobile promotional department. No.6000 was restored to main line standards by Messrs.A.R.Adams of Newport (Mon) and arrived at Hereford on 30 October 1968. It was first steamed there on 13 November.

In 1971 No.6000 was given the go-ahead by BR for work on the main line, and in October of that year it undertook several special workings, thus effectively inaugurating an era of main line steam working which continues to this day. In BR days the Kings were prohibited west of Cardiff, but on four weekends in September 1987 - after the track between Cardiff and Carmarthen had been upgraded to accept heavy oil tank wagons - No.6000 belatedly broke new ground by working through to Carmarthen. No.6000 returned to Swindon in April 1990, and moved to the GWR Museum two years later pending a decision on its future use.

Of the two other Kings saved for preservation, No.6023 KING EDWARD II was initially sold for scrap to Messrs T.W.Ward of Briton Ferry, but as Kings were not then permitted west of Cardiff, Messrs Ward couldn't take delivery of their purchase and so the engine was sold instead to Woodham Brothers of Barry. It was res-

cued - almost intact - from Barry by Messrs Harveys of Bristol and delivered to Temple Meads station in December 1984, where it was ensconced adjacent to the parcels dock at the south end of Platform Nine. However, little restoration was done, and the engine was dispatched in pieces to the GWR Society at Didcot during February and March 1990. The remainder of the restoration work is now well in hand, although some £11,000 has been required to manufacture a new pair of driving wheels, the original ones having been cut away at Barry, in order to move the locomotive.

The third surviving King is No.6024 KING EDWARD I. It was purchased from Woodham Brothers by the Buckinghamshire Railway Centre, where it arrived in March 1973. It was restored to full working order by April 1989 and, with the mothballing of No.6000 in 1992, became the only King with main line authorisation from BR. No.6024 subsequently moved to Tyseley and then to the GWR Society headquarters at Didcot. After completing its main-line duties on the 'Welsh Dragon' on 1 March 1995, it was withdrawn from traffic and taken to a secure private site in the Midlands for an overhaul. It is expected to be back in action during the summer of 1996.

Chapter Five

THE REGISTERS

On 4 April 1958, No.6012 KING EDWARD VI enters Banbury with the 1.10pm Paddington-Wolverhampton. PHOTOGRAPH: R.C.RILEY

The following listings have been collated from the official Swindon registers. It is possible that the original documents included the occasional slip of the pen - witness the alleged allocation of No.6015 to Aylesbury in 1947, which has been discussed earlier - but, otherwise, accuracy can be virtually guaranteed. A few words of explanation regarding the presentation of the listings are in order.

Shed allocations: The Swindon allocation register for 1933 has long since been missing. The allocations for that year have, therefore, been deduced from works and repair records. Although that is a very reliable method, it fails to provide the exact day on which a move was made to the next depot.

'Wait': Many routine overhauls to locomotives were scheduled in advance, and a locomotive was often held at its running shed for the few days before the date of the works visit. Such instances are identified in the registers by the word 'wait'. The word 'wait' also crops up occasionally when an engine failed and had to be taken to the nearest running shed to await entry to Swindon Works. For example, No.6007 failed at Slough on 12.10.55 - the

registers show it 'waiting' at Slough shed on 13.10.55 and then entering Swindon Works on 14.10.55.

The period a locomotive spent waiting to enter the works was used for administrative purposes - once the word 'wait' had been entered against a locomotive it came under the jurisdiction of Swindon Works, even if it were physically at Laira, Old Oak or wherever. It was considered acceptable for up to 5% of GWR stock to be under the works's jurisdiction simultaneously, but some serious explaining had to be done by the Swindon management if more than 5% was booked against the works at any one time.

Types of repairs: The listings use the official repair code abbreviations which were in effect at the time. After 1928 these were: **G** - General; **H** - Heavy; **I** - Intermediate; **L** - Light; **R** - Running. After Nationalisation, BR adopted LMSR-style repair codes; they came into use on the Western Region in December 1948. They were: **HC** - Heavy casual; **HG** - Heavy General; **HI** - Heavy intermediate. **LC** - Light casual; **LI** - Light intermediate; **U** - Unclassified.

Places of repair: As a general guide, 'Factory' denotes works (such as Swindon and Newton Abbot etc), while 'Shops' denotes

During 1960, the engine which worked the down 'Cambrian Coast Express' usually returned to London from Shrewsbury with the 2.35pm from Birkenhead. On 4 June 1960 No.6003 KING GEORGE IV stands at Platform Seven of Shrewsbury Station waiting for the right away. PHOTOGRAPH: S.D. WAINWRIGHT

workshops at a running shed. The Swindon registers were sometimes confusing when it came to the categories of 'Factory' and 'Shop'. For example, they occasionally included references to 'Bath Road Factory' but, of course, those entries referred to the running shed workshops Bath Road had no 'locomotive works' in the accepted sense (at least, not since Bristol & Exeter Railway days!).

In the following listings, where neither 'Factory' nor 'Shop' were quoted in the original GWR documents, we have assumed that the repair in question was undertaken in the running shed itself.

Swindon/Swindon Stock: Some GWR locomotives arriving at Swindon for non-urgent repairs were recorded as entering 'Swindon Factory Pool'. That said, in the case of the Kings a prompt repair and an early return to traffic were usually essential, and so they rarely spent time languishing in 'Swindon F.Pool' (as it was written). Due to the erratic (and invariably brief) appearance of Kings in 'Swindon F.Pool', that designation has been completely omitted from our listings for the class. The 'Swindon Works' dates given here are for a locomotive's arrival at Swindon be it the date of entry into 'Swindon F.Pool' or the date of reception at the works themselves.

When a repair at Swindon Works had been completed, the engine usually spent a couple of days or so at Swindon Stock shed (a building almost alongside the running shed) before being dispatched to its designated home. The 'Swindon Stock' dates are shown here, albeit only until August/September 1944 when they ceased to be recorded in the official registers. After that date, the entire time spent at Swindon in 'Swindon F.Pool' (if applicable), in the Works and then in 'Swindon Stock' - are shown together as 'Swindon Factory'.... N.B. (*Due to the destruction of certain official documents, the 'Swindon Stock' dates prior to 1929 are unknown*).

Boilers: An asterisk (*) denotes that the boiler was brand new.

Tenders: Some 90% of tender record cards were destroyed by British Railways and, to make things even more complicated for the researcher, the pre-1929 cards for the Kings have been removed from the ledgers. However, research undertaken (by Mr Bill Peto) has revealed which tenders were built for each of the Kings when new, and details of tender changes from then can be gleaned from other official documents.

Having arrived at Wolverhampton with the 'Inter-City' on 20 July 1954, No.6000 KING GEORGE V is turned on the Stafford Road 'table.PHOTOGRAPH: BRIAN MORRISON

6000 KING GEORGE V
To stock: 29 June 1927

Summary of sheds:

30.6.27	Old Oak Common
9.11.39	Exeter
3.40	Newton Abbot
4.40	Exeter
14.6.41	Laira
9.41	Exeter
2.42	Laira
30.12.48	Bath Road
10.52	Old Oak Common

Engine history:

29.6.27	Swindon Factory
	ATC fitted
30.6.27	Old Oak Common
2.8.27	U.S.A.
28.11.27	Swindon Factory **L**
12.12.27	Old Oak Common
7.2.28	Swindon Factory **L**
16.2.28	Swindon Stock
21.2.28	Swindon Factory **L**
24.2.28	Old Oak Common
5.6.28	Swindon Factory **L**
28.6.28	Old Oak Common
21.2.29	Swindon Factory **I**
17.5.29	Swindon Stock
21.5.29	Old Oak Common
27.5.29	Swindon
	Tender change
12.6.29	Swindon Factory **L**
20.6.29	Swindon Stock
22.6.29	Old Oak Common
5.10.29	Swindon Factory **L**
7.11.29	Swindon Stock
14.11.29	Old Oak Common
22.11.29	Old Oak Common Shps
25.11.29	Old Oak Common
2.12.29	Swindon Factory **R**
7.12.29	Old Oak Common
15.3.30	Reading *(wait)*
18.3.30	Swindon Factory **L**
12.4.30	Swindon Stock
15.4.30	Old Oak Common
12.6.30	Old Oak Common Shps
21.6.30	Old Oak Common

22.10.30	Old Oak Common *(wait)*
28.10.30	Swindon Factory **G**
23.12.30	Swindon Stock
17.1.31	Old Oak Common
22.7.31	Swindon Factory **R**
23.7.31	Swindon Stock
24.7.31	Old Oak Common
31.12.31	Swindon Factory
1.1.32	Old Oak Common
12.3.32	Old Oak Common *(wait)*
1.4.32	Swindon Factory **G**
5.5.32	Swindon Stock
12.5.32	Old Oak Common
13.2.33	Swindon Factory **I**
30.3.33	Swindon Stock
4.33	Old Oak Common
21.11.33	Old Oak Common Shps **R**
6.12.33	Old Oak Common
4.4.34	Old Oak Common *(wait)*
9.4.34	Swindon Factory **G**
29.6.34	Old Oak Common
23.7.34	Swindon Factory **L**
31.7.34	Swindon Stock
9.8.34	Old Oak Common
11.1.35	Swindon Factory **L**
15.1.35	Swindon Stock
16.1.35	Old Oak Common
8.5.35	Swindon Factory **I**
28.6.35	Swindon Stock
6.7.35	Old Oak Common
26.9.35	Swindon Factory **L**
28.9.35	Old Oak Common
12.6.36	Swindon Factory **I**
10.7.36	Swindon Stock
19.7.36	Old Oak Common
2.12.36	Old Oak Common Shps **L**
16.12.36	Old Oak Common
9.1.37	Swindon Factory **L**
12.2.37	Swindon Stock
14.2.37	Old Oak Common
1.3.37	Swindon Factory **R**
11.3.37	Swindon Stock
14.3.37	Old Oak Common
20.4.37	Old Oak Common Shps **R**
5.5.37	Old Oak Common
29.11.37	Swindon Factory **G**
20.1.38	Swindon Stock
23.1.38	Old Oak Common

9.5.38	Swindon Factory **L**
13.5.38	Swindon Stock
15.5.38	Old Oak Common
20.5.38	Old Oak Comn Shps **R**
16.6.38	Old Oak Common
5.8.38	Swindon Factory **L**
16.8.38	Swindon Stock
20.8.38	Old Oak Common
1.2.39	Old Oak Common *(wait)*
2.2.39	Swindon Factory **I**
22.3.39	Swindon Stock
26.3.39	Old Oak Common
27.10.39	Newton Abbot F'ty **L**
9.11.39	Exeter
23.12.39	Swindon Factory **I**
19.2.40	Swindon Stock
2.3.40	Exeter
3.40	Newton Abbot
4.40	Exeter
22.3.41	Swindon Factory **G**
6.6.41	Swindon Stock
14.6.41	Laira
10.41	Exeter
2.42	Laira
23.3.42	Laira *(wait)*
7.4.42	Swindon Factory **L**
19.5.42	Swindon Stock
21.5.42	Laira
31.8.42	Laira Shops **R**
17.9.42	Laira
3.10.42	Bath Road *(wait)*
8.10.42	Swindon Factory **I**
21.11.42	Swindon Stock
25.11.42	Laira
8.3.43	Laira *(wait)*
19.3.43	Swindon Factory **L**
22.4.43	Swindon Stock
29.4.43	Laira
14.6.43	Laira Shops **R**
5.7.43	Laira
20.10.43	Old Oak Common **R**
18.11.43	Laira
26.11.43	Laira Shops **R**
7.1.44	Laira
19.1.44	Old Oak Common *(wait)*
2.2.44	Swindon Factory **L**
24.2.44	Swindon Stock
27.2.44	Laira

27.4.44	Laira Shops **R**
16.5.44	Laira
25.5.44	Laira *(wait)*
20.6.44	Swindon Factory **I**
5.8.44	Swindon Stock
7.8.44	Laira
4.10.44	Laira Shops **R**
24.10.44	Laira
1.1.45	Laira Shops **R**
2.2.45	Laira
9.4.45	Laira Shops **R**
27.4.45	Laira
9.6.45	Laira Shops **R**
25.6.45	Laira
3.7.45	Laira *(wait)*
12.7.45	Swindon Factory **L**
31.8.45	Laira
1.10.45	Laira *(wait)*
16.10.45	Swindon Factory **L**
26.11.45	Laira
17.1.46	Laira Shops **R**
9.2.46	Laira
8.3.46	Swindon Factory **G**
18.4.46	Laira
15.5.46	Laira Shops **R**
31.5.46	Laira
16.9.46	Laira Shops **R**
5.10.46	Laira
7.11.46	Laira Shops **R**
28.11.46	Laira
14.1.47	Laira *(wait)*
12.2.47	Swindon Factory **L**
21.3.47	Laira
5.6.47	Laira *(wait)*
20.6.47	Swindon Factory **L**
8.8.47	Laira
10.9.47	Newton Abbot F'ty **L**
10.9.47	Laira
30.12.47	Taunton *(wait)*
26.1.48	Swindon Factory **I**
1.3.48	Laira
16.3.48	Laira Shops **R**
24.3.48	Laira
17.4.48	Laira Shops **R**
5.5.48	Laira
8.12.48	Old Oak Common **R**
30.12.48	Bath Road
5.5.49	Bath Road *(wait)*

12.5.49	Swindon Factory **HG** (start)
20.6.49	Swindon Stock
23.6.49	Swindon Factory **HG** (finish)
27.6.49	Bath Road
9.8.49	Old Oak Comn Shps **LC**
28.8.49	Bath Road
20.10.49	Bath Road Shops **U**
6.11.49	Bath Road
17.11.49	Bath Road *(wait)*
25.11.49	Swindon Factory **LC**
21.12.49	Bath Road
15.2.50	Bath Road *(wait)*
16.2.50	Swindon Factory **U**
2.3.50	Bath Road
2.8.50	Bath Road Shops **U**
16.8.50	Bath Road
28.11.50	Swindon Factory **HI**
5.1.51	Bath Road
7.8.51	Swindon Factory **U**
21.8.51	Bath Road
15.11.51	Shrewsbury LM R **U**
21.12.51	Bath Road
25.2.52	Bath Road *(wait)*
5.3.52	Swindon Factory **HG**
10.4.52	Bath Road
10.52	Old Oak Common
6.2.53	Old Oak Common *(wait)*
20.2.53	Swindon Factory **LC**
27.4.53	Old Oak Common
13.10.53	Taunton Shops **U**
2.11.53	Old Oak Common
5.2.54	Bath Road Shops **U**
2.3.54	Old Oak Common
12.3.54	Swindon Factory **HI**
26.4.54	Old Oak Common
24.12.54	Laira *(wait)*
30.12.54	Laira Shops **LC**
27.1.55	Old Oak Common
9.2.55	Old Oak Common Shps **U**
25.2.55	Old Oak Common
4.8.55	Old Oak Common *(wait)*
6.8.55	Swindon Factory **HG**
13.9.55	Old Oak Common
30.1.56	Laira Shops **LC**
12.2.56	Old Oak Common
25.2.56	Swindon Factory **LC**
29.3.56	Old Oak Common
28.6.56	Taunton Shops **U**
4.8.56	Old Oak Common
26.9.56	Old Oak Common *(wait)*
17.10.56	Swindon Factory **HI**
4.12.56	Old Oak Common
12.7.57	Old Oak Common Shps **U**
25.7.57	Old Oak Common
24.3.58	Old Oak Common *(wait)*
28.3.58	Swindon Factory **HG**
24.6.58	Old Oak Common
5.7.59	Old Oak Common Shps **U**
23.7.59	Old Oak Common
8.10.59	Swindon Factory **HI**
4.12.59	Old Oak Common
14.12.59	Old Oak Common *(wait)*
16.12.59	Swindon Factory **HI**
23.12.59	Old Oak Common
7.9.60	Old Oak Common Shps **U**
26.9.60	Old Oak Common
3.1.61	Old Oak Common Shps **U**
3.2.61	Old Oak Common
31.5.61	Old Oak Common *(wait)*
5.6.61	Swindon Factory **LI**
22.8.61	Old Oak Common
8.9.61	Old Oak Common *(wait)*
22.9.61	Old Oak Common
21.6.62	Swindon Factory **U**
18.7.62	Old Oak Common
3.12.62	Wthdrwn (Alternatively stated to be 4.12.62)
8.68	To Messr Adams, Newport;
11.68	To Messrs Bulmers, Hereford;
4.90	To Swindon
3.92	To Swindon Museum

Boilers and mileages:

First	4662 *	
23.12.30	4663	(161,083)
5.5.32	4666	(250,145)
30.3.33	..	(316,938)
29.6.34	4680	(394,172)
28.6.35	..	(457,071)
10.7.36	..	(535,276)
20.1.38	4686	(632,713)
22.3.39	..	(705,343)
19.2.40	..	(767,980)
6.6.41	4675	(841,970)
21.11.42	..	(924,818)
5.8.44	..	(1,000,678)
18.4.46	4678	(1,078,179)
1.3.48	..	(1,160,947)
27.6.49	4677	(1,222,797)
5.1.51	4668	(1,293,688)
10.4.52	8600 *	(1,357,573)
26.4.54	..	(1,448,421)
13.9.55	8624	(1,532,795)
4.12.56	..	(1,596,025)
24.6.58	8610	(1,686,164)
4.12.59	8616	(1,763,428)
22.8.61	..	(1,850,242)
Final mileage:		1,910,424

Tenders:

First	2389
17.5.29	2430
27.5.29	2392
20.6.29	2400
10.30	2388
30.6.31	2556
5.5.32	2547
30.3.33	2556
19.2.40	2704
7.6.41	2726
21.11.42	2642
24.2.44	2704
15.6.44	2563
5.8.44	2847
31.8.45	2694
18.4.46	2606
1.3.48	2630
5.1.51	2759
22.5.54	2849
13.9.55	2870
4.12.56	2732
24.6.58	2743
11.7.59	2768
4.12.59	2909
28.1.61	2889
22.8.61	2727

.....................ooo..........................

6001 KING EDWARD VII
To stock: July 1927

Summary of sheds:

9.7.27	Old Oak Common
10.54	Stafford Road

Engine history:

7.27	Swindon Factory *ATC fitted*
9.7.27	Old Oak Common
22.8.27	Swindon Factory **L**
23.8.27	Old Oak Common
16.9.27	Swindon Factory **L**
23.9.27	Old Oak Common
5.3.28	Swindon Factory **L**
28.3.28	Old Oak Common
6.6.28	Swindon Factory **L**
2.7.28	Old Oak Common
28.8.28	Swindon Factory **L**
13.9.28	Old Oak Common
15.1.29	Old Oak Common *(wait)*
18.1.29	Swindon Factory **L**
23.2.29	Swindon Stock
1.3.29	Old Oak Common
1.5.29	Swindon Factory **L**
14.5.29	Swindon Stock
17.5.29	Old Oak Common
22.7.29	Swindon Factory **R**
27.7.29	Swindon Stock
1.8.29	Old Oak Common
1.8.29	Swindon Factory **L**
2.8.29	Old Oak Common
11.2.30	Swindon Factory **L**
28.2.30	Swindon Stock
4.3.30	Old Oak Common
10.3.30	Swindon Factory **H**
24.5.30	Swindon Stock

No.6001 KING EDWARD VII, newly fitted with a double chimney, is attended at Old Oak Common on 5 May 1956.PHOTOGRAPH: BRIAN MORRISON

31.5.30	Reading (repair ?)
5.6.30	Old Oak Common
15.8.30	Exeter (repair?) R
3.9.30	Old Oak Common
16.11.30	Old Oak Common Shps R
28.11.30	Old Oak Common
10.1.31	Swindon Factory L
9.2.31	Swindon Stock
14.2.31	Old Oak Common
11.4.31	Swindon Factory L
4.5.31	Swindon Stock
5.5.31	Old Oak Common
27.5.31	Swindon Factory L
5.6.31	Swindon Stock
20.6.31	Old Oak Common
6.1.32	Swindon Factory G
29.2.32	Swindon Stock
5.3.32	Old Oak Common
10.3.32	Swindon Factory
	Speedometer fitted
11.3.32	Old Oak Common
30.3.32	Swindon Factory
	Speedometer removed
1.4.32	Old Oak Common
12.4.32	Swindon Factory
	Speedometer refitted
19.4.32	Old Oak Common
18.5.32	Swindon Factory
	Speedometer adjusted
21.5.32	Old Oak Common
7.11.32	Old Oak Common Shps R
25.11.32	Old Oak Common
18.1.33	Swindon Factory I
10.3.33	Swindon Stock
3.33	Old Oak Common
13.11.33	Old Oak Common Shps R
25.11.33	Old Oak Common
5.12.33	Old Oak Common Shps R
20.12.33	Old Oak Common
17.1.34	Swindon Factory G
13.3.34	Swindon Stock
16.3.34	Old Oak Common
7.4.34	Swindon Factory
	For experiments
9.4.34	Swindon Stock
10.4.34	Old Oak Common
11.6.34	Swindon Factory L
20.6.34	Swindon Stock
22.6.34	Old Oak Common
27.2.35	Swindon Factory I
23.4.35	Swindon Stock
4.5.35	Old Oak Common
1.6.35	Swindon Factory L
14.6.35	Swindon Stock
22.6.35	Old Oak Common
28.4.36	Swindon Factory G
7.7.36	Swindon Stock
17.7.36	Old Oak Common
13.8.36	Swindon Factory L
21.8.36	Swindon Stock
24.8.36	Old Oak Common
16.10.36	Old Oak Common (wait)
27.10.36	Swindon Factory L
7.11.36	Swindon Stock
12.11.36	Old Oak Common
8.9.37	Old Oak Common Shps R
30.9.37	Old Oak Common
1.11.37	Swindon Factory I
10.12.37	Swindon Stock
21.12.37	Old Oak Common
22.8.38	Stafford Road F'cty L
9.9.38	Old Oak Common
22.11.38	Stafford Road F'cty L
28.11.38	Old Oak Common
29.11.38	Swindon Factory G
17.1.39	Swindon Stock
22.1.39	Old Oak Common
30.3.39	Swindon Factory L
6.5.39	Swindon Stock
11.5.39	Old Oak Common
2.10.39	Old Oak Common Shps R
25.10.39	Old Oak Common
28.12.39	Old Oak Common Shps R
3.2.40	Swindon Factory I
20.3.40	Swindon Stock
31.3.40	Old Oak Common
18.3.41	Old Oak Common (wait)
20.3.41	Swindon Factory I
6.5.41	Swindon Stock
8.5.41	Old Oak Common
22.7.41	Taunton Shops R
25.8.41	Old Oak Common
8.10.41	Reading (wait)
13.10.41	Swindon Factory R
29.10.41	Swindon Stock
30.10.41	Old Oak Common
8.7.42	Old Oak Common (wait)
13.7.42	Swindon Factory G
1.9.42	Swindon Stock
3.9.42	Old Oak Common
15.3.43	Old Oak Common (wait)
23.3.43	Swindon Factory L
3.5.43	Swindon Stock
7.5.43	Old Oak Common
28.7.43	Old Oak Common (wait)
29.7.43	Stafford Road F'cty L
12.8.43	Stafford Road (failed ?)
10.43	Old Oak Common
4.12.43	Old Oak Common (wait)
15.12.43	Swindon Factory I
21.1.44	Swindon Stock
28.1.44	Old Oak Common
19.3.44	Old Oak Common Shps R
29.4.44	Old Oak Common
24.5.44	Old Oak Common Shps L
1.7.44	Old Oak Common
11.8.44	Reading Shops R
23.8.44	Old Oak Common
5.2.45	Old Oak Common R
21.2.45	Old Oak Common
28.3.45	Old Oak Common Shps R
21.4.45	Old Oak Common
24.7.45	Old Oak Common R
29.8.45	Old Oak Common
13.12.45	Swindon Factory G
19.1.46	Old Oak Common
18.7.46	Old Oak Common Shps R
2.8.46	Old Oak Common
6.10.46	Reading Shops R
31.10.46	Old Oak Common
12.11.46	Old Oak Common Shps R
2.12.46	Old Oak Common
25.2.47	Swindon Factory I
29.3.47	Old Oak Common
31.10.47	Old Oak Common R
23.11.47	Old Oak Common
29.4.48	Old Oak Common (wait)
5.5.48	Swindon Factory G
21.6.48	Old Oak Common
10.4.49	Reading Shops U
5.5.49	Old Oak Common
20.5.49	Newton Abbot (wait)
25.5.49	Laira Shops U
1.7.49	Old Oak Common
21.7.49	Old Oak Common U
12.8.49	Old Oak Common
25.9.49	Old Oak Common Shps U
12.10.49	Old Oak Common
16.11.49	Old Oak Common (wait)
22.11.49	Swindon Factory HG
23.12.49	Old Oak Common
9.3.50	Old Oak Common U
23.3.50	Old Oak Common
23.10.50	Taunton Shops U
2.12.50	Old Oak Common
29.1.51	Old Oak Common (wait)
2.2.51	Swindon Factory HG
13.3.51	Old Oak Common
5.4.51	Swindon Factory HG
18.4.51	Old Oak Common
9.11.51	Bath Road Shops U
13.12.51	Old Oak Common
27.12.51	Old Oak Common Shps U
14.1.52	Old Oak Common
22.1.52	Newton Abbot (wait)
24.1.52	Taunton Shops U
12.2.52	Old Oak Common
16.4.52	Old Oak Common Shps U
8.5.52	Old Oak Common
10.7.52	Old Oak Common Shps U
28.7.52	Old Oak Common
13.8.52	Old Oak Common (wait)
20.8.52	Stafford Road F'cty U
28.8.52	Old Oak Common
1.9.52	Stafford Road F'cty U
18.9.52	Old Oak Common
13.11.52	Laira Shops U
13.1.53	Old Oak Common
26.1.53	Swindon Factory HG
9.3.53	Old Oak Common
16.4.53	Swindon Factory
	On test plant
26.6.53	Old Oak Common
23.7.53	Swindon Factory
	On test plant
20.8.53	Old Oak Common
18.1.54	Old Oak Common Shps U
5.2.54	Old Oak Common
3.8.54	Old Oak Common (wait)
10.8.54	Swindon Factory HI
29.9.54	Old Oak Common
10.54	Stafford Road
31.12.54	Stafford Road U
31.1.55	Stafford Road
14.3.55	Stafford Road F'cty LC
25.3.55	Stafford Road
20.5.55	Stafford Road U
25.5.55	Stafford Road
26.9.55	Stafford Road U
20.10.55	Stafford Road
12.11.55	Banbury (wait)
19.11.55	Swindon Factory HG
26.6.56	Stafford Road
30.6.56	Swindon Factory LC
14.9.56	Stafford Road
9.7.57	Stafford Road F'cty U
23.7.57	Stafford Road
21.8.57	Stafford Road U
9.9.57	Stafford Road
9.10.57	Stafford Road (wait)
17.10.57	Swindon Factory LI
3.12.57	Stafford Road
24.2.58	Stafford Road (wait)
3.3.58	Swindon Factory LC
24.5.58	Banbury (wait)
3.6.58	Stafford Road F'cty LC
26.6.58	Stafford Road
7.9.59	Swindon Factory LI
13.11.59	Stafford Road
25.4.60	Stafford Road U
11.5.60	Stafford Road
1.10.60	Stafford Road U
25.10.60	Stafford Road
27.3.61	Swindon Factory LI
25.5.61	Stafford Road
8.9.61	Stafford Road U
11.10.61	Stafford Road
18.3.62	Stafford Road U
14.4.62	Stafford Road
4.9.62	Wthdrwn (Alternatively stated to be 6.9.62)
17.12.62	Sold as scrap to Cox & Danks of Langley Green

Boilers and mileages:

First	4663 *	
24.5.30	4680	(149,916)
29.2.32	4667	(245,536)
10.3.33	..	(312,363)
13.3.34	4689	(373,315)
23.4.35	..	(445,779)
7.7.36	4671	(523,615)
10.12.37	..	(615,971)
17.1.39	4681	(694,050)
20.3.40	..	(768,219)
6.5.41	..	(851,048)
1.9.42	4664	(935,629)
21.1.44	..	(1,021,691)
19.1.46	4682	(1,122,133)
29.3.47	4694	(1,190,496)
21.6.48	4674	(1,263,590)
23.12.49	4669	(1,336,862)
12.3.51	4691	(1,418,165)
9.3.53	8608 *	(1,510,364)
29.9.54	..	(1,580,147)
24.2.56	8627	(1,629,809)
13.11.59	..	(1,796,436)
Final mileage:		1,878,179

Tenders:

First	2387
23.2.28	2399
14.5.29	2388
10.30	2400
23.4.35	2609
17.1.39	2548
6.5.39	2434
20.3.40	2554
6.5.41	2704
1.9.42	2665
7.11.42	2629
19.1.46	2800
21.6.48	2772
23.12.49	2710
12.3.51	2728
30.1.54	4015
29.9.54	2695
24.2.56	2829
14.9.57	2742
22.2.58	2556
14.5.58	2742
28.6.58	2646
13.11.59	2809
25.5.61	2838

........................ooo........................

6002 KING WILLIAM IV
To stock: July 1927

Summary of sheds:

22.7.27	Laira
11.1.38	Newton Abbot
5.38	Laira
11.39	Exeter
5.6.40	Laira
7.40	Exeter
8.40	Laira
26.9.41	Exeter
28.1.42	Laira
12.48	Stafford Road
7.50	Old Oak Common
22.6.59	Laira
13.9.60	Old Oak Common
15.6.62	Stafford Road

Engine history:

9.7.27	Swindon Factory
	ATC fitted
22.7.27	Laira
25.8.27	Swindon Factory L
26.8.27	Laira
30.9.27	Swindon Factory L
5.10.27	Laira
14.11.28	Swindon Factory L
10.12.28	Laira
15.2.29	Newton Abbot F'cty R

A fine view of the more-stylish elliptical pattern double chimney - No.6002 KING WILLIAM IV at Acocks Green with the 'Cambrian Coast' in 1961. PHOTOGRAPH: MICHAEL MENSING

25.2.29	Laira
9.4.29	Laira Shops **L**
16.4.29	Laira
18.4.29	Swindon Factory **H**
13.6.29	Swindon Stock
20.6.29	Laira
11.12.29	Laira Shops **L**
20.12.29	Laira
19.3.30	Laira Shops **L**
28.3.30	Laira
28.4.30	Laira *(wait)*
7.5.30	Swindon Factory **L**
23.6.30	Swindon Stock
27.6.30	Laira
3.12.30	Newton Abbot F'cty **R**
18.12.30	Laira
3.3.31	Laira *(wait)*
4.3.31	Swindon Factory **G**
23.4.31	Swindon Stock
1.5.31	Laira
5.5.31	Swindon Factory **R**
22.5.31	Laira
4.4.32	Swindon Factory **L**
29.4.32	Swindon Stock
7.5.32	Laira
14.6.32	Swindon Factory **L**
21.6.32	Swindon Stock
23.6.32	Laira
3.8.32	Laira Shops **R**
25.8.32	Laira
17.10.32	Swindon Factory **I**
6.12.32	Swindon Stock
10.12.32	Laira
31.3.33	Swindon Factory **L**
1.3.33	Laira
20.7.33	Laira Shops **R**
3.8.33	Laira
12.1.34	Laira Shops **R**
29.1.34	Laira
7.2.34	Swindon Factory **G**
10.4.34	Swindon Stock
19.4.34	Laira
8.10.34	Swindon Factory **L**
6.11.34	Swindon Stock
7.11.34	Laira
14.11.34	Newton Abbot F'cty **R**
27.11.34	Laira
21.1.35	Laira Shops **R**
6.2.35	Laira
5.4.35	Laira *(wait)*
8.5.35	Swindon Factory **I**
25.6.35	Swindon Stock
6.7.35	Laira
7.11.35	Laira Shops **R**
25.11.35	Laira
21.7.36	Swindon Factory **L**
24.7.36	Swindon Stock
26.7.36	Laira (or Old Oak?)
4.8.36	Old Oak Common Shps **R**
28.8.36	Laira (or Old Oak?)
22.9.36	Swindon Factory **G**
2.11.36	Swindon Stock
9.11.36	Laira
12.36	Newton Abbot F'cty
12.36	Laira
9.9.37	Laira Shops **R**
24.9.37	Laira
16.10.37	Old Oak Common *(wait)*
13.11.37	Swindon Factory **I**
7.1.38	Swindon Stock
11.1.38	Newton Abbot
28.2.38	Newton Abbot *(wait)*
7.3.38	Swindon Factory **L**
17.3.38	Swindon Stock
23.3.38	Newton Abbot
5.38	Laira
5.9.38	Laira *(wait)*
7.9.38	Swindon Factory **L**
8.10.38	Swindon Stock
14.10.38	Laira
8.3.39	Swindon Factory **I**
28.4.39	Swindon Stock
6.5.39	Laira
5.7.39	Swindon Factory **L**
13.7.39	Swindon Stock
14.7.39	Laira
11.39	Exeter
7.2.40	Old Oak Common Shps **L**
9.3.40	Exeter
13.4.40	Swindon Factory **I**
28.5.40	Swindon Stock
5.6.40	Laira
7.40	Exeter
8.40	Laira
8.4.41	Laira Shops **R**
22.4.41	Laira
21.6.41	Laira *(wait)*
23.6.41	Swindon Factory **G**
19.9.41	Swindon Stock
26.9.41	Exeter
9.1.42	Exeter Shops **L**
25.1.42	Exeter (possibly idle?)
28.1.42	Laira
22.4.42	Laira *(wait)*
6.5.42	Swindon Factory **L**
4.6.42	Swindon Stock
7.6.42	Laira
22.7.42	Laira *(wait)*
27.7.42	Swindon Factory **L**
28.8.42	Swindon Stock
30.8.42	Laira
16.11.42	Laira Shops **R**
1.12.42	Laira
3.5.43	Swindon Factory **I**
8.6.43	Swindon Stock
13.6.43	Laira
23.9.43	Laira *(wait)*
27.9.43	Swindon Factory **L**
23.10.43	Swindon Stock
29.10.43	Laira
21.2.44	Laira *(wait)*
8.3.44	Swindon Factory **L**
21.4.44	Swindon Stock
29.4.44	Laira
16.10.44	Laira *(wait)*
24.10.44	Swindon Factory **I**
19.12.44	Laira
20.2.45	Laira Shops **R**
12.3.45	Laira
24.3.45	Swindon Factory **L**
18.4.45	Laira
24.10.45	Newton Abbot *(wait)*
9.11.45	Swindon Factory **L**
11.12.45	Laira
1.46	Newton Abbot *(wait)*
8.2.46	Swindon Factory **L**
9.3.46	Laira
22.3.46	Laira Shops **R**
13.4.46	Laira
8.5.46	Laira *(wait)*
15.4.46	Swindon Factory **G**
22.6.46	Laira
1.7.46	Laira Shops **R**
26.7.46	Laira
28.10.46	Laira Shops **R**
15.11.46	Laira
20.1.47	Laira Shops **R**
9.2.47	Laira
7.4.47	Laira Shops **R**
23.4.47	Laira
15.5.47	Laira Shops **R**
18.5.47	Laira
27.8.47	Laira Shops **R**
27.9.47	Laira
5.11.47	Laira *(wait)*
18.11.47	Swindon Factory **I**
1.1.48	Laira
4.3.48	Laira Shops **R**
18.3.48	Laira
6.5.48	Swindon Factory
7.5.48	Laira
12.48	Stafford Road
17.1.49	Stafford Road F'cty **LC**
27.1.49	Stafford Road
16.4.49	Stafford Road **LC**
26.4.49	Stafford Road
6.9.49	Old Oak Common *(wait)*
13.9.49	Swindon Factory **HG**
21.10.49	Stafford Road
7.50	Old Oak Common
6.9.50	Old Oak Common Shps **U**
25.9.50	Old Oak Common
6.3.51	Old Oak Common *(wait)*
13.3.51	Swindon Factory **HI**
23.4.51	Old Oak Common
25.10.51	Old Oak Common *(wait)*
29.10.51	Swindon Factory **LC**
23.11.51	Old Oak Common
19.1.52	Old Oak Common *(wait)*
20.2.52	Swindon Factory **HC**
27.3.52	Old Oak Common
19.11.52	Old Oak Common *(wait)*
27.11.52	Swindon Factory **HI**
2.1.53	Old Oak Common
20.1.53	Old Oak Common *(wait)*
23.1.53	Swindon Factory **U**
10.2.53	Old Oak Common
27.8.53	Old Oak Common *(wait)*
8.10.53	Swindon Factory **LC**
10.12.53	Old Oak Common
31.12.53	Leamington Shops **U**
4.1.54	Old Oak Common
23.3.54	Old Oak Common *(wait)*
2.4.54	Swindon Factory **HC**
20.5.54	Old Oak Common
9.8.54	Taunton Shops **U**
2.9.54	Old Oak Common
29.10.54	Old Oak Common *(wait)*
5.11.54	Swindon Factory **HI**
16.12.54	Old Oak Common
1.6.55	Old Oak Common *(wait)*
17.6.55	Swindon Factory **LC**
28.7.55	Old Oak Common
5.9.55	Old Oak Common *(wait)*
8.9.55	Swindon Factory **LC**
6.10.55	Old Oak Common
31.10.55	Old Oak Common *(wait)*
3.11.55	Swindon Factory **HG**
1.3.56	Old Oak Common
23.5.56	Swindon Factory **U**
26.5.56	Old Oak Common
12.2.57	Old Oak Common **U**
6.3.57	Old Oak Common
15.4.57	Laira Shops **U**
16.5.57	Old Oak Common
12.9.57	Old Oak Common *(wait)*
20.9.57	Swindon Factory **HI**
14.11.57	Old Oak Common
18.11.57	Swindon Factory **U**
4.12.57	Old Oak Common
2.6.58	Westbury (wait)
6.6.58	Swindon Factory **LC**
3.7.58	Old Oak Common
20.4.59	Exeter *(wait)*
24.4.59	Swindon Factory **HG**
22.6.59	Laira
6.4.60	Laira Shops **U**
22.4.60	Laira
11.8.60	Laira Shops **U**

Date	Shed	
4.9.60	Laira	
13.9.60	Old Oak Common	
26.9.60	Stafford Road	U
30.9.60	Old Oak Common	
15.11.60	Old Oak Common	U
8.12.60	Old Oak Common	
10.12.60	Swindon Factory	LI
2.2.61	Old Oak Common	
18.5.61	Old Oak Common Shps	U
2.6.61	Old Oak Common	
16.9.61	Stafford Road	U
21.10.61	Old Oak Common	
14.11.61	Old Oak Common Shps	U
4.12.61	Old Oak Common	
14.2.62	Old Oak Common	HC
15.6.62	Stafford Road	
20.6.62	Stafford Road	U
9.8.62	Stafford Road	
7.9.62	Wthdrwn (alternatively stated to be 21.9.62)	
28.1.63	Sold as scrap to Cox & Danks of Langley Green Both nameplates had been reserved for private buyers.	

Boilers and mileages:

Date	Boiler	Mileage
First	4664 *	
13.6.29	..	(100,583)
23.4.31	4678	(211,757)
6.12.32	..	(295,963)
10.4.34	4667	(360,747)
25.6.35	..	(432,082)
2.11.36	4678	(521,571)
7.1.38	..	(607,901)
28.4.39	..	(682,146)
28.5.40	..	(747,156)
19.9.41	4676	(830,177)
8.6.43	..	(934,205)
19.12.44	..	(1,015,460)
22.6.46	4693	(1,088,623)
1.1.48	4663	(1,171,565)
21.10.49	4665	(1,267,256)
23.4.51	4693	(1,342,339)
27.3.52	4671	(1,389,101)
2.1.53	4690	(1,432,483)

Date	Boiler	Mileage
20.5.54	4691	(1,492,051)
16.12.54	4661	(1,518,485)
1.3.56	8626 *	(1,565,334)
14.11.57	..	(1,659,451)
22.6.59	8607	(1,746,876)
2.2.61	..	(1,836,406)
Final mileage:		1,891,952

Tenders:

Date	Tender
First	2388
25.2.29	2403
23.6.30	2398
12.11.37	2391 #
28.4.39	2442
28.5.40	2743
19.9.41	2642
14.6.42	2790
8.6.43	2776
19.12.44	2742
23.11.51	2694
2.1.53	2763
20.5.54	2710
9.10.54	2905
1.3.56	2838
14.11.57	2786
18.4.59	2613
22.6.59	2386
30.12.61	2728
15.6.62	2841
11.8.62	2818

Swindon registers state that this change was made at Ebbw Junction. We have doubts.

.........................ooo.......................

6003 KING GEORGE IV
To stock: July 1927

Summary of sheds:

Date	Shed
22.7.27	Old Oak Common
13.9.60	Canton
15.2.62	Old Oak Common

Engine history:

7.27	Swindon Factory	
	ATC fitted	
9.7.27	Swindon Stock	
22.7.27	Old Oak Common	
10.8.27	Swindon Factory	L
18.8.27	Old Oak Common	
24.8.27	Old Oak Common Shps	L
25.8.27	Old Oak Common	
5.10.27	Swindon Factory	L
13.10.27	Old Oak Common	
16.2.28	Swindon Factory	L
21.2.28	Old Oak Common	
11.6.28	Swindon Factory	L
23.6.28	Old Oak Common	
6.7.28	Swindon Factory	L
10.7.28	Old Oak Common	
22.9.28	Swindon Factory	L
13.10.28	Old Oak Common	
8.12.28	Swindon Factory	L
26.1.29	Old Oak Common	
11.4.29	Swindon Factory	R
16.4.29	Old Oak Common	
23.5.29	Swindon Factory	H
27.6.29	Swindon Stock	
12.7.29	Old Oak Common	
20.2.30	Swindon Factory	H
28.4.30	Swindon Stock	
2.5.30	Old Oak Common	
25.7.30	Swindon Factory	L
22.8.30	Swindon Stock	
27.8.30	Old Oak Common	
15.1.31	Swindon Factory	L
16.2.31	Swindon Stock	
21.2.31	Old Oak Common	
3.6.31	Swindon Factory	L
4.6.31	Swindon Stock	
6.6.31	Old Oak Common	
25.11.31	Swindon Factory	I
29.1.32	Swindon Stock	
6.2.32	Old Oak Common	
13.6.32	Swindon Factory	L
14.6.32	Old Oak Common	
27.10.32	Laira Shops	R
16.11.32	Old Oak Common	
25.1.33	Swindon Factory	G

21.3.33	Swindon Stock	
3.33	Old Oak Common	
16.1.34	Old Oak Common	(wait)
30.1.34	Swindon Factory	I
21.3.34	Swindon Stock	
28.3.34	Old Oak Common	
3.12.34	Swindon Factory	L
27.12.34	Swindon Stock	
4.1.35	Old Oak Common	
13.2.35	Swindon Factory	I
13.4.35	Swindon Stock	
18.4.35	Old Oak Common	
10.1.36	Swindon Factory	L
30.1.36	Swindon Stock	
1.2.36	Old Oak Common	
16.2.36	Old Oak Common	(wait)
4.3.36	Swindon Factory	L
23.3.36	Old Oak Common	
3.4.36	Old Oak Common	(wait)
6.4.36	Swindon Factory	G
16.5.36	Swindon Stock	
21.5.36	Old Oak Common	
14.10.36	Taunton	(repair)
10.36	Old Oak Common	
2.3.37	Old Oak Common Shps	R
22.3.37	Old Oak Common	
6.4.37	Swindon Factory	I
26.5.37	Swindon Stock	
30.5.37	Old Oak Common	
30.8.37	Old Oak Common Shps	R
23.9.37	Old Oak Common	
22.1.38	Old Oak Common	(wait)
31.3.38	Swindon Factory	L
17.2.38	Swindon Stock	
20.2.38	Old Oak Common	
7.5.38	Swindon Factory	I
1.7.38	Swindon Stock	
4.7.38	Old Oak Common	
3.8.38	Old Oak Common	(wait)
4.8.38	Swindon Factory	L
16.8.38	Swindon Stock	
21.8.38	Old Oak Common	
27.1.39	Old Oak Common	(wait)
28.1.39	Swindon Factory	L
13.2.39	Swindon Stock	
16.2.39	Old Oak Common	
22.5.39	Swindon Factory	G
6.7.39	Swindon Stock	
23.7.39	Old Oak Common	
22.12.39	Swindon Factory	L
12.1.40	Swindon Stock	
18.1.40	Old Oak Common	
6.9.40	Swindon Factory	I
21.10.40	Swindon Stock	
25.10.40	Old Oak Common	
7.7.41	Old Oak Common Shps	R
25.7.41	Old Oak Common	
12.10.41	Old Oak Common	(wait)
13.10.41	Swindon Factory	I
2.12.41	Swindon Stock	
5.12.41	Old Oak Common	
30.4.42	Old Oak Common Shps	R
23.5.42	Old Oak Common	
26.1.43	Swindon Factory	G
20.3.43	Swindon Stock	
28.3.43	Old Oak Common	
31.1.44	Laira	(wait)
22.2.44	Swindon Factory	L
31.3.44	Swindon Stock	
5.4.44	Old Oak Common	
4.7.44	Old Oak Common Shps	R
1.8.44	Old Oak Common	
27.10.44	Old Oak Common Shps	R
31.10.44	Old Oak Common	
21.3.45	Taunton	(wait)
24.3.45	Swindon Factory	I
12.5.45	Swindon Stock	
25.1.46	Westbury	(wait)
28.1.46	Swindon Factory	L

Having brought in the down 'Cambrian Coast' to Shrewsbury on 4 June 1960, No.6003 KING GEORGE IV has been uncoupled and the lamps changed. The engine will reverse into Coleham shed as soon as the train has departed (in the same direction) for the rest of its journey to Aberystwyth.
PHOTOGRAPH: S.D.WAINWRIGHT

1.3.46	Old Oak Common	18.9.56	Old Oak Common Shps **U**
6.8.46	Laira Shops **R**	18.10.56	Old Oak Common
22.8.46	Old Oak Common	25.11.56	Old Oak Common Shps **U**
22.9.46	Reading Shops **R**	20.12.56	Old Oak Common
12.10.46	Swindon Factory **G**	31.1.57	Reading *(wait)*
18.11.46	Old Oak Common	1.2.57	Swindon Factory **HI**
25.11.46	Laira Shops **R**	4.4.57	Old Oak Common
6.12.46	Old Oak Common	9.10.57	Old Oak Common Shps **U**
16.3.47	Old Oak Common Shps **R**	29.10.57	Old Oak Common
30.4.47	Old Oak Common	17.4.58	Old Oak Common *(wait)*
24.6.47	Old Oak Common Shps **R**	3.5.58	Swindon Factory **HI**
8.7.47	Old Oak Common	30.7.58	Old Oak Common
9.10.47	Old Oak Common Shps **R**	7.10.59	Old Oak Common Shps **U**
23.10.47	Old Oak Common	22.10.59	Old Oak Common
13.1.48	Old Oak Common *(wait)*	18.12.59	Swindon Factory **HG**
30.1.48	Swindon Factory **I**	30.3.60	Old Oak Common
10.3.48	Old Oak Common	13.9.60	Canton
18.8.48	Old Oak Common Shps **R**	14.1.61	St.Philips Marsh *(wait)*
9.5.48	Old Oak Common	1.2.61	Swindon Factory **LC**
26.6.48	Taunton Shops **R**	19.5.61	Canton
13.7.48	Old Oak Common	28.10.61	Swindon **U**
15.8.48	Old Oak Common Shps **L**	12.11.61	Canton
13.9.48	Old Oak Common	17.1.62	Old Oak Comn Shps **LC**
12.11.48	Old Oak Common Shps **R**	15.2.62	Old Oak Common
26.11.48	Old Oak Common	10.4.62	In store (Old Oak?)
14.1.49	Taunton Shops **U**	**25.6.62**	Wthdrwn (alternatively
19.1.49	Old Oak Common		stated to be 19.6.62)
27.1.49	Old Oak Common Shps **U**	17.7.62	Swindon Factory
24.2.49	Old Oak Common	8.9.62(w/e)	Cut up at Swindon
24.6.49	Old Oak Common *(wait)*		
19.7.49	Swindon Factory **LC**	**Boilers and mileages:**	
17.8.49	Old Oak Common	First	4665 *
19.10.49	Old Oak Common *(wait)*	27.6.29	..	(106,236)
31.10.49	Swindon Factory **LC**	28.4.30	4682	(152,100)
2.12.49	Old Oak Common	29.1.32	..	(252,039)
16.1.50	Taunton Shops **U**	21.3.33	4671	(321,058)
16.2.50	Old Oak Common	21.3.34	..	(384,855)
27.2.50	Old Oak Common *(wait)*	13.4.35	..	(451,971)
2.3.50	Swindon Factory **HG**	16.5.36	4684	(519,995)
13.4.50	Old Oak Common	26.5.37	..	(591,551)
14.2.51	Old Oak Common *(wait)*	1.7.38	..	(666,202)
21.2.51	Swindon Factory **HI**	6.7.39	4691	(727,569)
3.4.51	Old Oak Common	21.10.40	..	(813,900)
4.9.51	Taunton Shops **U**	2.12.41	..	(896,868)
2.10.51	Old Oak Common	20.3.43	4680	(981,894)
10.10.51	Old Oak Common Shps **U**	12.5.45	..	(1,101,381)
5.11.51	Old Oak Common	18.11.46	4676	(1,195,108)
30.11.51	Laira Shops **U**	10.3.48	4664	(1,251,678)
6.12.51	Old Oak Common	13.4.50	4674	(1,330,692)
25.1.52	Old Oak Common *(wait)*	3.4.51	..	(1,391,543)
1.2.52	Swindon Factory **LC**	28.10.52	8604 *	(1,469,386)
5.3.52	Old Oak Common	2.2.54	..	(1,527,590)
3.9.52	Newton Abbot *(wait)*	19.5.55	8614	(1,594,701)
12.9.52	Swindon Factory **HG**	4.4.57	4699	(1,673,746)
28.10.52	Old Oak Common	30.7.58	8619	(1,745,987)
6.11.52	Reading Shops **U**	30.3.60	8602	(1,828,621)
1.12.52	Old Oak Common	Final mileage:		1,920,479
9.9.53	Old Oak Common Shps **U**			
25.9.53	Old Oak Common	**Tenders:**		
16.11.53	Laira *(wait)*	First	2391	
4.12.53	Swindon Factory **HI**	28.4.30	2393	
2.2.54	Old Oak Common	16.2.31	2428	
6.9.54	Old Oak Common **U**	29.1.32	2425	
7.10.54	Old Oak Common	11.8.33	2442	
19.2.55	Laira Shops **U**	27.12.34	2547	
24.3.55	Old Oak Common	6.2.37	2402	
31.3.55	Old Oak Common *(wait)*	7.1.39	2557	
14.4.55	Swindon Factory **HI**	21.10.40	2772	
19.5.55	Old Oak Common	2.12.41	2815	
15.6.55	Laira Shops **U**	31.3.44	2726	
20.7.55	Old Oak Common	12.5.45	2788	
28.9.55	Old Oak Common Shps **U**	18.11.46	2905	
13.10.55	Old Oak Common	22.3.47	2733	
20.1.56	Old Oak Comn Shps **LC**	28.10.52	2849	
10.2.56	Old Oak Common	2.2.54	2649	
6.4.56	Swindon Factory **LC**	9.10.54	2883	
17.5.56	Old Oak Common	26.3.55	2630 #	
28.5.56	Taunton Shops **U**	26.3.55	2612 #	
2.7.56	Old Oak Common	19.5.55	2776	

17.5.56	2531
4.4.57	2565
30.11.57	2717
30.7.58	2632
29.12.59	2901
30.3.60	2864
19.5.61	2875

Probably explained by
No.2630 being returned
to Swindon for essential
repairs.

........................ooo........................

6004 KING GEORGE III
To stock: July 1927

Summary of sheds:

25.8.27	Laira
10.41	Exeter
1.42	Laira
12.48	Stafford Road
3.54	Laira
18.12.59	Old Oak Common
13.9.60	Canton

Engine history:

16.7.27	Swindon Factory
	ATC fitted
25.8.27	Laira
27.8.27	Swindon Factory **L**
1.9.27	Laira
20.9.27	Swindon Factory **L**
22.9.27	Laira
21.11.27	Laira Shops **R**
28.11.27	Laira
9.4.28	Swindon Factory **L**
29.5.28	Laira
11.8.28	Swindon Factory **L**
22.8.28	Laira
28.11.28	Swindon Factory **L**
29.12.28	Laira
6.2.29	Laira Shops **R**
19.2.29	Laira
17.4.29	Swindon Factory **H**
21.6.29	Swindon Stock
22.6.29	Laira
29.10.29	Swindon Factory **L**
18.11.29	Swindon Stock
21.11.29	Laira
28.3.30	Laira Shops **L**
3.4.30	Laira
5.4.30	Swindon Factory **L**
14.4.30	Swindon Stock
17.4.30	Laira
28.6.30	Laira *(wait)*
30.6.30	Swindon Factory **R**
12.7.30	Swindon Stock
15.7.30	Laira
13.8.30	Newton Abbot *(wait)*
14.8.30	Swindon Factory **L**
15.8.30	Swindon Stock
19.8.30	Laira
12.11.30	Laira Shops **L**
12.12.30	Laira
30.12.30	Newton Abbot F'cty **L**
9.1.31	Laira
2.2.31	Swindon Factory **L**
10.3.31	Swindon Stock
14.3.31	Laira
15.4.31	Swindon Factory **I**
8.6.31	Swindon Stock
13.6.31	Laira
2.9.31	Swindon Factory **L**
10.9.31	Swindon Stock
12.9.31	Laira
16.12.31	Laira *(wait)*
31.12.31	Swindon Factory **G**
11.2.32	Swindon Stock

17.2.32	Newton Abbot
3.32	Laira
12.4.32	Laira Shops **R**
30.4.32	Laira
9.6.32	Laira Shops **R**
7.7.32	Laira
23.3.33	Swindon Factory **L**
27.3.33	Laira
2.5.33	Swindon Factory **I**
3.7.33	Swindon Stock
7.33	Laira
14.5.34	Swindon Factory **I**
6.7.34	Swindon Stock
19.7.34	Laira
24.9.34	Swindon Factory **L**
5.10.34	Swindon Stock
13.10.34	Laira
8.3.35	Laira Shops **R**
23.3.35	Laira
20.7.35	Swindon Factory **L**
1.8.35	Swindon Stock
3.8.35	Laira
3.10.35	Swindon Factory **G**
18.11.35	Swindon Stock
11.35	Laira
5.12.35	Swindon Factory **L**
18.12.35	Swindon Stock
20.12.35	Laira
18.4.36	Laira Shops **R**
4.5.36	Laira
26.9.36	Laira Shops **R**
14.10.36	Laira
16.2.37	Swindon Factory **I**
2.4.37	Swindon Stock
6.4.37	Laira
28.4.37	Swindon Factory **L**
13.5.37	Swindon Stock
17.5.37	Laira
21.9.37	Swindon Factory **L**
2.10.37	Swindon Stock
10.10.37	Newton Abbot
11.11.37	Swindon Factory **L**
3.12.37	Swindon Stock
11.12.37	Laira
6.1.38	Laira Shops **R**
22.1.38	Laira
1.4.38	Laira Shops **R**
18.4.38	Laira
28.6.38	Swindon Factory **I**
30.8.38	Swindon Stock
12.9.38	Laira
2.3.39	Swindon Factory **L**
5.4.39	Swindon Stock
6.4.39	Laira
13.6.39	Swindon Factory **L**
13.7.39	Swindon Stock
25.7.39	Laira
5.12.39	Swindon Factory **I**
30.1.40	Swindon Stock
13.2.40	Laira
12.4.40	Swindon Factory **L**
6.5.40	Swindon Stock
12.5.40	Laira
18.7.40	Swindon Factory **L**
13.8.40	Swindon Stock
17.8.40	Laira
3.4.41	Swindon Factory **G**
17.6.41	Swindon Stock
28.6.41	Laira
10.41	Exeter
1.42	Laira
19.3.42	Old Oak Common Shps **R**
5.4.42	Laira
14.4.42	Laira Shops **R**
1.5.42	Laira
16.9.42	Swindon Factory **I**
6.11.42	Swindon Stock
10.11.42	Laira
27.11.42	Laira Shops **R**

6.11.42	..	(877,942)
14.3.44	..	(962,721)
28.9.45	4674	(1,049,240)
14.12.46	4661	(1,125,654)
12.11.48	..	(1,222,949)
23.9.49	4675	(1,261,993)
22.9.50	4685	(1,309,779)
12.2.52	4694	(1,375,860)
23.1.53	4663	(1,426,160)
9.9.53	8612 *	(1,452,811)
19.5.55	8623	(1,533,852)
21.11.56	..	(1,621,595)
24.4.58	4696	(1,727,016)
18.12.59	8620	(1,820,789)
3.8.61	8624	(1,871,922)
Final mileage:		1,917,258

The 11am ex-Paddington, hauled by No.6004 KING GEORGE III, sets a cracking pace near Westbury on Sunday 22 July 1956. PHOTOGRAPH: R.C.RILEY

Tenders:

First	2393
6.2.29	2401
21.6.29	2391
14.4.30	2413
12.7.30	2392
10.3.31	2393
8.6.31	2425
11.2.32	2399
19.11.32	2434
6.7.34	2440
5.4.39	2609
17.6.41	2707
6.11.42	2695
14.3.44	2788
14.10.44	2743
2.11.46	2759
12.11.48	2629
8.9.54	2612
19.5.56	2398
21.11.56	2870
10.8.57	2913
24.4.58	2868
6.9.58	2789
18.12.59	2875
22.4.61	2846
3.8.61	2813

........................ooo........................

6005 KING GEORGE II
To stock: July 1927

Summary of sheds:

6.8.27	Old Oak Common
8.30	Stafford Road
3.5.34	Old Oak Common
6.34	Stafford Road
7.9.62	Old Oak Common

Engine history:

7.27	Swindon Factory
	ATC fitted
6.8.27	Old Oak Common
23.8.27	Swindon Factory **L**
24.8.27	Old Oak Common
21.9.27	Old Oak Common Shps **L**
27.9.27	Old Oak Common
5.1.28	Swindon Factory **L**
3.2.28	Old Oak Common
1.5.28	Swindon Factory **L**
30.5.28	Old Oak Common
4.6.28	Swindon Factory **L**
20.6.28	Old Oak Common
29.8.28	Newton Abbot Shops
9.28	Old Oak Common
3.1.29	Swindon Factory **L**
20.3.29	Swindon Stock
26.3.29	Old Oak Common
1.6.29	Swindon Factory **L**
20.6.29	Swindon Stock
24.6.29	Old Oak Common

30.11.42	Laira
8.1.43	Taunton Shops **R**
28.1.43	Laira
5.7.43	Laira Shops **R**
15.7.43	Laira
6.9.43	Laira Shops **R**
25.9.43	Laira
8.2.44	Swindon Factory **I**
14.3.44	Swindon Stock
22.3.44	Laira
16.8.44	Laira *(wait)*
5.9.44	Swindon Factory **L**
14.10.44	Laira
24.12.44	Laira Shops **R**
29.1.45	Laira
18.4.45	Laira Shops **R**
2.5.45	Laira
3.7.45	Laira Shops **R**
20.7.45	Laira
28.7.45	Laira *(wait)*
1.8.45	Swindon Factory **G**
28.9.45	Laira
8.4.46	Laira Shops **R**
30.4.46	Laira
7.10.46	Laira Shops **R**
1.11.46	Laira *(wait)*
2.11.46	Swindon Factory **I**
14.12.46	Laira
20.2.47	Laira Shops **R**
11.3.47	Laira
8.5.47	Laira Shops **R**
24.5.47	Laira
22.9.47	Laira Shops **R**
8.10.47	Laira
19.11.47	Laira Shops **R**
5.12.47	Laira
31.12.47	Reading Shops **R**
21.2.48	Laira
18.3.48	Laira Shops **R**
8.4.48	Laira
26.4.48	Newton Abbot F'cty
	(Tender work)
29.4.48	Laira
10.8.48	Laira Shops **R**
28.8.48	Laira
24.9.48	Reading *(wait)*

6.10.48	Swindon Factory **I**
12.11.48	Laira
12.48	Stafford Road
21.6.49	Stafford Road **U**
5.7.49	Stafford Road
15.8.49	Stafford Road *(wait)*
25.8.49	Swindon Factory **HC**
23.9.49	Stafford Road
21.8.50	Swindon Factory **HG**
22.9.50	Stafford Road
24.7.51	Stafford Road **LC**
13.9.51	Stafford Road
4.10.51	Stafford Road **U**
12.10.51	Stafford Road
7.1.52	Swindon Factory **HI**
12.2.52	Stafford Road
31.10.52	Stafford Road **U**
11.11.52	Stafford Road
28.11.52	Banbury *(wait)*
9.12.52	Swindon F'cty **HC**
23.1.53	Stafford Road
16.7.53	Stafford Road *(wait)*
23.7.53	Swindon Factory **HG**
9.9.53	Stafford Road
3.54	Laira
1.4.54	Laira Shops **U**
3.5.54	Laira
23.7.54	Laira *(wait)*
12.8.54	Swindon Factory **LC**
8.9.54	Laira
31.12.54	Laira Shops **U**
6.1.55	Laira
20.1.55	Laira Shops **U**
1.2.55	Laira
23.2.55	Swindon Factory **HG**
19.5.55	Laira
18.7.55	Westbury Shops *(wait)*
19.7.55	Swindon Factory **LC**
29.8.55	Laira
19.1.56	Laira Shops **LC**
23.2.56	Laira
22.6.56	Taunton Shops **U**
12.7.56	Laira
11.10.56	Swindon Factory **HI**
21.11.56	Laira
21.2.57	Laira Shops **U**

28.2.57	Laira
11.6.57	Laira Shops **U**
21.6.57	Laira
10.7.57	Laira Shops **U**
30.7.57	Laira
31.10.57	Laira *(wait)*
5.11.57	Newton Abbot F'cty **LC**
16.11.57	Laira
10.3.58	Swindon Factory **HG**
24.4.58	Laira
11.9.58	Laira Shops **U**
29.9.58	Laira
7.10.58	Laira Shops **U**
4.10.58	Laira
30.1.59	Newton Abbot F'cty **U**
13.2.59	Laira
5.6.59	Bath Road Shops **U**
3.7.59	Laira
20.10.59	Swindon Factory **HI**
18.12.59	Old Oak Common
16.5.60	Old Oak Common *(wait)*
7.6.60	Swindon Factory **LC**
29.7.60	Old Oak Common
15.8.60	Old Oak Common **U**
30.8.60	Old Oak Common
13.9.60	Canton
16.1.61	Canton Shops **U**
2.2.61	Canton
23.3.61	Canton *(wait)*
5.4.61	Swindon Factory **HC**
3.8.61	Canton
19.9.62	**Wthdrwn**
3.11.62	Cut up at Swindon

Boilers and mileages:

First	4666 *	
21.6.29	..	(97,573)
8.6.31	..	(207,659)
11.2.32	4669	(242,026)
3.7.33	..	(318,473)
6.7.34	..	(376,904)
18.11.35	4682	(465,903)
2.4.37	..	(544,360)
30.8.38	..	(627,276)
30.1.40	..	(713,445)
17.6.41	4688	(790,873)

17.10.29	Swindon Factory L
6.12.29	Swindon Stock
9.12.29	Swindon Factory L
16.1.30	Swindon Stock
22.1.30	Old Oak Common
28.4.30	Swindon Factory H
30.6.30	Swindon Stock
15.7.30	Old Oak Common
8.30	Stafford Road
4.10.30	Swindon Shops R
10.10.30	Swindon Stock
20.10.30	Swindon Shops L
27.10.30	Swindon Stock
11.30	Swindon Shops
20.12.30	Old Oak Common (on loan)
9.1.31	Swindon Factory D.O. "experiments"
30.3.31	Swindon Stock
31.3.31	Stafford Road
2.7.31	Stafford Road (wait)
7.7.31	Swindon Factory G
11.9.31	Swindon Stock
9.31	Swindon Factory More D.O. tests
30.9.31	Swindon (on exhibition)
17.12.31	Swindon Stock
19.12.31	Stafford Road
7.7.32	Stafford Road (wait)
18.7.32	Swindon Factory L
19.8.32	Swindon Stock
27.8.32	Stafford Road
25.1.33	Swindon Factory I
23.3.33	Swindon Stock
3.33	Stafford Road
7.8.33	Stafford Road F'cty L
11.8.33	Stafford Road
6.9.33	Stafford Road F'cty R
9.9.33	Stafford Road
4.11.33	Swindon Factory G
22.12.33	Swindon Stock
1.1.34	Stafford Road
3.5.34	Old Oak Common
6.34	Stafford Road
24.9.34	Stafford Road
19.11.34	Stafford Road F'cty L
11.12.34	Stafford Road
31.12.34	Stafford Road (wait)
1.1.35	Swindon Factory I
22.2.35	Swindon Stock
1.3.35	Stafford Road
2.9.35	Stafford Road F'cty L
13.9.35	Stafford Road
30.1.36	Stafford Road (wait)
7.2.36	Swindon Factory G
20.3.36	Swindon Stock
26.3.36	Stafford Road
19.6.37	Stafford Road (wait)
28.6.37	Swindon Factory I
26.8.37	Swindon Stock
28.8.37	Stafford Road
23.8.38	Stafford Road (wait)
5.9.38	Swindon Factory G
25.10.38	Swindon Stock
6.11.38	Stafford Road
2.11.39	Stafford Road (wait)
3.11.39	Swindon Factory I
9.12.39	Swindon Stock
16.12.39	Stafford Road
8.11.40	Swindon Factory L
19.12.40	Swindon Stock
23.12.40	Stafford Road
27.1.41	Swindon Factory L
12.3.41	Swindon Stock
21.3.41	Stafford Road
22.11.41	Swindon Factory L
8.1.42	Swindon Stock
10.1.42	Stafford Road
26.1.42	Stafford Road (wait)
28.1.42	Stafford Road F'cty L
7.2.42	Stafford Road
25.7.42	Stafford Road F'cty R
17.8.42	Stafford Road (wait)
1.9.42	Swindon Factory L
22.9.42	Swindon Stock
23.9.42	Stafford Road
15.3.43	Stafford Road (wait)
23.3.43	Swindon Factory L
11.5.43	Swindon Stock
15.5.43	Stafford Road
25.1.44	Old Oak Common (wait)
8.2.44	Swindon Factory G
25.3.44	Swindon Stock
30.3.44	Stafford Road
30.9.44	Stafford Road R
19.10.44	Stafford Road
18.2.45	Stafford Road R
13.3.45	Stafford Road
17.5.45	Stafford Road (wait)
31.5.45	Swindon Factory I
17.7.45	Stafford Road
27.3.46	Stafford Road (wait)
9.4.46	Swindon Factory L
14.5.46	Stafford Road
15.6.46	Leamington (wait)
24.6.46	Swindon Factory L
23.7.46	Stafford Road
29.10.46	Stafford Road R
15.11.46	Stafford Road
25.1.47	Stafford Road R
14.2.47	Stafford Road
21.3.47	Swindon Factory G
28.4.47	Stafford Road
5.4.48	Stafford Road R
19.4.48	Stafford Road
31.8.48	Stafford Road (wait)
7.9.48	Swindon Factory I
14.10.48	Stafford Road
11.9.49	Old Oak Common Shps U
29.9.49	Stafford Road
17.1.50	Swindon Factory HG
22.2.50	Stafford Road
28.2.51	Stafford Road F'cty U
9.3.51	Stafford Road
3.5.51	Banbury (wait)
15.5.51	Swindon Factory HG
5.7.51	Stafford Road
3.8.51	Old Oak Common Shps U
21.8.51	Stafford Road
22.5.52	Old Oak Common Shps U
11.6.52	Stafford Road
3.9.52	Old Oak Common Shps U
25.9.52	Stafford Road
2.12.52	Swindon Factory HG
16.1.53	Stafford Road
14.3.53	Stafford Road U
23.3.53	Stafford Road
28.9.53	Stafford Road F'cty U
30.10.53	Stafford Road
27.1.54	Old Oak Common Shps U
24.2.54	Stafford Road
9.4.54	Stafford Road (wait)
27.4.54	Swindon Factory LC
23.6.54	Stafford Road
9.10.54	Stafford Road (wait)
21.10.54	Swindon Factory HG (start)
4.2.55	Stafford Road
3.3.35	Stafford Road (wait)
4.3.35	Swindon Factory HG (finish)
15.3.55	Stafford Road
24.1.56	Stafford Road (wait)
30.1.56	Stafford Road F'cty LC
18.2.56	Stafford Road
29.5.56	Stafford Road (wait)
2.6.56	Swindon Factory HI
16.7.56	Stafford Road

It's the turn of No.6005 KING GEORGE II to have the slotted bogie - 7 August 1959 at Wolverhampton (Low Level), waiting to depart with the 8.55am Birkenhead-Paddington. PHOTOGRAPH: S.D. WAINWRIGHT

6.11.56	Stafford Road U
27.11.56	Stafford Road
12.3.57	Stafford Road U
27.3.57	Stafford Road
14.11.57	Shrewsbury Shops U
2.12.57	Stafford Road
6.3.58	Swindon Factory LI
21.4.58	Stafford Road
19.6.58	Stafford Road (wait)
21.6.58	Swindon Factory LC
3.9.58	Stafford Road
26.1.59	Stafford Road U
17.2.59	Stafford Road
14.3.59	Stafford Road (wait)
19.3.59	Swindon Factory LI
28.5.59	Stafford Road
29.10.59	Stafford Road U
18.11.59	Stafford Road
12.2.60	Stafford Road U
9.3.60	Stafford Road
24.5.60	Stafford Road (wait)
30.5.60	Swindon Factory HG
25.8.60	Stafford Road
26.12.60	Stafford Road U
20.1.61	Stafford Road
9.5.61	Stafford Road U
19.6.61	Stafford Road
22.12.61	Stafford Road U
14.3.62	Stafford Road (wait)
28.3.62	Swindon Factory LI
28.5.62	Stafford Road
7.9.62	Old Oak Common
19.11.62	Wthdrwn (alternatively stated to be 20.11.62)
17.10.63	Sold as scrap to J.Cashmore of Newport

Boilers and mileages:

First	4661 *	
30.6.30	..	(135,072)
11.9.31	4673	(173,295)
23.3.33	..	(236,477)
22.12.33	4684	(275,895)
22.2.35	..	(335,671)
20.3.36	4690	(396,215)
26.8.37	..	(476,784)
25.10.38	4676	(547,187)
9.12.39	..	(608,672)
12.3.41	4674	(665,378)
8.1.42	..	(699,113)
11.5.43	4670	(761,017)
25.3.44	4661	(796,949)
17.7.45	..	(858,513)
14.5.46	4668	(902,032)
28.4.47	4688	(941,914)
14.10.48	4681	(1,020,088)
22.2.50	4687	(1,091,801)
5.7.51	4663	(1,161,946)
16.1.53	8606 *	(1,233,518)
4.2.55	8620 *	(1,309,292)
16.7.56	8615	(1,376,773)
28.5.59		(1,512,075)
25.8.60	8601	(1,571,562)
28.5.62	..	1,655,227
Final mileage:		1,679,275

Tenders:

First	2390
4.29	2393
20.6.29	2384
11.9.31	2440
3.34	2394
2.36	2401
6.12.39	2548
12.3.41	2643
8.1.42	2788
25.3.44	2642
14.5.46	2790
14.10.48	2743
5.7.51	2763
16.1.53	2694
23.6.54	2763
4.2.55	2913
16.7.56	2556
22.2.58	2742
21.4.58	2556
28.5.62	2787

........................ooo........................

6006 KING GEORGE I
To stock: February 1928

Summary of sheds

8.3.28	Laira
10.4.30	Old Oak Common
5.30	Laira
25.7.30	Old Oak Common
8.30	Stafford Road

Engine history

25.2.28	Swindon Factory
	ATC fitted
8.3.28	Laira
12.5.28	Old Oak Common
4.6.28	Swindon Factory **L**
11.6.28	Swindon Stock
6.28	Laira
10.12.28	Swindon Factory **L**
21.1.29	Laira
24.4.29	Swindon Factory **L**
22.6.29	Swindon Stock
28.6.29	Laira
29.11.29	Laira Shops **L**
11.12.29	Laira
3.3.30	Swindon Factory **L**
8.4.30	Laira
10.4.30	Old Oak Common
5.30	Laira
26.5.30	Swindon Factory **H**
16.7.30	Swindon Stock
25.7.30	Old Oak Common
8.30	Stafford Road
25.8.31	Swindon Factory **G**
6.11.31	Swindon Stock
19.11.31	Stafford Road
19.7.32	Stafford Road *(wait)*
22.7.32	Swindon Factory **L**
12.8.32	Swindon Stock
18.8.32	Stafford Road
14.11.32	Swindon Factory **L**
21.12.32	Swindon Stock
22.12.32	Stafford Road
19.4.33	Swindon Factory **G**
29.6.33	Swindon Stock
7.33	Stafford Road
5.3.34	Stafford Road F'cty **L**
29.3.34	Stafford Road
9.5.34	Swindon Factory **I**
4.7.34	Swindon Stock
14.7.34	Stafford Road
5.2.35	Swindon Factory **L**
21.2.35	Swindon Stock
23.3.35	Stafford Road
9.10.35	Swindon Factory **G**
21.11.35	Swindon Stock
3.12.35	Stafford Road
13.10.36	Stafford Road *(wait)*
20.10.36	Swindon Factory **L**
1.12.36	Swindon Stock
5.12.36	Stafford Road
25.1.37	Swindon Factory **L**
31.1.37	Swindon Stock
2.37	Stafford Road
2.9.37	Stafford Road *(wait)*
3.9.37	Swindon Factory **G**
23.10.37	Swindon Stock
5.11.37	Stafford Road
8.12.38	Stafford Road *(wait)*
23.12.38	Swindon Factory **I**
11.2.39	Swindon Stock
19.2.39	Stafford Road
25.3.39	Stafford Road *(wait)*
4.4.39	Swindon Factory **L**
24.4.39	Swindon Stock
30.4.39	Stafford Road
15.2.40	Swindon Factory **L**
16.3.40	Swindon Stock
26.3.40	Stafford Road
13.5.40	Stafford Road F'cty **L**
15.5.40	Stafford Road
24.10.40	Swindon Factory **I**
7.12.40	Swindon Stock
23.12.40	Stafford Road
17.7.41	Stafford Road *(wait)*
2.8.41	Swindon Factory **L**
3.9.41	Swindon Stock
4.9.41	Stafford Road
29.5.42	Stafford Road *(wait)*

31.5.42	Stafford Road F'cty **R**
5.6.42	Stafford Road
11.8.42	Swindon Factory **I**
2.10.42	Swindon Stock
7.10.42	Stafford Road
13.4.43	Swindon Factory **L**
23.7.43	Swindon Stock
26.7.43	Stafford Road
8.12.43	Stafford Road *(wait)*
5.1.44	Swindon Factory **R**
5.2.44	Swindon Stock
8.2.44	Stafford Road
16.2.44	Stafford Road *(wait)*
2.3.44	Swindon Factory **L**
3.4.44	Swindon Stock
7.4.44	Stafford Road
19.4.44	Stafford Road **R**
6.5.44	Stafford Road
6.8.44	Old Oak Common Shps **R**
28.9.44	Stafford Road
16.11.44	Stafford Road *(wait)*
17.11.44	Swindon Factory **G**
8.1.45	Stafford Road
3.10.45	Stafford Road *(wait)*
23.10.45	Swindon Factory **L**
13.12.45	Stafford Road
14.1.46	Leamington *(wait)*
27.1.46	Stafford Road **R**
10.2.46	Stafford Road
13.9.46	Old Oak Common **R**
1.10.46	Stafford Road
2.11.46	Stafford Road *(wait)*
7.11.46	Swindon Factory **I**
19.12.46	Stafford Road
15.5.47	Old Oak Common Shps **R**
3.6.47	Stafford Road
13.11.47	Stafford Road *(wait)*
11.12.47	Swindon Factory **L**
21.1.48	Stafford Road
16.3.48	Stafford Road F'cty **R**
24.3.48	Stafford Road
27.4.48	Old Oak Common Shps **R**
20.5.48	Stafford Road
12.9.48	Stafford Road *(wait)*
22.9.48	Swindon Factory **I**
29.10.48	Stafford Road

28.8.49	Stafford Road **LC**
26.9.49	Stafford Road
2.2.50	Stafford Road *(wait)*
13.2.50	Swindon Factory **HG**
22.3.50	Stafford Road
12.4.51	Old Oak Common Shps **U**
10.5.51	Stafford Road
12.6.51	Swindon Factory **HI**
13.8.51	Stafford Road
28.5.52	Old Oak Common *(wait)*
4.6.52	Swindon Factory **HC**
3.7.52	Stafford Road
9.9.52	Stafford Road F'cty **U**
1.10.52	Stafford Road
18.2.53	Banbury *(wait)*
24.2.53	Swindon Factory **HG**
23.4.53	Stafford Road
23.11.53	Swindon Factory **LC**
28.12.53	Stafford Road
11.8.54	Stafford Road *(wait)*
20.8.54	Swindon Factory **HC**
15.10.54	Stafford Road
4.1.55	Old Oak Common Shps **U**
25.1.55	Stafford Road
7.2.55	Stafford Road *(wait)*
10.2.55	Swindon Factory **HI**
5.4.55	Stafford Road
12.11.55	Banbury Shops **U**
26.11.55	Stafford Road
31.1.56	Old Oak Comn Shps **LC**
16.2.56	Stafford Road
7.5.56	Stafford Road *(wait)*
10.5.56	Swindon Factory **HG**
27.6.56	Stafford Road
1.5.57	Stafford Road **U**
18.5.57	Stafford Road
15.6.57	Stafford Road **U**
1.7.57	Stafford Road
5.10.57	Stafford Road **U**
21.10.57	Stafford Road
12.11.57	Old Oak Common Shps **U**
29.11.57	Stafford Road
15.1.58	Swindon Factory **LI**
24.2.58	Stafford Road
17.7.58	Stafford Road **U**
6.8.58	Stafford Road

6.10.58	Old Oak Common Shps **U**
24.10.58	Stafford Road
1.11.58	Stafford Road **U**
20.11.58	Stafford Road
24.2.59	Stafford Road **U**
20.3.59	Stafford Road
21.4.59	Stafford Road **U**
25.5.59	Stafford Road
23.11.59	Swindon Factory **LI**
5.2.60	Stafford Road
1.7.60	Stafford Road F'cty **LC**
14.7.60	Stafford Road
29.8.60	Stafford Road **U**
27.9.60	Stafford Road
3.11.60	Tyseley Shops **U**
23.11.60	Stafford Road
16.12.60	Stafford Road F'cty **U**
1.4.61	Stafford Road **U**
21.4.61	Stafford Road
14.8.61	Tyseley Shops **U**
26.9.61	Stafford Road
21.11.61	Stafford Road **U**
10.12.61	Stafford Road
15.2.62	Withdrawn
26.2.62	Swindon Factory
21.4.62	Cut up at Swindon

Boilers and mileages

Date	Boiler	Mileage
First	4667 *	
16.7.30	..	(120,535)
6.11.31	4661	(191,283)
29.3.34	4690	(271,533)
4.7.34	..	(327,644)
21.11.35	4686	(410,824)
23.10.37	4661	(522,139)
11.2.39	..	(596,527)
16.3.40	4684	(651,349)
7.12.40	..	(684,465)
2.10.42	..	(771,151)
23.7.43	4674	(799,456)
8.1.45	4682	(849,508)
13.12.45	4689	(886,322)
19.12.46	..	(928,277)
21.1.48	4685	(972,701)
29.10.48	..	(1,006,149)
22.3.50	4681	(1,073,356)

The Birmingham line in 1957 - double-chimney No.6006 KING GEORGE I approaches Hatton station on 16 February. PHOTOGRAPH: NATIONAL RAILWAY MUSEUM

Fresh from the works and complete with its new blue livery, No.6007 KING WILLIAM III was photographed on a test run at Bath on 14 January 1950. PHOTOGRAPH: IVO PETERS

13.8.51	4692	(1,135,686)	7.3.28	Old Oak Common	
3.7.52	4675	(1,186,201)	26.3.28	Swindon Factory L	
23.4.53	8609 *	(1,222,955)	31.3.28	Old Oak Common	
5.4.55	8607	(1,299,182)	15.6.28	Swindon Factory L	
27.6.56	4695	(1,357,863)	22.6.28	Old Oak Common	
5.2.60	..	(1,511,174)	24.9.28	Swindon Factory L	
Final mileage:		1,593,367	18.10.28	Old Oak Common	
			16.2.29	Old Oak Common *(wait)*	

13.10.33	Swindon Factory I
13.12.33	Old Oak Common
24.2.34	Swindon Factory
	(for experiments)
27.2.34	Swindon Stock
28.2.34	Old Oak Common
2.7.34	Swindon Factory L

4.12.38	Old Oak Common
11.1.39	Old Oak Common Shps L
3.2.39	Old Oak Common
30.5.39	Swindon Factory L
26.6.39	Swindon Stock
2.7.39	Old Oak Common
18.11.39	Swindon Factory G

Tenders:

First	2392
11.12.29	2389
16.7.30	2401
6.11.31	2394
3.34	2440
4.7.34	2434
24.4.39	2550
7.12.40	2742
8.1.45	2776
19.12.46	2763
29.10.48	2726
13.8.51	2612
15.10.54	2648
5.4.55	2710
27.6.56	2875
5.2.60	2842

........................ooo........................

6007 KING WILLIAM III
To stock: March 1928

Summary of sheds:

7.3.28	Old Oak Common
18.3.59	Laira
22.9.59	Stafford Road

Engine history:

3.3.28	Swindon Factory
	ATC fitted

20.2.29	Swindon Factory L
9.4.29	Swindon Stock
17.4.29	Old Oak Common
13.8.29	Swindon Factory L
23.8.29	Swindon Stock
26.8.29	Old Oak Common
8.1.30	Swindon Factory H
2.4.30	Swindon Stock
12.4.30	Old Oak Common
22.9.30	Swindon Factory L
2.10.30	Swindon Stock
4.10.30	Old Oak Common
1.1.31	Old Oak Common Shps R
22.1.31	Old Oak Common
10.3.31	Swindon Factory G
13.5.31	Swindon Stock
20.5.31	Old Oak Common
25.11.31	Old Oak Common Shps R
15.12.31	Old Oak Common
31.12.31	Old Oak Common *(wait)*
11.1.32	Swindon Factory L
4.2.32	Swindon Stock
6.2.32	Old Oak Common
1.7.32	Old Oak Common Shps R
19.7.32	Old Oak Common
12.8.32	Swindon Factory G
27.9.32	Swindon Stock
15.10.32	Old Oak Common
10.7.33	Swindon Factory L
12.7.33	Swindon Stock
7.33	Old Oak Common

4.7.34	Swindon Stock
5.7.34	Old Oak Common
27.8.34	Swindon Factory L
29.8.34	Swindon Stock
2.9.34	Old Oak Common
23.11.34	Old Oak Common Shps R
12.12.34	Old Oak Common
14.1.35	Swindon Factory G
5.4.35	Swindon Stock
12.4.35	Old Oak Common
15.1.36	Swindon Factory
	Officially withdrawn after
	Shrivenham accident, but
	in practice was repaired
	(see text)
24.3.36	Old Oak Common
15.6.36	Laira Shops R
30.6.36	Old Oak Common
1.2.37	Stafford Road F'cty L
3.2.37	Old Oak Common
19.4.37	Swindon Factory G
5.6.37	Swindon Stock
13.6.37	Old Oak Common
4.10.37	Old Oak Common Shps R
27.10.37	Old Oak Common
19.6.38	Old Oak Common *(wait)*
20.6.38	Swindon Factory I
17.8.38	Swindon Stock
28.8.38	Old Oak Common
5.11.38	Old Oak Common *(wait)*
9.11.38	Swindon Factory L
23.11.38	Swindon Stock

5.1.40	Swindon Stock
13.1.40	Old Oak Common
24.11.40	Old Oak Common *(wait)*
28.11.40	Swindon Factory I
25.1.41	Swindon Stock
31.1.41	Old Oak Common
2.2.42	Old Oak Common Shps R
23.2.42	Old Oak Common
6.7.42	Swindon Factory I
26.8.42	Swindon Stock
30.8.42	Old Oak Common
22.10.42	Old Oak Common Shps R
4.11.42	Old Oak Common
28.4.43	Old Oak Common Shps R
13.5.43	Old Oak Common
9.6.43	Old Oak Common Shps R
29.6.43	Old Oak Common
2.11.43	Old Oak Common Shps L
16.11.43	Old Oak Common
15.12.43	Laira *(wait)*
12.1.44	Swindon Factory G
26.2.44	Swindon Stock
5.3.44	Old Oak Common
14.3.45	Old Oak Common Shps L
18.4.45	Old Oak Common
4.7.45	Laira *(wait)*
20.7.45	Swindon Factory I
12.9.45	Old Oak Common
15.5.46	Swindon Factory L
14.6.46	Old Oak Common
27.8.46	Old Oak Common *(wait)*
11.9.46	Swindon Factory G

1.11.46	Old Oak Common
3.3.47	Laira (wait)
7.3.47	Swindon Factory **L**
25.3.47	Old Oak Common
24.4.47	Laira Shops **L**
27.5.47	Old Oak Common
3.10.47	Old Oak Common (wait)
22.10.47	Swindon Factory **I**
28.11.47	Old Oak Common
30.3.48	Laira Shops **R**
17.4.48	Old Oak Common
4.5.48	Swindon Factory **R**
27.5.48	Old Oak Common
14.6.48	Laira (wait)
24.6.48	Swindon Factory **L**
30.7.48	Old Oak Common
13.9.48	Old Oak Common (wait)
29.9.48	Swindon Factory **L**
25.10.48	Old Oak Common
16.2.49	Old Oak Common (wait)
23.2.49	Swindon Factory **LC**
25.3.49	Old Oak Common
7.6.49	Old Oak Common (wait)
10.6.49	Swindon Factory **LC**
4.7.49	Old Oak Common
15.7.49	Taunton Shops **U**
12.8.49	Old Oak Common
6.12.49	Swindon Factory **HG**
12.1.50	Old Oak Common
1.6.50	Old Oak Common (wait)
1.6.50	Swindon Factory **U**
14.6.50	Old Oak Common
21.9.50	Old Oak Common Shps **U**
19.10.50	Old Oak Common
22.11.50	Laira (wait)
4.12.50	Swindon Factory **HI**
29.1.51	Old Oak Common
24.4.51	Old Oak Common Shps **U**
8.5.51	Old Oak Common
8.6.51	Old Oak Common (wait)
19.6.51	Swindon Factory **LC**
2.7.51	Old Oak Common
27.8.51	Old Oak Comn Shps **LC**
3.10.51	Old Oak Common
12.2.52	Taunton Shops **U**
1.4.52	Old Oak Common
28.7.52	Old Oak Common (wait)
6.8.52	Swindon Factory **HG**
1.10.52	Old Oak Common
13.10.53	Old Oak Common Shps **U**
16.11.53	Old Oak Common
14.1.54	Old Oak Common **U**
27.1.54	Old Oak Common
8.2.54	Swindon Factory **HI**
1.4.54	Old Oak Common
8.4.54	Taunton Shops **U**
1.5.54	Old Oak Common
30.9.54	Old Oak Comon Shps **LC**
29.10.54	Old Oak Common
13.12.54	Old Oak Common Shps **U**
12.1.55	Old Oak Common
2.2.55	Old Oak Common **U**
25.2.55	Old Oak Common
4.5.55	Old Oak Common (wait)
12.5.55	Swindon Factory **HG**
27.6.55	Old Oak Common
12.8.55	Swindon Factory **U**
1.9.55	Old Oak Common
13.10.55	Slough (wait)
14.10.55	Swindon Factory **HC**
17.11.55	Old Oak Common
26.11.55	Westbury Shops **U**
24.12.55	Old Oak Common
27.1.56	Bath Road Shops **LC**
24.2.56	Old Oak Common
23.4.56	Taunton (wait)
28.4.56	Swindon Factory **HG**
21.9.56	Old Oak Common
22.7.57	Old Oak Common Shps **U**

21.8.57	Old Oak Common (wait)
26.8.57	Swindon Factory **HI**
28.10.57	Old Oak Common
25.1.58	Old Oak Common Shps **U**
31.1.58	Old Oak Common
7.5.58	Bath Road Shops **U**
29.5.58	Old Oak Common
31.7.58	Old Oak Common Shps **U**
15.8.58	Old Oak Common
22.8.58	Old Oak Common **U**
8.9.58	Old Oak Common
29.9.58	Old Oak Common Shps **U**
17.10.58	Old Oak Common
13.1.59	Swindon Factory **HG**
25.2.59	Old Oak Common
3.3.59	Swindon Factory **U**
18.3.59	Laira
21.4.59	Laira Shops **U**
8.5.59	Laira
27.7.59	Laira Shops **U**
20.8.59	Laira
22.9.59	Stafford Road
1.3.60	Stafford Road **U**
9.4.60	Stafford Road
1.5.60	Old Oak Common Shps **U**
27.5.60	Stafford Road
9.9.60	Banbury Shops **U**
26.9.60	Stafford Road
25.11.60	Stafford Road F'cty **U**
9.12.60	Stafford Road
20.10.60	Tyseley Shops **U**
18.11.60	Stafford Road
19.1.61	Stafford Road **U**
4.2.61	Stafford Road
20.3.61	Stafford Road **U**
20.4.61	Stafford Road
30.5.61	Stafford Road (wait)
12.6.61	Swindon Factory **LI**
18.8.61	Stafford Road
7.2.62	Stafford Road **U**
3.3.62	Stafford Road
12.3.62	Tyseley Shops **U**
28.3.62	Stafford Road
3.5.62	Stafford Road **U**
12.6.62	Stafford Road
7.9.63	**Withdrawn** (alternatively stated to be 21.9.63)
27.2.63	Sold as scrap to Cox & Danks of Langley Green

Boilers and mileages:

First	4668 *	
2.4.30	..	(107,132)
13.5.31	4676	(164,385)
27.9.32	4662	(243,614)
13.12.33	..	(320.030)
5.4.35	4661	(393,119)
'renewed' after accident		
24.3.36	4661	
5.6.37	4667	(81,209)
17.8.38	..	(175,211)
5.1.40	4669	(266,617)
25.1.41	..	(339,685)
26.8.42	..	(449,303)
26.2.44	4667	(530,387)
12.9.45	..	(616,835)
1.11.46	4691	(687,065)
28.11.47	4687	(742,228)
12.1.50	4662	(836,241)
29.1.51	..	(897,557)
1.10.52	4683	(978,241)
1.4.54	..	(1,067,779)
27.6.55	8606	(1,124,419)
21.9.56	8607	(1,157,768)
28.10.57	..	(1,225,159)
25.2.59	8600	(1,295,741)
18.8.61	..	(1,389,004)
Final mileage:		1,437,609
Total mileage from 3.28:1,830,728		

Tenders:

First	2387
2.10.30	2395
13.5.31	2392
19.7.32	2465
27.9.32	2392
13.12.33	2388
5.4.35	2572
'renewed' after accident	
24.3.36	2572
23.11.38	2715
25.1.41	2790
25.4.42	2665
4.11.42	2704
26.2.44	2695
12.9.45	2710
27.5.48	2612
2.7.51	2726
1.10.52	2815
1.4.54	2428
1.6.54	2630
29.1.55	2723
27.6.55	2531
21.9.56	2923
28.10.57	2838
25.2.59	2854
18.8.61	2597

........................ooo........................

6008 KING JAMES II
To stock: March 1928

Summary of sheds:

27.4.28	Laira
15.7.30	Old Oak Common
8.30	Stafford Road
11.6.52	Laira
2.2.59	Stafford Road

Engine history:

3.28	Swindon Factory
	ATC fitted
10.3.28	Swindon Stock
12.4.28	Swindon Factory **L**
27.4.28	Laira
11.6.28	Swindon Factory **L**
18.6.28	Laira
15.10.28	Swindon Factory **L**
6.11.28	Laira
9.4.29	Swindon Factory **L**
8.6.29	Swindon Stock
20.6.29	Laira
4.12.29	Laira Shops **L**
16.12.29	Laira
20.2.30	Swindon Factory **L**
22.2.30	Swindon Stock
26.3.30	Laira
30.4.30	Swindon Factory **H**
30.6.30	Swindon Stock
15.7.30	Old Oak Common
8.30	Stafford Road
7.8.31	Stafford Road (wait)
12.8.31	Swindon Factory **G**
15.10.31	Swindon Stock
24.10.31	Stafford Road
21.1.32	Swindon Factory **L**
22.1.32	Swindon Stock
24.1.32	Stafford Road
19.2.32	Swindon Factory **L**
7.3.32	Stafford Road
23.7.32	Stafford Road (wait)
27.7.32	Swindon Factory **L**
30.8.32	Swindon Stock
3.9.32	Stafford Road
10.12.32	Stafford Road (wait)
21.12.32	Swindon Factory **I**
10.2.33	Swindon Stock

2.33	Stafford Road
24.10.33	Swindon Factory **L**
16.11.33	Swindon Stock
11.33	Stafford Road
2.1.34	Stafford Road (wait)
6.1.34	Swindon Factory **G**
27.3.34	Swindon Stock
5.4.34	Stafford Road
27.10.34	Stafford Road Shops **L**
16.11.34	Stafford Road
27.3.35	Swindon Factory **G**
27.5.35	Swindon Stock
1.6.35	Stafford Road
9.8.35	Stafford Road F'cty **L**
13.8.35	Stafford Road
11.9.35	Swindon Factory **L**
1.10.35	Swindon Stock
5.10.35	Stafford Road
26.2.36	Swindon Factory **L**
15.4.36	Swindon Stock
22.4.36	Stafford Road
2.9.36	Stafford Road F'cty **L**
4.9.36	Stafford Road
26.10.36	Stafford Road (wait)
26.10.36	Swindon Factory **I**
5.12.36	Swindon Stock
12.12.36	Stafford Road
13.12.37	Stafford Road (wait)
31.12.37	Swindon Factory **G**
21.2.38	Swindon Stock
10.3.38	Stafford Road
20.3.39	Stafford Road (wait)
29.3.39	Swindon Factory **I**
22.5.39	Stafford Road
6.6.40	Stafford Road (wait)
14.6.40	Swindon Factory **G**
7.8.40	Swindon Stock
18.8.40	Stafford Road
31.8.41	Stafford Road (wait)
6.9.41	Swindon Factory **L**
31.10.41	Swindon Stock
4.11.41	Stafford Road
23.1.42	Stafford Road (wait)
24.2.42	Swindon Factory **L**
14.4.42	Swindon Stock
14.4.42	Stafford Road
28.4.42	Stafford Road (wait)
5.5.42	Swindon Factory **L**
23.5.42	Swindon Stock
24.5.42	Stafford Road
2.10.42	Stafford Road (wait)
13.10.42	Swindon Factory **I**
23.11.42	Swindon Stock
30.11.42	Stafford Road
6.1.43	Swindon Factory **L**
18.1.43	Swindon Stock
21.1.43	Stafford Road
3.3.43	Stafford Road F'cty **L**
26.3.43	Stafford Road
5.6.43	Leamington (wait)
25.6.43	Swindon Factory **L**
27.8.43	Swindon Stock
1.9.43	Stafford Road
4.10.43	Stafford Road (wait)
25.10.43	Swindon Factory **L**
13.12.43	Swindon Stock
17.12.43	Stafford Road
11.5.44	Stafford Road (wait)
24.5.44	Swindon Factory **L**
30.6.44	Swindon Stock
3.7.44	Stafford Road
17.11.44	Stafford Road **R**
19.12.44	Stafford Road
3.1.45	Stafford Road (wait)
13.1.45	Swindon Factory **I**
28.2.45	Stafford Road
10.4.45	Stafford Road F'cty **R**
27.4.45	Stafford Road
3.7.45	Stafford Road F'cty **L**

1.9.45	Stafford Road
28.9.45	Stafford Road (wait)
21.11.45	Swindon Factory L
28.12.45	Stafford Road
3.1.46	Stafford Road R
21.1.46	Stafford Road
7.8.46	Stafford Road (wait)
14.8.46	Swindon Factory L
9.9.46	Stafford Road
21.9.46	Stafford Road R
16.10.46	Stafford Road
31.10.46	Stafford Road F'cty L
14.12.46	Stafford Road
30.12.46	Stafford Road (wait)
9.1.47	Swindon Factory L
22.2.47	Stafford Road
1.3.47	Old Oak Common R
22.3.47	Stafford Road
31.5.47	Stafford Road F'cty R
3.6.47	Stafford Road
6.8.47	Old Oak Common R
20.8.47	Stafford Road
23.10.47	Stafford Road (wait)
31.10.47	Swindon Factory I
17.12.47	Stafford Road
12.7.48	Stafford Road (wait)
11.8.48	Swindon Factory L
21.9.48	Stafford Road
5.10.49	Stafford Road (wait)
10.10.49	Swindon Factory HG
16.11.49	Stafford Road
5.6.50	Stafford Road (wait)
12.6.50	Swindon Factory LC
17.7.50	Stafford Road
19.11.50	Old Oak Common Shps U
8.1.51	Stafford Road
12.2.51	Stafford Road (wait)
14.2.51	Swindon Factory HG
22.3.51	Stafford Road
7.9.51	Stafford Road U
24.9.51	Stafford Road
27.11.51	Stafford Road (wait)
5.12.51	Swindon Factory LC
23.1.52	Stafford Road
8.4.52	Stafford Road (wait)
29.4.52	Swindon Factory LC
11.6.52	Laira
16.9.52	Laira Shops U
9.10.52	Laira
10.11.52	Laira (wait)
18.11.52	Swindon Factory HI
9.1.53	Laira
19.6.53	Laira Shops U
11.7.53	Laira
20.10.53	Old Oak Common (wait)
9.11.53	Swindon Factory LC
16.12.53	Laira
27.4.54	Exeter (wait)
4.5.54	Swindon Factory HI
18.6.54	Laira
1.10.54	Laira Shops U
31.10.54	Laira
31.1.55	Laira (wait)
8.2.55	Swindon Factory LC
30.3.55	Laira
31.10.55	Swindon Factory HG
13.12.55	Laira
31.1.56	Old Oak Comn Shps LC
17.2.56	Laira
27.8.56	Bath Road Shops U
18.9.56	Laira
2.10.56	Laira Shops U
9.10.56	Laira
24.11.56	Laira Shops U
6.12.56	Laira
18.1.57	Laira Shops U
4.2.57	Laira
8.4.57	Swindon Factory HG
11.7.57	Laira

Heading a Liverpool-Plymouth train, No.6008 KING JAMES II restarts from Newton Abbot on 10 May 1958. PHOTOGRAPH: BRIAN MORRISON

23.10.57	Laira Shops U
6.11.57	Laira
13.2.58	Laira Shops U
25.2.58	Laira
9.6.58	Laira Shops U
27.6.58	Laira
13.11.58	Swindon Factory HG
30.12.58	Laira
2.2.59	Stafford Road
16.10.59	Stafford Road U
10.11.59	Stafford Road
18.1.60	Stafford Road U
5.2.60	Stafford Road
13.6.60	Stafford Road (wait)
25.6.60	Swindon Factory LI
22.9.60	Stafford Road
23.2.61	Stafford Road U
22.3.61	Stafford Road
28.12.61	Stafford Road U
19.1.62	Stafford Road
23.1.62	Stafford Road U
23.2.62	Stafford Road
19.6.62	Wthdrwn
26.6.63	Cut up at Swindon

Boilers and mileages:

First 4669 *		
30.6.30	..	(109,671)
15.10.31	4674	(178,973)
10.2.33	..	(239,016)
27.3.34	4673	(295,875)
27.5.35	4663	(359,794)
5.12.36	..	(441,862)
21.2.38	4673	(510,795)
22.5.39	..	(581,236)
7.8.40	4661	(640,453)
23.11.42	..	(733,697)
13.12.43	4684	(761,992)
28.12.45	4686	(835,021)
22.2.47	4672	(867,490)
17.12.47	..	(895,774)
21.9.48	4669	(932,207)
16.11.49	4693	(988,363)
22.3.51	4679	(1,057,531)
9.1.53	4673	(1,143,490)
18.6.54	4687	(1,230,307)
13.12.55	8600	(1,328,750)

11.7.57	8611	(1,405,184)
30.12.58	4699	(1,509,100)
22.9.60	..	(1,598,699)
Final mileage:		1,695,925

Tenders:

First	2396
4.28	2401
16.12.29	2392
22.3.30	2398
30.6.30	2394
15.10.31	2401
15.4.36	2394
22.5.39	2629
14.4.42	2642
23.11.42	2606
18.1.43	2762
28.2.45	2775
22.2.47	2629
21.7.48	2728
22.3.51	2772
11.6.52	2743
1.1.52	2762
30.3.55	2715
13.12.55	2931
1.12.56	2398
11.7.57	2569
30.12.58	2775
23.2.62	2436

........................ooo.......................

6009 KING CHARLES II
To stock: March 1928

Summary of sheds:

3.4.28	Old Oak Common

Engine history:

24.3.28	Swindon Factory
	ATC fitted
3.4.28	Old Oak Common
18.6.28	Swindon Factory L
26.6.28	Old Oak Common
15.10.28	Swindon Factory L
20.11.28	Old Oak Common
20.11.28	Swindon Factory L

28.11.28	Old Oak Common
9.4.29	Swindon Factory L
23.5.29	Swindon Stock
29.5.29	Old Oak Common
23.11.29	Laira Shops L
2.12.29	Old Oak Common
24.12.29	Swindon Factory H
6.3.30	Swindon Stock
15.3.30	Reading (wait)
17.3.30	Swindon Factory L
8.4.30	Swindon Stock
14.4.30	Old Oak Common
9.7.30	Swindon Factory L
15.7.30	Old Oak Common
21.1.31	Old Oak Common Shps R
9.2.31	Old Oak Common
6.3.31	Old Oak Common Shps R
18.3.31	Old Oak Common
22.4.31	Swindon Factory G
19.6.31	Swindon Stock
27.6.31	Old Oak Common
14.1.32	Swindon Factory L
23.3.32	Swindon Stock
23.3.32	Old Oak Common
26.7.32	Swindon Factory L
19.8.32	Swindon Stock
27.8.32	Old Oak Common
1.2.33	Swindon Factory I
11.4.33	Swindon Stock
4.33	Old Oak Common
11.9.33	Old Oak Common (wait)
19.9.33	Swindon Factory L
13.10.33	Old Oak Common
3.4.34	Swindon Factory G
30.5.34	Swindon Stock
10.6.34	Old Oak Common
28.7.34	Swindon Factory L
1.8.34	Swindon Stock
2.8.34	Old Oak Common
13.2.35	Old Oak Common Shps R
7.3.35	Old Oak Common
30.4.35	Swindon Factory I
20.6.35	Swindon Stock
4.7.35	Old Oak Common
22.6.36	Old Oak Common (wait)
29.6.36	Swindon Factory G
17.8.36	Swindon Stock

23.8.36	Old Oak Common	23.11.44	Old Oak Common	27.6.50	Old Oak Common U	20.11.55	Old Oak Common
12.10.37	Swindon Factory **I**	15.2.45	Old Oak Common Shps **L**	22.7.50	Old Oak Common	29.12.55	Old Oak Common (*wait*)
27.11.37	Swindon Stock	17.3.45	Old Oak Common	21.10.50	Taunton Shops **U**	2.1.56	Swindon Factory **HG**
6.12.37	Old Oak Common	12.4.45	Old Oak Common Shps **R**	20.12.50	Old Oak Common	25.5.56	Old Oak Common
18.4.38	Old Oak Common Shps **R**	4.5.45	Old Oak Common	30.12.50	Old Oak Common **U**	4.3.57	Old Oak Common Shps **U**
7.5.38	Old Oak Common	23.9.45	Old Oak Common (*wait*)	11.1.51	Old Oak Common	19.3.57	Old Oak Common
22.1.39	Old Oak Common (*wait*)	3.10.45	Swindon Factory **G**	25.2.51	Old Oak Comn Shps **LC**	26.4.57	Taunton Shops **U**
24.1.39	Swindon Factory **I**	15.11.45	Old Oak Common	21.3.51	Old Oak Common	20.5.57	Old Oak Common
7.3.39	Swindon Stock	12.7.46	Old Oak Common **R**	2.5.51	Swindon Factory **HG**	8.8.57	Swindon Factory **HI**
12.3.39	Old Oak Common	27.7.46	Old Oak Common **R**	5.6.51	Old Oak Common	27.9.57	Old Oak Common
30.3.40	Swindon Factory **G**	26.9.46	Old Oak Common **R**	18.1.52	Old Oak Common (*wait*)	29.5.58	Old Oak Common Shps **U**
27.5.40	Swindon Stock	17.10.46	Old Oak Common	25.1.52	Swindon Factory **LC**	12.6.58	Old Oak Common
3.6.40	Old Oak Common	8.11.46	Old Oak Common (*wait*)	27.2.52	Old Oak Common	8.9.58	Reading (*wait*)
30.12.40	Old Oak Common (*wait*)	19.11.46	Swindon Factory **I**	4.6.52	Taunton Shops **U**	12.9.58	Swindon Factory **LC**
10.1.41	Swindon Factory **L**	31.12.46	Old Oak Common	17.6.52	Old Oak Common	21.11.58	Old Oak Common
7.3.41	Swindon Stock	11.2.47	Old Oak Common Shps **R**	16.7.52	Old Oak Common (*wait*)	20.2.59	Swindon Factory **HI**
15.3.41	Old Oak Common	1.3.47	Old Oak Common	29.7.52	Swindon Factory **LC**	16.4.59	Old Oak Common
8.7.41	Old Oak Common (*wait*)	27.5.47	Old Oak Common **R**	3.9.52	Old Oak Common	25.12.59	Stafford Road F'cty **U**
12.7.41	Swindon Factory **R**	13.6.47	Old Oak Common	2.10.52	Old Oak Common Shps **U**	14.1.60	Old Oak Common
2.8.41	Swindon Stock	26.9.47	Old Oak Common Shps **R**	6.11.52	Old Oak Common	5.2.60	Old Oak Common Shps **U**
2.8.41	Old Oak Common	13.10.47	Old Oak Common	23.1.53	Swindon Factory **HI**	29.2.60	Old Oak Common
30.1.42	Old Oak Common (*wait*)	2.11.47	Old Oak Common Shps **R**	19.3.53	Old Oak Common	6.7.60	Old Oak Common Shps **U**
18.2.42	Swindon Factory **I**	25.11.47	Old Oak Common Shps **R**	21.9.53	Old Oak Common Shps **U**	15.9.60	Old Oak Common
1.4.42	Swindon Stock	15.12.47	Old Oak Common Shps **R**	13.10.53	Old Oak Common	7.3.61	Swindon Factory **HG**
5.4.42	Old Oak Common	31.12.47	Old Oak Common	19.11.53	Old Oak Common Shps **U**	12.5.61	Old Oak Common
26.11.42	Old Oak Common Shps **R**	22.1.48	Old Oak Common Shps **R**	3.12.53	Old Oak Common	5.3.62	Old Oak Common (*wait*)
30.12.42	Old Oak Common	17.2.48	Old Oak Common	15.2.54	Laira Shops **U**	16.3.62	Swindon Factory **LC**
9.2.43	Swindon Factory **I**	12.4.48	Old Oak Common (*wait*)	14.3.54	Old Oak Common	18.6.62	Old Oak Common
25.3.43	Swindon Stock	23.4.48	Swindon Factory **G**	22.4.54	Old Oak Common Shps **U**	3.8.62	In store
30.3.43	Old Oak Common	28.5.58	Old Oak Common	6.5.54	Old Oak Common	**7.9.62**	**Wthdrwn**
4.12.43	Old Oak Common (*wait*)	11.10.48	Old Oak Common (*wait*)	1.6.54	Swindon Factory **HG**	14.9.62	Sold as scrap to
16.12.43	Swindon Factory **L**	22.10.48	Swindon Factory **L**	28.7.54	Old Oak Common		J.Cashmore;
25.1.44	Swindon Pool	12.11.48	Old Oak Common	1.10.54	Laira Shops **U**		probably cut up at Great
29.1.44	Swindon Factory **L**	17.3.49	Old Oak Common **U**	27.10.54	Old Oak Common		Bridge.
3.2.44	Swindon Stock	1.4.49	Old Oak Common	27.1.55	Old Oak Common Shps **U**		
4.2.44	Old Oak Common	22.5.49	Old Oak Comn Shps **LC**	18.2.55	Old Oak Common		
24.6.44	Old Oak Common Shps **L**	27.6.49	Old Oak Common	22.9.55	Laira Shops **U**		
28.7.44	Old Oak Common	14.9.49	Old Oak Common (*wait*)	14.10.55	Old Oak Common		
22.8.44	Old Oak Common (*wait*)	22.9.49	Swindon Factory **HG**	21.10.55	Westbury (*wait*)		
27.9.44	Swindon Factory **L**	4.11.49	Old Oak Common	28.10.55	Bath Road Shops **U**		

Boilers and mileages:

First	4670 *	
6.3.30	..	(99,071)
19.6.31	4664	(167,259)
11.4.33	..	(267,305)

No.6009 KING CHARLES II at Old Oak Common on 7 August 1955. PHOTOGRAPH: ERIC SAWFORD

Only a few weeks out of Swindon after a heavy general, immaculately-groomed No.6010 KING CHARLES I stands at Old Oak Common on 20 March 1955. We're not too sure why the smokebox numberplate is edged in white - such an adornment was more usually associated with Scottish Region engines! PHOTOGRAPH: BRIAN MORRISON

30.5.34	4678	(339,193)
20.6.35	..	(409,733)
17.8.36	4670	(493,861)
27.11.37	..	(590,274)
7.3.39	..	(681,599)
27.5.40	4692	(761,225)
1.4.42	..	(879,304)
25.3.43	..	(947,120)
15.11.45	4665	(1,091,500)
31.12.46	4674	(1,162,488)
28.5.48	4673	(1,230,724)
4.11.49	4676	(1,301,199)
5.6.51	4669	(1,373,490)
19.3.53	4677	(1,467,149)
28.7.54	8615 *	(1,541,390)
25.5.56	4697	(1,617,561)
27.9.57	..	(1,711,198)
16.4.59	8623	(1,790,290)
12.5.61	8615	(1,887,913)
Final mileage:		1,935,102

Tenders:

First	2384
23.5.29	2390
9.2.31	2389
18.3.31	2390
19.6.31	2402
13.10.33	2548
26.7.34	2428
17.11.34	2642
7.2.41	2759
23.11.44	2763
31.12.46	2788
12.4.48	2800
19.3.53	2695
28.7.54	2564
25.5.56	2805
26.1.57	2913
10.8.57	2870
21.11.58	2727
12.5.61	2929
18.6.62	2818
11.8.62	2841

6010 KING CHARLES I
To stock: April 1928

Summary of sheds:

21.4.28	Laira
21.12.29	Newton Abbot
2.30	Laira
2.4.59	Old Oak Common

Engine history:

11.4.28	Swindon Factory
	ATC fitted
21.4.28	Laira
22.6.28	Swindon Factory L
26.6.28	Laira
29.12.28	Swindon Factory
22.1.29	Swindon Stock
16.2.29	Laira
15.6.29	Swindon Factory R
22.6.29	Swindon Stock
24.6.29	Laira
24.7.29	Laira Shops L
9.8.29	Laira
25.10.29	Swindon Factory H
14.12.29	Swindon Stock
21.12.29	Newton Abbot
2.30	Laira
3.5.30	Swindon Factory L
7.6.30	Swindon Stock
15.6.30	Laira
25.8.30	Laira Shops L
1.9.30	Laira
11.11.30	Newton Abbot F'cty L
3.12.30	Laira
22.12.30	Swindon Factory L
24.12.30	Laira
5.5.31	Laira *(wait)*
6.5.31	Swindon Factory I
29.6.31	Swindon Stock
3.7.31	Laira
20.2.32	Swindon Factory I
14.3.32	Swindon Stock
16.3.32	Laira

22.6.32	Laira Shops R
15.7.32	Laira
10.10.32	Swindon Factory G
7.12.32	Swindon Stock
14.12.32	Laira
11.1.33	Swindon Factory L
10.2.33	Swindon Stock
2.33	Laira
24.5.33	Swindon Factory L
2.6.33	Swindon Stock
6.33	Laira
2.9.33	Swindon Factory
	(speedometer)
6.9.33	Swindon Stock
9.33	Laira
14.9.33	Laira Shops R
29.9.33	Laira
2.1.34	Swindon Factory I
15.2.34	Swindon Stock
22.2.34	Laira
23.3.34	Swindon Factory
29.3.34	Laira
5.6.34	Swindon Factory L
8.6.34	Swindon Stock
11.6.34	Laira
10.11.34	Laira Shops R
24.11.34	Laira
7.1.35	Swindon Factory
11.1.35	Laira
8.2.35	Laira Shops L
23.2.35	Laira
4.4.35	Swindon Factory G
1.6.35	Swindon Stock
7.6.35	Laira
28.8.35	Swindon Factory L
27.9.35	Swindon Stock
2.10.35	Laira
12.10.35	Swindon Factory L
25.10.35	Swindon Stock
10.35	Laira
7.2.36	Taunton Shops
2.36	Laira
1.5.36	Newton Abbot F'cty

5.36	Laira
15.7.36	Swindon Factory L
25.7.36	Swindon Stock
31.7.36	Laira
17.11.36	Swindon Factory I
30.12.36	Swindon Stock
6.1.37	Laira
16.6.37	Swindon Factory L
8.7.37	Swindon Stock
11.7.37	Laira
29.10.37	Laira Shops R
18.11.37	Laira
29.12.37	Swindon Factory G
16.2.38	Swindon Stock
2.3.38	Laira
19.7.38	Swindon Factory L
13.8.38	Swindon Stock
18.8.38	Laira
30.3.39	Swindon Factory I
18.5.39	Swindon Stock
21.5.39	Laira
9.6.39	Swindon Factory L
17.6.39	Swindon Stock
24.6.39	Laira
6.10.39	Laira Shops R
26.10.39	Laira
16.11.39	Swindon Factory L
13.12.39	Swindon Stock
19.12.39	Laira
8.2.40	Swindon Factory L
1.3.40	Swindon Stock
6.3.40	Laira
30.10.40	Swindon Factory I
30.12.40	Swindon Stock
2.1.41	Laira
10.9.41	Laira Shops R
3.10.41	Laira
14.4.42	Swindon Factory I
1.6.42	Swindon Stock
3.6.42	Laira
25.9.42	Laira Shops R
18.10.42	Laira
16.3.43	Laira Shops R

8.4.43	Laira		
6.5.43	Laira *(wait)*		
26.5.43	Swindon Factory **G**		
6.7.43	Swindon Stock		
10.7.43	Laira		
11.11.43	Laira Shops **L**		
31.12.43	Laira		
16.5.44	Laira Shops **R**		
6.6.44	Laira		
31.7.44	Swindon Factory **I**		
8.9.44	Laira		
1.2.45	Laira Shops **R**		
16.2.45	Laira		
23.4.45	Laira Shops **R**		
7.5.45	Laira		
26.7.45	Laira Shops **R**		
10.8.45	Laira		
22.9.45	Laira Shops **R**		
17.10.45	Laira		
7.1.46	Swindon Factory **G**		
14.2.46	Laira		
19.6.46	Laira Shops **R**		
11.7.46	Laira		
23.9.46	Laira Shops **R**		
24.10.46	Laira		
27.12.46	Laira Shops **R**		
22.1.47	Laira		
25.1.47	Exeter *(wait)*		
8.2.47	Swindon Factory **I**		
17.3.47	Laira		
7.7.47	Laira Shops **R**		
16.7.47	Laira		
12.9.47	Taunton Shops **R**		
3.10.47	Laira		
1.3.48	Laira Shops **R**		
23.4.48	Laira		
27.7.48	Newton Abbot *(wait)*		
3.8.48	Swindon Factory **L**		
13.8.48	Laira		
28.9.48	Laira Shops **L**		
16.10.48	Laira		
17.12.48	Swindon Factory **HG**		
31.1.49	Laira		
9.5.49	Laira *(wait)*		
17.5.49	Swindon Factory **HC**		
31.5.49	Laira		
8.8.49	Laira Shops **U**		
26.8.49	Laira		
22.11.49	Laira Shops **U**		
15.12.49	Laira		
17.3.50	Laira Shops **U**		
30.3.50	Laira		
2.5.50	Swindon Factory **HG**		
5.6.50	Laira		
5.9.50	Laira Shops **U**		
15.9.50	Laira		
6.10.50	Laira *(wait)*		
20.10.50	Swindon Factory **LC**		
13.11.50	Laira		
19.2.51	Laira *(wait)*		
27.2.51	Swindon Factory **LC**		
21.3.51	Laira		
10.8.51	Laira *(wait)*		
17.8.51	Swindon Factory **HG**		
9.10.51	Laira		
15.10.51	Swindon Factory **U**		
17.10.51	Laira		
3.11.51	Old Oak Common *(wait)*		
7.11.51	Swindon Factory **LC**		
5.12.51	Laira		
25.2.52	Laira Shops **U**		
12.3.52	Laira		
5.4.52	Laira *(wait)*		
22.4.52	Swindon Factory **LC**		
14.5.52	Laira		
11.8.52	Laira *(wait)*		
16.9.52	Swindon Factory **LC**		
15.10.52	Laira		
31.12.52	Laira *(wait)*		

9.1.53	Swindon Factory **HI**
23.2.53	Laira
9.4.53	Swindon Factory **HI**
25.5.53	Laira
16.7.53	Laira *(wait)*
5.8.53	Swindon Factory **LC**
15.10.53	Laira
6.11.53	Laira *(wait)*
17.12.53	Swindon Factory **LC**
7.1.54	Laira
16.3.54	Laira *(wait)*
5.4.54	Swindon Factory **LC**
25.5.54	Laira
6.7.54	Laira Shops **U**
23.7.54	Laira
11.9.54	Laira Shops **U**
3.10.54	Laira
23.10.54	Laira Shops **U**
19.11.54	Laira
20.1.55	Laira *(wait)*
26.1.55	Swindon Factory **HG**
2.3.55	Laira
1.9.55	Taunton Shops **U**
21.9.55	Laira
21.10.55	Laira Shops **U**
5.11.55	Laira
24.1.56	Laira *(wait)*
28.1.56	Swindon Factory **HI**
27.3.56	Laira
3.1.57	Bath Road Shops **U**
31.1.57	Laira
17.6.57	Swindon Factory **HI**
12.9.57	Laira
26.9.57	Swindon Factory **LC**
10.10.57	Laira
22.11.57	Laira Shops **U**
3.12.57	Laira
1.5.58	Taunton Shops **U**
21.5.58	Laira
6.8.58	Laira Shops **U**
23.8.58	Laira
22.11.58	Laira Shops **U**
10.12.58	Laira
12.1.59	Taunton *(wait)*
15.1.59	Swindon Factory **HI**
2.4.59	Old Oak Common
27.4.60	Old Oak Common Shps **U**
12.5.60	Old Oak Common
19.7.60	Old Oak Common Shps **U**
5.8.60	Old Oak Common
7.9.60	Swindon Factory **HG**
31.10.60	Old Oak Common
6.5.61	Banbury Shops **U**
1.6.61	Old Oak Common
7.7.61	Reading Shops **U**
26.7.61	Old Oak Common
12.3.62	Canton Shops **U**
2.4.62	Old Oak Common
1.5.62	Ebbw Jctn Shops **U**
21.5.62	Old Oak Common
22.6.62	Wthdrwn
	Cut up at Swindon

Boilers and mileages:

First	4671 *	
14.12.29	..	(92,950)
29.6.31	..	(170,284)
7.12.32	4676	(244,377)
15.2.34	..	(307,157)
1.6.35	4668	(383,765)
30.12.36	..	(477,919)
16.2.38	4662	(553,302)
18.5.39	..	(640,246)
30.12.40	..	(736,802)
1.6.42	..	(829,503)
6.7.43	4685	(894,287)
8.9.44	..	(969,800)
14.2.46	4692	(1,061,543)
17.3.47	..	(1,125,239)

31.1.49	4680	(1,216,808)
31.5.49	4683	(1,239,222)
5.6.50	4672	(1,303,891)
9.10.5	4696 *	(1,381,345)
23.2.53	..	(1,439,893)
2.3.55	8622 *	(1,522,407)
27.3.56	..	(1,594,275)
12.9.57	8625	(1,682,902)
2.4.59	8611	(1,779,147)
31.10.60	8628	(1,859,765)
Final mileage:		1,928,258

Tenders:

First	2394
22.6.29	2399
14.12.29	2402
29.6.31	2403
7.12.32	2555
14.9.40	2710
1.6.42	2629
18.10.42	2665
6.7.43	2763
14.8.43	2678
11.9.43	2763
8.9.44	2649
31.5.49	2648
9.10.51	2849
15.10.52	2733
24.11.53	2428
7.1.54	2726
2.3.55	2762
27.3.56	2569
12.9.57	2394
2.4.59	2768
11.7.59	2743
31.10.60	2802

........................ooo........................

6011 KING JAMES I
To stock: April 1928

Summary of sheds:

1.5.28	Old Oak Common
11.39	Bath Road
6.43	Old Oak Common
17.1.46	Stafford Road
7.9.62	Old Oak Common

Engine history:

4.28	Swindon Factory
	ATC fitted
14.4.28	Swindon Stock
1.5.28	Old Oak Common
30.5.28	Swindon Factory **L**
5.6.28	Old Oak Common
6.7.28	Swindon Factory **L**
20.7.28	Old Oak Common
14.1.29	Swindon Factory **L**
6.3.29	Swindon Stock
11.3.29	Old Oak Common
15.6.29	Swindon Factory **R**
21.6.29	Swindon Stock
26.6.29	Old Oak Common
27.6.29	Swindon Factory **L**
12.7.29	Swindon Stock
19.7.29	Old Oak Common
19.11.29	Swindon Factory **L**
5.12.29	Swindon Stock
7.12.29	Old Oak Common
16.1.30	Swindon Factory **H**
15.4.30	Swindon Stock
28.4.30	Old Oak Common
21.11.30	Old Oak Common Shps **L**
20.12.30	Old Oak Common
13.1.31	Swindon Factory **L**
20.2.31	Swindon Stock
28.2.31	Old Oak Common

5.5.31	Swindon Factory **G**
24.6.31	Swindon Stock
30.6.31	Old Oak Common
6.4.32	Old Oak Common Shps **R**
22.4.32	Old Oak Common
6.10.32	Swindon Factory **I**
22.11.32	Swindon Stock
26.11.32	Old Oak Common
7.8.33	Old Oak Common *(wait)*
12.8.33	Swindon Factory **L**
25.8.33	Swindon Stock
8.33	Old Oak Common
31.10.33	Old Oak Common *(wait)*
18.11.33	Swindon Factory **I**
11.1.34	Swindon Stock
21.1.34	Old Oak Common
8.6.34	Old Oak Common *(wait)*
11.6.34	Swindon Factory **L**
12.7.34	Swindon Stock
25.7.34	Old Oak Common
10.10.34	Swindon Factory **L**
5.11.34	Swindon Stock
9.11.34	Old Oak Common
18.2.35	Swindon Factory **G**
26.4.35	Swindon Stock
7.5.35	Old Oak Common
2.10.35	Old Oak Common Shps **R**
18.10.35	Old Oak Common
28.2.36	Old Oak Common Shps **R**
24.3.36	Old Oak Common
24.3.36	Swindon Factory **I**
15.5.36	Swindon Stock
26.5.36	Old Oak Common
19.9.36	Swindon Factory **L**
30.9.36	Swindon Stock
6.10.36	Old Oak Common
4.11.36	Swindon Factory **L**
28.11.36	Swindon Stock
2.12.36	Old Oak Common
25.9.37	Swindon Factory **G**
10.11.37	Swindon Stock
14.11.37	Old Oak Common
11.4.38	Swindon Factory **L**
4.5.38	Swindon Stock
8.5.38	Old Oak Common
12.11.38	Swindon Factory **I**
30.12.38	Swindon Stock
8.1.39	Old Oak Common
11.39	Bath Road
11.12.39	Swindon Factory **I**
24.1.40	Swindon Stock
3.2.40	Bath Road
3.4.40	Bath Road Shops **R**
20.4.40	Bath Road
29.7.40	Swindon Factory **L**
3.9.40	Swindon Stock
7.9.40	Bath Road
21.10.40	Old Oak Common Shps **R**
23.11.40	Bath Road
26.1.41	Bath Road Shops **R**
11.3.41	Bath Road
28.4.41	Taunton Shops **R**
23.5.41	Bath Road
24.7.41	Bath Road Shops **R**
8.8.41	Bath Road
25.8.41	Old Oak Common Sops **R**
13.9.41	Bath Road
4.12.41	Swindon Factory **G**
24.1.42	Swindon Stock
3.2.42	Bath Road
10.2.42	Bath Road *(wait)*
14.2.42	Swindon Factory **L**
30.3.42	Swindon Stock
31.3.42	Bath Road
12.4.42	Taunton Shops **R**
6.5.42	Bath Road
14.5.42	Swindon Factory **R**
30.5.42	Swindon Stock
2.6.42	Bath Road

Old Oak shed, 5 May 1956. No.6011 KING JAMES I, having brought a cup final special into London, has been inscribed with the legend: 'Brum 0 Man 5' - a trifle optimistic, the result being a more modest 3-1 in Manchester City's favour. Note the fabricated double chimney. PHOTOGRAPH: BRIAN MORRISON

16.10.42	Bath Road Shops **R**		*Tender work only*	9.10.54	Stafford Road	**Boilers and mileages:**	
10.11.42	Bath Road	30.1.48	Stafford Road	20.10.54	Stafford Road *(wait)*	First	4673 *
11.12.42	Swindon Factory **L**	26.2.48	Stafford Road *(wait)*	2.11.54	Swindon Factory **HI**	15.4.30	..	(100,838)
16.1.43	Swindon Stock	10.3.48	Swindon Factory **L**	21.12.54	Stafford Road	24.6.31	4668	(165,733)
20.1.43	Bath Road	12.4.48	Stafford Road	19.2.55	Stafford Road *(wait)*	22.11.32	..	(243,155)
20.4.43	Old Oak Common Shps **R**	28.4.48	Stafford Road *(wait)*	26.2.55	Swindon Factory **U**	11.1.34	..	(307,902)
5.5.43	Bath Road	5.5.48	Swindon Factory **L**	11.3.55	Stafford Road	26.4.35	4662	(372,819)
6.43	Old Oak Common	11.6.48	Stafford Road	16.5.55	Tyseley Shops **U**	15.5.36	..	(440,189)
9.1.44	Swindon Factory **I**	19.9.48	Stafford Road **R**	23.5.55	Stafford Road	10.11.37	4664	(537,466)
17.2.44	Swindon Stock	5.10.48	Stafford Road	29.9.55	Old Oak Common Shps **U**	30.12.38	..	(623,268)
23.2.44	Old Oak Common	9.11.48	Stafford Road F'cty **L**	26.10.55	Stafford Road	24.1.40	..	(698,095)
9.3.44	Old Oak Common Shps **L**	10.12.48	Stafford Road	14.1.56	Stafford Road *(wait)*	24.1.42	4678	(786,161)
10.3.44	Old Oak Common	10.5.49	Old Oak Common Shps **U**	26.1.56	Swindon Factory **HG**	17.2.44	..	(892,033)
2.7.44	Old Oak Common *(wait)*	26.5.49	Stafford Road	26.3.56	Stafford Road	17.1.46	4688	(985,710)
26.7.44	Swindon Factory **L**	27.5.49	Swindon Factory **HI**	8.3.57	Old Oak Common *(wait)*	6.2.47	4666	(1,037,901)
8.8.44	Old Oak Common	1.7.49	Stafford Road	16.3.57	Swindon Factory **LI**	11.6.48	4689	(1,083,252)
15.11.44	Old Oak Common *(wait)*	28.2.50	Old Oak Common Shps **U**	7.6.57	Stafford Road	1.7.49	..	(1,124,055)
2.12.44	Swindon Factory **L**	29.3.50	Stafford Road	8.7.57	Stafford Road F'cty **U**	10.8.50	4688	(1,176,312)
29.12.44	Old Oak Common	8.6.50	Stafford Road *(wait)*	19.7.57	Stafford Road	16.10.51	4672	(1,232,482)
20.4.45	Old Oak Common Shps **R**	16.6.50	Swindon Factory **HC**	7.4.58	Old Oak Common Shps **U**	3.12.52	8605 *	(1,292,833)
10.5.45	Old Oak Common	10.8.50	Stafford Road	21.4.58	Stafford Road	21.12.54	4695	(1,359,584)
10.6.45	Old Oak Common Shps **R**	10.11.50	Old Oak Common Shps **U**	20.5.58	Stafford Road F'cty **U**	26.3.56	8608	(1,413,714)
11.7.45	Old Oak Common	30.11.50	Stafford Road	8.6.58	Stafford Road	20.5.60	..	(1,595,247)
26.9.45	Old Oak Common Shps **R**	15.3.51	Stafford Road *(wait)*	20.9.58	Swindon Factory **LI**	23.2.62	..	(1,679,040)
12.10.45	Old Oak Common	22.3.51	Swindon Factory **LC**	14.11.58	Stafford Road	Final mileage:		1,718,295
23.11.45	Old Oak Common *(wait)*	17.4.51	Stafford Road	17.3.59	Stafford Road F'cty **U**			
8.12.45	Swindon Factory **G**	7.9.51	Swindon Factory **HI**	10.4.59	Stafford Road	**Tenders:**	
17.1.46	Stafford Road	16.10.51	Stafford Road	5.12.59	Stafford Road **U**	First	2395
29.12.46	Didcot *(wait)*	29.9.52	Stafford Road *(wait)*	2.1.60	Stafford Road	15.4.30	2547
8.1.47	Swindon Factory **I**	23.10.52	Swindon Factory **HG**	1.3.60	Swindon Factory **LI**	24.6.31	2442
6.2.47	Stafford Road	3.12.52	Stafford Road	20.5.60	Stafford Road	25.8.33	2425
27.2.47	Swindon Factory	5.1.53	Swindon Factory	18.11.60	Stafford Road **U**	24.1.40	2710
13.3.47	Stafford Road		*On test plant*	16.12.60	Stafford Road	3.9.40	2775
18.3.47	Westbury *(wait)*	28.4.53	Swindon Factory **U**	14.8.61	Stafford Road **U**	24.1.42	2643
21.3.47	Swindon Factory	5.6.53	Stafford Road	6.9.61	Stafford Road	16.1.43	2728
2.4.47	Stafford Road	10.11.53	Stafford Road F'cty **U**	28.10.61	Swindon Factory **HI**	8.8.44	2409
26.5.47	Stafford Road **R**	6.1.54	Stafford Road	23.2.62	Stafford Road	29.12.44	2800
11.6.47	Stafford Road	11.1.54	Stafford Road *(wait)*	7.9.62	Old Oak Common	17.1.46	2629
10.1.48	Stafford Road **R**	30.1.54	Swindon Factory **LC**	**18.12.62**	Wthdrwn (alternatively	6.2.47	2775
26.1.48	Stafford Road	24.3.54	Stafford Road		stated to be 21.12.62)	16.10.51	2808
28.1.48	Banbury	25.9.54	Stafford Road **U**	25.1.64	Cut up at Swindon	21.12.54	2715

11.3.55	2815
7.6.57	2922
8.57	2815
14.9.57	2829
14.6.58	2742
23.2.62	2386

.......................ooo..........................

6012 KING EDWARD VI
To stock: April 1928

Summary of sheds:

21.4.28	Newton Abbot
5.7.28	Laira
6.54	Old Oak Common
16.10.59	Laira (loan?)
4.11.59	Old Oak Common
3.4.62	Stafford Road

Engine history:

21.4.28	Swindon Stock	27.4.31	Swindon Factory **R**	3.6.39	Laira	23.4.46	Laira Shops **R**
26.4.28	Newton Abbot	28.4.31	Swindon Stock	22.8.39	Laira Shops **R**	8.5.46	Laira
16.6.28	Swindon Factory **L**	2.5.31	Laira	7.9.39	Laira	5.7.46	Laira Shops **R**
5.7.28	Laira	2.6.31	Newton Abbot *(wait)*	7.11.39	Swindon Factory **I**	26.7.46	Laira
1.9.28	Swindon Factory **L**	10.6.31	Swindon Factory **L**	13.12.39	Swindon Stock	21.10.46	Laira *(wait)*
30.10.28	Laira	31.7.31	Swindon Stock	21.12.39	Laira	28.10.46	Swindon Factory **G**
3.1.29	Laira Shops **L**	8.8.31	Laira	11.12.40	Swindon Factory **I**	12.12.46	Laira
14.1.29	Laira	21.9.31	Laira *(wait)*	30.1.41	Swindon Stock	18.12.46	Laira Shops **R**
19.2.29	Swindon Factory **L**	3.11.31	Swindon Factory **L**	2.2.41	Laira	12.2.47	Laira
28.3.29	Swindon Stock	26.11.31	Swindon Stock	11.8.41	Old Oak Common Shps **R**	4.6.47	Laira Shops **R**
2.4.29	Laira	2.12.31	Laira	25.9.41	Laira	27.6.47	Laira
20.6.29	Swindon Factory **R**	3.3.32	Laira Shops **R**	3.10.41	Laira Shops **R**	28.10.47	Laira *(wait)*
24.6.29	Swindon Stock	23.3.32	Laira	13.10.41	Laira	18.11.47	Swindon Factory **L**
29.6.29	Laira	25.4.32	Swindon Factory **G**	3.12.41	Exeter *(wait)*	24.12.47	Laira
26.8.29	Laira Shops **L**	6.7.32	Swindon Stock	6.12.41	Swindon Factory **R**	2.1.48	Swindon Factory **L**
6.9.29	Laira	12.7.32	Laira	13.1.42	Swindon Stock	8.1.48	Laira
11.11.29	Laira Shops **L**	7.6.33	Laira Shops **R**	18.1.42	Laira	16.3.48	Laira Shops **R**
22.11.29	Laira	27.6.33	Laira	8.2.42	Laira Shops **R**	2.4.48	Laira
1.1.30	Swindon Factory **H**	3.10.33	Swindon Factory **I**	19.3.42	Laira	9.7.48	Laira Shops **R**
19.3.30	Swindon Stock	24.11.33	Laira	5.9.42	Swindon Factory **I**	23.7.48	Laira
25.3.30	Swindon Factory **R**	8.6.34	Laira Shops **R**	21.10.42	Swindon Stock	21.9.48	Swindon Factory **I**
4.4.30	Swindon Stock	27.6.34	Laira	24.10.42	Laira	2.11.48	Laira
17.4.30	Laira	11.11.34	Laira *(wait)*	16.12.42	Laira Shops **R**	22.12.48	Swindon Factory
27.8.30	Swindon Factory **R**	13.11.34	Swindon Factory **G**	21.1.43	Laira	5.1.49	Laira
28.8.30	Laira	8.1.35	Swindon Stock	29.6.43	Laira Shops **R**	16.1.49	Old Oak Common Shps **U**
10.10.30	Newton Abbot F'cty **R**	18.1.35	Laira	13.7.43	Laira	31.1.49	Laira
29.10.30	Laira	19.9.35	Laira *(wait)*	23.9.43	Laira Shops **R**	13.7.49	Laira Shops **U**
19.1.31	Newton Abbot F'cty **R**	19.11.35	Swindon Factory **I**	14.10.43	Laira	11.8.49	Laira
5.2.31	Laira	7.1.36	Swindon Stock	13.11.43	Stafford Road **R**	2.11.49	Old Oak Common Shps **U**
		19.1.36	Laira	3.12.43	Laira	23.11.49	Laira
		14.5.36	Swindon Factory **L**	14.12.43	Laira *(wait)*	6.12.49	Laira Shops **U**
		25.5.36	Swindon Stock	31.12.43	Swindon Factory **G**	9.4.50	Laira *(wait)*
		30.5.36	Laira	1.2.44	Swindon Stock	14.4.50	Swindon Factory **HG**
		9.10.36	Laira *(wait)*	8.2.44	Laira	23.5.50	Laira
		3.2.37	Swindon Factory **I**	21.6.44	Laira Shops **R**	2.10.50	Laira Shops **U**
		23.3.37	Swindon Stock	5.7.44	Laira	12.10.50	Laira
		28.3.37	Laira	20.11.44	Laira Shops **R**	3.12.50	Laira Shops **U**
		2.9.37	Stafford Road F'cty **L**	30.11.44	Laira	11.1.51	Laira
		12.9.37	Laira	12.2.45	Laira Shops **R**	13.2.51	Laira Shops **U**
		21.10.37	Taunton Shops **R**	6.3.45	Laira	2.3.51	Laira
		3.12.37	Laira	4.5.45	Laira *(wait)*	2.5.51	Laira Shops **U**
		8.2.38	Laira Shops **R**	24.5.45	Newton Abbot Shops **L**	8.6.51	Laira
		23.2.38	Laira	6.6.45	Laira	18.9.51	Swindon Factory **HG**
		21.4.38	Laira Shops **R**	16.6.45	Westbury *(wait)*		(start)
		5.5.38	Laira	19.6.45	Swindon Factory **I**	25.10.51	Swindon Stock
		19.7.38	Swindon Factory **G**	23.8.45	Laira	9.11.51	Swindon Factory **HG**
		13.9.38	Swindon Stock	10.1.46	Newton Abbot F'cty **L**		(finish)
		22.9.38	Laira	8.2.46	Laira	27.11.51	Laira
		28.4.39	Swindon Factory **L**	1.4.46	Laira Shops **R**	28.4.52	Laira Shops **U**
		26.5.39	Swindon Stock	19.4.46	Laira	11.5.52	Laira
						18.8.52	Laira Shops **U**
						9.9.52	Laira
						25.11.52	Laira Shops **U**
						15.12.52	Laira
						28.1.53	Laira Shops **U**
						13.2.53	Laira
						10.3.53	Swindon Factory **HI**
						21.4.53	Laira
						11.7.53	Laira *(wait)*
						29.7.53	Swindon Factory **LC**
						23.9.53	Laira
						26.12.53	Laira Shops **U**
						29.12.53	Laira
						18.5.54	Laira Shops **U**
						4.6.54	Laira
						6.54	Old Oak Common
						13.9.54	Old Oak Common *(wait)*
						20.9.54	Swindon Factory **HG**
						28.10.54	Old Oak Common
						25.2.55	Old Oak Common *(wait)*
						26.2.55	Swindon Factory **LC**
						19.4.55	Old Oak Common
						4.9.55	Taunton Shops **U**
						30.9.55	Old Oak Common
						2.11.55	Laira *(wait)*
						5.11.55	Swindon Factory **LC**
						30.12.55	Old Oak Common
						9.1.56	Swindon Factory **LC**
						7.2.56	Old Oak Common

No.6012 KING EDWARD VI, not long out of Swindon, it would appear, after receiving its new blue livery (applied May 1950) hauls the 'Riviera' through Sonning Cutting. PHOTOGRAPH: NATIONAL RAILWAY MUSEUM

14.3.56	Old Oak Common Shps U
6.4.56	Old Oak Common
19.4.56	Old Oak Common Shps U
4.5.56	Old Oak Common
24.7.56	Old Oak Common (wait)
27.7.56	Swindon Factory HI
10.9.56	Old Oak Common
15.9.56	Old Oak Common (wait)
20.9.56	Swindon Factory U
5.10.56	Old Oak Common
16.8.57	Bath Road Shops U
7.9.57	Old Oak Common
1.10.57	Old Oak Common Shps U
15.10.57	Old Oak Common
27.11.57	Old Oak Common (wait)
29.11.57	Swindon Factory HG
12.2.58	Old Oak Common
21.7.58	Old Oak Comn Shps LC
8.8.58	Old Oak Common
2.1.59	Old Oak Common Shps U
6.1.59	Old Oak Common
8.5.59	Old Oak Common Shps U
2.6.59	Old Oak Common
15.8.59	Swindon Factory HG
16.10.59	Laira (on loan)
4.11.59	Old Oak Common
13.1.60	Old Oak Common (wait)
25.1.60	Swindon Factory LC
12.2.60	Old Oak Common
26.2.60	Swindon Factory LC
11.4.60	Old Oak Common
24.10.60	Old Oak Common Shps U
10.11.60	Old Oak Common
9.3.61	Old Oak Common (wait)
18.3.61	Swindon Factory LI
12.5.61	Old Oak Common
1.8.61	Stafford Road U
31.8.61	Old Oak Common
14.12.61	Old Oak Common (wait)
12.1.62	Swindon Factory LC
14.3.62	Old Oak Common
20.3.62	Old Oak Common Shps U
3.4.62	Stafford Road
20.8.62	In store (Stafford Road)
7.9.62	Wthdrwn
9.10.63	Sold as scrap to Cox & Danks of Langley Green

Boilers and mileages:

First	4672 *	
19.3.30	..	(103,618)
6.7.32	4679	(215,099)
24.11.33	..	(303,075)
8.1.35	4681	(372,480)
7.1.36	..	(443,494)
23.3.37	..	(520,729)
13.9.38	4663	(618,950)
13.12.39	..	(704,639)
30.1.41	..	(779,648)
21.10.42	..	(879,232)
1.2.44	4694	(953,754)
23.8.45	..	(1,041,250)
12.12.46	4680	(1,117,311)
2.11.48	4666	(1,201,139)
23.5.50	4661	(1,277,968)
25.10.51	4687	(1,356,948)
21.4.53	4669	(1,448,053)
28.10.54	8619	(1,539,048)
10.9.56	..	(1,614,698)
12.2.58	8617	(1,691,805)
16.10.59	8603	(1,786,212)
12.5.61	..	(1,858,321)
Final mileage:		1,910,525

Tenders:

First	2396
28.4.31	2548
31.7.31	2554
26.11.31	2550

23.3.37	2547
30.1.41	2695
21.10.42	2707
23.8.45	2695
3.11.45	2759
12.12.46	2743
2.11.48	2763
5.1.49	2716
28.10.54	2395
19.4.55	2775
13.8.55	2931
30.12.55	2544
10.9.56	2717
30.11.57	2620
12.2.58	2846
16.10.59	2646
12.5.61	2564
14.3.62	2413

.....................ooo.........................

6013 KING HENRY VIII
To stock: April 1928

Summary of sheds:

15.5.28	Old Oak Common
2.4.59	Laira
4.3.60	Old Oak Common
16.6.61	Stafford Road

Engine history:

4.28	Swindon Factory ATC fitted
28.4.28	Swindon Stock
15.5.28	Old Oak Common
20.6.28	Swindon Factory L
29.6.28	Old Oak Common
15.9.28	Swindon Factory L
28.9.28	Old Oak Common
6.3.29	Swindon Factory L
24.4.29	Swindon Stock
1.5.29	Old Oak Common
24.6.29	Swindon Factory R
27.6.29	Swindon Stock
3.7.29	Old Oak Common
31.10.29	Swindon Factory L
25.11.29	Swindon Stock
29.11.29	Old Oak Common
8.1.30	Swindon Factory H
7.4.30	Swindon Stock
15.4.30	Old Oak Common
8.5.30	Taunton Shops R
27.5.30	Old Oak Common
15.9.30	Old Oak Common Shps R
1.10.30	Old Oak Common
7.11.30	Old Oak Common (wait)
18.11.30	Swindon Factory L
16.1.31	Swindon Stock
22.1.31	Old Oak Common
20.6.31	Swindon Factory R
24.6.31	Swindon Stock
26.6.31	Old Oak Common
11.1.32	Old Oak Common Shps L
17.2.32	Old Oak Common
21.4.32	Swindon Factory I
17.6.32	Swindon Stock
24.6.32	Old Oak Common
10.3.33	Swindon Factory G
18.5.33	Swindon Stock
5.33	Old Oak Common
5.10.33	Old Oak Common Shps R
27.10.33	Old Oak Common
17.4.34	Swindon Factory I
31.5.34	Swindon Stock
7.6.34	Old Oak Common
11.8.34	Swindon Factory L
4.9.34	Swindon Stock
9.9.34	Old Oak Common
14.9.34	Taunton Shops R

10.10.34	Old Oak Common
4.3.35	Old Oak Common Shps R
23.3.35	Old Oak Common
18.5.35	Swindon Factory G
11.7.35	Swindon Stock
20.7.35	Old Oak Common
14.9.35	Swindon Factory L
18.9.35	Swindon Stock
18.9.35	Old Oak Common
28.9.35	Swindon Factory L
2.10.35	Swindon Stock
14.10.35	Old Oak Common
28.1.36	Old Oak Common Shps R
15.2.36	Old Oak Common
14.4.36	Old Oak Common Shps R
15.5.36	Old Oak Common
23.9.36	Swindon Factory I
5.11.36	Swindon Stock
13.11.36	Old Oak Common
5.7.37	Old Oak Common Shps L
20.7.37	Old Oak Common
23.7.37	Swindon Factory L
6.8.37	Swindon Stock
8.8.37	Old Oak Common
30.8.37	Taunton Shops R
25.9.37	Old Oak Common
10.1.38	Old Oak Common (wait)
11.1.38	Swindon Factory G
18.3.38	Swindon Stock
27.3.38	Old Oak Common
13.8.38	Reading (wait)
22.8.38	Swindon Factory L
6.9.38	Swindon Stock
11.9.38	Old Oak Common
16.1.39	Old Oak Common (wait)
31.1.39	Swindon Factory I
14.3.39	Swindon Stock
19.3.39	Old Oak Common
12.10.39	Old Oak Common Shps R
24.10.39	Old Oak Common
13.3.40	Old Oak Common Shps R
2.4.40	Old Oak Common
8.4.40	Swindon Factory I
16.5.40	Swindon Stock
23.5.40	Old Oak Common
21.4.41	Old Oak Common (wait)
23.4.41	Swindon Factory I
16.6.41	Swindon Stock
22.6.41	Old Oak Common
19.5.42	Old Oak Common Shps R
24.6.42	Old Oak Common
4.8.42	Swindon Factory G
25.9.42	Swindon Stock
28.9.42	Old Oak Common
1.6.43	Old Oak Common R
21.6.43	Old Oak Common
1.10.43	Swindon Factory I
24.11.43	Swindon Stock
28.11.43	Old Oak Common
23.12.43	Swindon Factory R
1.1.44	Swindon Stock
8.1.44	Old Oak Common
19.1.44	Exeter (wait)
23.1.44	Swindon Factory R
2.2.44	Swindon Stock
6.2.44	Old Oak Common
25.5.44	Old Oak Common Shps R
15.6.44	Old Oak Common
15.9.44	Old Oak Common Shps R
24.10.44	Old Oak Common
9.2.45	Old Oak Common Shps R
23.2.45	Old Oak Common
6.4.45	Old Oak Common (wait)
24.4.45	Swindon Factory I
14.6.45	Old Oak Common
31.10.45	Old Oak Common (wait)
23.11.45	Swindon Factory L
12.12.45	Old Oak Common
16.12.45	Old Oak Common Shps R

16.1.46	Old Oak Common
22.5.46	Swindon Factory L
29.6.46	Old Oak Common
2.11.46	Old Oak Common Shps L
15.12.46	Old Oak Common
25.1.47	Old Oak Common (wait)
29.1.47	Swindon Factory G
4.3.47	Old Oak Common
11.3.47	Swindon Factory G
22.3.47	Old Oak Common
17.4.47	Laira Shops R
14.5.47	Old Oak Common
12.9.47	Old Oak Common Shps L
15.10.47	Old Oak Common
13.11.47	Old Oak Common R
4.12.47	Old Oak Common
6.1.48	Old Oak Common Shps L
5.2.48	Old Oak Common
2.3.48	Old Oak Common (wait)
15.3.48	Swindon Factory L
14.4.48	Old Oak Common
11.6.48	Old Oak Common Shps R
8.7.48	Old Oak Common
28.10.48	Old Oak Common Shps R
26.11.48	Old Oak Common
7.1.49	Swindon Factory HG
10.2.49	Old Oak Common
10.6.49	Old Oak Common Shps U
24.6.49	Old Oak Common
26.8.49	Old Oak Comn Shps LC
9.9.49	Old Oak Common
25.10.49	Westbury (wait)
28.10.49	Swindon Factory LC
25.11.49	Old Oak Common
3.3.50	Laira Shops U
30.3.50	Old Oak Common
12.5.50	Swindon Factory HG
19.6.50	Old Oak Common
15.3.51	Old Oak Common U
2.4.51	Old Oak Common
23.4.51	Laira (wait)
26.4.51	Swindon Factory LC
11.5.51	Old Oak Common
17.8.51	Old Oak Common (wait)
22.8.51	Swindon Factory HG
10.10.51	Old Oak Common
6.3.52	Old Oak Common (wait)
10.3.52	Swindon Factory LC
18.4.52	Old Oak Common
10.9.52	Old Oak Common U
30.9.52	Old Oak Common
24.11.52	Old Oak Common U
11.12.52	Old Oak Common
20.1.53	Old Oak Common (wait)
26.1.53	Swindon Factory HI
13.3.53	Old Oak Common
15.7.53	Old Oak Common (wait)
12.8.53	Swindon Factory LC
21.9.53	Old Oak Common
13.5.54	Old Oak Common Shps U
29.5.54	Old Oak Common
16.6.54	Old Oak Common (wait)
30.6.54	Swindon Factory HG
22.9.54	Old Oak Common
9.11.54	Old Oak Common (wait)
18.11.54	Swindon Factory U
1.12.54	Old Oak Common
26.5.55	Laira Shops U
27.6.55	Old Oak Common
19.7.55	Old Oak Common Shps U
19.8.55	Old Oak Common
29.8.55	Bath Road Shops U
11.10.55	Old Oak Common
26.1.56	Old Oak Comn Shps LC
17.2.56	Old Oak Common
1.5.56	Swindon Factory HI
27.6.56	Old Oak Common
15.6.57	Taunton Shops U
16.6.57	Old Oak Common

The down 'Riviera', headed by No.6013 KING HENRY VIII, passes through Wellington on 29 June 1957. PHOTOGRAPH: R.E. TOOP

26.7.57	Old Oak Common *(wait)*	18.3.38	4680	(596,455)
27.7.57	Swindon Factory **U**	14.3.39	..	(664,920)
15.8.57	Old Oak Common	16.5.40	..	(752,850)
28.8.57	Old Oak Common *(wait)*	16.6.41	..	(825,770)
4.9.57	Swindon Factory **HI**	25.9.42	4679	(908,197)
17.10.57	Old Oak Common	24.11.43	..	(983,833)
23.10.58	Old Oak Common Shps **U**	14.6.45	..	(1,060,125)
12.11.58	Old Oak Common	22.3.47	4667	(1,149,519)
2.12.58	Old Oak Common Shps **U**	10.2.49	4682	(1,239,835)
18.12.58	Old Oak Common	19.6.50	4686	(1,318,911)
22.12.58	Taunton Shops **U**	10.10.51	4697 *	(1,398,986)
21.1.59	Old Oak Common	13.3.53	..	(1,486,161)
3.2.59	Swindon Factory **HG**	22.9.54	8616 *	(1,536,060)
18.3.59	Old Oak Common	27.6.56	..	(1,618,928)
2.4.59	Laira	17.10.57	8622	(1,705,808)
4.3.60	Old Oak Common	18.3.59	8621	(1,785,249)
6.5.60	Old Oak Common Shps **U**			
25.5.60	Old Oak Common	8.8.60	..	(1,862,985)
27.5.60	Old Oak Common *(wait)*	Final mileage:		1,950,462
3.6.60	Swindon Factory **LI**			
8.8.60	Old Oak Common	**Tenders:**		
8.5.61	Stafford Road F'cty **LC**	First	2397	
16.6.61	Stafford Road	24.4.29	2398	
8.8.61	Stafford Road **U**	7.4.30	2428	
24.8.61	Stafford Road	1.10.30	2398	
1.3.62	Stafford Road **U**	16.1.31	2387	
21.3.62	Stafford Road	6.8.37	2557	
12.6.62	Wthdrwn (alternatively	1.38	2695	
	stated to be 19.6.62)	2.4.40	2726	
29.12.62	Cut up at Swindon	16.6.41	2609	
		25.9.42	2849	
Boilers and mileages:		10.10.51	2775	
First	4675 *	18.4.52	2695	
7.4.30	..	13.3.53	2800	
(104,476)		27.2.54	2695	
16.1.31	4665	22.9.54	2629	
(146,440)		5.10.54	2931	
17.6.32	..	13.8.55	2775	
(232,808)		27.6.56	2710	
18.5.33	4682	3.11.56	2934	
(291,138)		17.10.57	2540	
31.5.34	..	18.3.59	2795	
(361,742)		1.62	2436	
11.7.35	4676	2.62	2775	
(427,691)				
5.11.36	..			
(513,129)				

........................ooo........................

6014 KING HENRY VII
To stock: May 1928

Summary of sheds:

18.6.28	Newton Abbot
3.6.29	Laira
30.7.30	Old Oak Common
8.30	Stafford Road
26.3.35	Old Oak Common
10.52	Laira
16.2.54	Stafford Road

Engine history:

5.28	Swindon Factory	
	ATC fitted	
8.5.28	Swindon Stock	
2.6.28	Swindon Factory **L**	
18.6.28	Newton Abbot	
28.11.28	Newton Abbot F'cty **L**	
12.12.28	Newton Abbot	
3.4.29	Swindon Factory **L**	
27.5.29	Swindon Stock	
3.6.29	Laira	
7.10.29	Swindon Factory **L**	
7.11.29	Swindon Stock	
9.11.29	Laira	
7.3.30	Laira Shops **L**	
19.3.30	Laira	
16.6.30	Swindon Factory **H**	
17.7.30	Swindon Stock	
30.7.30	Old Oak Common	
8.30	Stafford Road	
6.10.30	Swindon Factory **L**	
3.11.30	Swindon Stock	
8.11.30	Stafford Road	
18.11.30	Swindon Factory **L**	
26.11.30	Swindon Stock	
5.12.30	Stafford Road	
11.6.31	Swindon Factory **L**	
13.8.31	Swindon Stock	
18.8.31	Stafford Road	
20.2.32	Swindon Factory **L**	
10.3.32	Swindon Stock	
18.3.32	Stafford Road	
30.5.32	Swindon Factory **L**	
6.7.32	Swindon Stock	
9.7.32	Stafford Road	

25.10.32	Swindon Factory **I**	
16.12.32	Swindon Stock	
21.12.32	Stafford Road	
19.6.33	Stafford Road F'cty **L**	
23.6.33	Stafford Road	
15.7.33	Swindon Factory **G**	
26.9.33	Swindon Stock	
29.6.34	Stafford Road F'cty **L**	
26.7.34	Stafford Road	
15.10.34	Stafford Road F'cty **L**	
19.10.34	Stafford Road	
19.1.35	Swindon Factory **G**	
	'Streamlined'	
11.3.35	Swindon Stock	
26.3.35	Old Oak Common	
20.8.35	Swindon Factory **L**	
22.8.35	Swindon Stock	
22.8.35	Old Oak Common	
10.12.35	Swindon Factory **L**	
20.12.35	Swindon Stock	
23.12.35	Old Oak Common	
13.3.36	Swindon Factory **I**	
29.4.36	Swindon Stock	
3.5.36	Old Oak Common	
3.8.36	Taunton *(wait)*	
31.8.36	Swindon Factory **L**	
11.9.36	Swindon Stock	
13.9.36	Old Oak Common	
13.10.36	Swindon Factory **L**	
9.11.36	Swindon Stock	
11.11.36	Old Oak Common	
14.1.37	Swindon Factory **L**	
2.2.37	Swindon Stock	
4.2.37	Old Oak Common	
4.3.37	Taunton Shops	
12.3.37	Old Oak Common	
28.4.37	Old Oak Common Shps **R**	
15.5.37	Old Oak Common	
6.7.37	Swindon Factory **L**	
12.7.37	Swindon Stock	
25.7.37	Old Oak Common	
8.11.37	Swindon Factory **G**	
24.12.37	Swindon Stock	
2.1.38	Old Oak Common	
17.1.38	Old Oak Common Shps **R**	
12.2.38	Old Oak Common	
17.10.38	Old Oak Common Shps **R**	
8.11.38	Old Oak Common	
14.3.39	Swindon Factory **I**	
4.5.39	Swindon Stock	
7.5.39	Old Oak Common	
10.9.39	Old Oak Common Shps **R**	
30.9.39	Old Oak Common	
25.12.39	Old Oak Common Shps **R**	
8.1.40	Old Oak Common	
13.4.40	Swindon Factory **I**	
31.5.40	Swindon Stock	
7.6.40	Old Oak Common	
30.9.41	Old Oak Common *(wait)*	
3.10.41	Swindon Factory **G**	
29.11.41	Swindon Stock	
3.12.41	Old Oak Common	
11.12.42	Swindon Factory **I**	
21.1.43	Swindon Stock	
25.1.43	Old Oak Common	
7.4.43	Old Oak Common Shps **R**	
11.5.43	Old Oak Common	
10.2.44	Old Oak Common Shps **R**	
29.2.44	Old Oak Common	
11.4.44	Old Oak Common Shps **R**	
26.4.44	Old Oak Common	
1.5.44	Old Oak Common Shps **R**	
16.6.44	Old Oak Common	
13.8.44	Old Oak Common *(wait)*	
23.8.44	Swindon Factory **G**	
19.10.44	Old Oak Common	
11.7.45	Old Oak Common Shps **R**	
27.7.45	Old Oak Common	
23.1.46	Swindon Factory **I**	

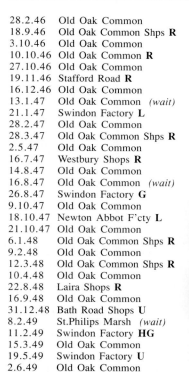

28.2.46	Old Oak Common
18.9.46	Old Oak Common Shps **R**
3.10.46	Old Oak Common
10.10.46	Old Oak Common **R**
27.10.46	Old Oak Common
19.11.46	Stafford Road **R**
16.12.46	Old Oak Common
13.1.47	Old Oak Common *(wait)*
21.1.47	Swindon Factory **L**
28.2.47	Old Oak Common
28.3.47	Old Oak Common Shps **R**
2.5.47	Old Oak Common
16.7.47	Westbury Shops **R**
14.8.47	Old Oak Common
16.8.47	Old Oak Common *(wait)*
26.8.47	Swindon Factory **G**
9.10.47	Old Oak Common
18.10.47	Newton Abbot F'cty **L**
21.10.47	Old Oak Common
6.1.48	Old Oak Common Shps **R**
9.2.48	Old Oak Common
12.3.48	Old Oak Common Shps **R**
10.4.48	Old Oak Common
22.8.48	Laira Shops **R**
16.9.48	Old Oak Common
31.12.48	Bath Road Shops **U**
8.2.49	St.Philips Marsh *(wait)*
11.2.49	Swindon Factory **HG**
15.3.49	Old Oak Common
19.5.49	Swindon Factory **U**
2.6.49	Old Oak Common
10.7.49	Old Oak Common Shps **U**
28.7.49	Old Oak Common
7.11.49	Old Oak Common Shps **U**
28.11.49	Old Oak Common
17.6.50	Westbury *(wait)*
20.6.50	Swindon Factory **HG**
18.8.50	Old Oak Common
30.11.50	Old Oak Common Shps **U**
2.1.51	Old Oak Common
9.4.51	Laira Shops **U**
24.4.51	Old Oak Common
2.10.51	Old Oak Common Shps **U**
16.10.51	Old Oak Common
13.11.51	Westbury *(wait)*
19.11.51	Swindon Factory **HG**
11.1.52	Old Oak Common
7.3.52	Old Oak Common *(wait)*
17.3.52	Swindon Factory **HG**
2.4.52	Old Oak Common
23.7.52	Old Oak Common Shps **U**
14.8.52	Old Oak Common
10.52	Laira
27.10.52	Laira Shops **U**
2.11.52	Laira
29.12.52	Laira Shops **U**
16.1.53	Laira
25.2.53	Taunton Shops **LC**
27.3.53	Laira
12.7.53	Reading Shops **U**
13.8.53	Laira
17.9.53	Laira Shops **U**
6.10.53	Laira
11.1.54	Swindon Factory **HG**
16.2.54	Stafford Road
17.2.54	Leamington *(wait)*
22.2.54	Stafford Road F'cty **U**
3.3.54	Stafford Road
29.9.54	Old Oak Common Shps **U**
5.11.54	Stafford Road
12.4.55	Stafford Road F'cty **U**
25.4.55	Stafford Road
4.7.55	Old Oak Common *(wait)*
19.7.55	Swindon Factory **LI**
25.8.55	Stafford Road
31.8.55	Stafford Road *(wait)*
6.9.55	Swindon Factory **HC**
1.11.55	Stafford Road
24.1.56	Stafford Road **LC**

The once-'streamlined' No.6014 KING HENRY VII retained its wedge-fronted cab until the end of its days. It is seen here passing through Widney Manor in 1957, double-heading with 'Hall' No.6960. PHOTOGRAPH: MICHAEL MENSING

14.2.56	Stafford Road
1.6.56	Stafford Road *(wait)*
8.6.56	Swindon Factory **HG**
11.10.56	Stafford Road
14.6.57	Stafford Road F'cty **U**
17.6.57	Stafford Road
19.7.57	Stafford Road *(wait)*
25.7.57	Swindon Factory **HG**
20.9.57	Stafford Road
9.10.57	Stafford Road F'cty **LC**
15.10.57	Stafford Road
28.6.58	Stafford Road **U**
19.7.58	Stafford Road
25.8.58	Old Oak Common Shps **U**
17.9.58	Stafford Road
8.10.58	Stafford Road **U**
22.10.58	Stafford Road
17.6.59	Swindon Factory **LI**
2.10.59	Stafford Road
14.10.59	Stafford Road **U**
30.10.59	Stafford Road
24.5.60	Stafford Road F'cty **LC**
7.7.60	Stafford Road
14.7.60	Banbury *(wait)*
3.8.60	Stafford Road F'cty **U**
19.8.60	Stafford Road
11.10.60	Banbury Shops **U**
3.11.60	Stafford Road
5.12.60	Stafford Road **U**
29.12.60	Stafford Road
8.9.61	Swindon Factory **HG**
6.12.61	Stafford Road
28.2.62	Old Oak Common Shps **U**
16.3.62	Stafford Road
23.5.62	Old Oak Common Shps **U**
18.6.62	Stafford Road
20.8.62	In store (Stafford Road)
7.9.62	Wthdrwn (alternatively stated to be 21.9.62)
7.3.63	Sold as scrap to Cox & Danks of Langley Green

Boilers and mileages:

First	4674 *	
17.7.30	..	(112,531)
13.8.31	4670	(155,755)
16.12.32	..	(216,546)
26.9.33	4661	(255,639)

11.3.35	4679	(337,637)
29.4.36	..	(417,908)
24.12.37	4666	(512,685)
4.5.39	..	(608,165)
31.5.40	..	(683,749)
29.11.41	4682	(787,300)
21.1.43	..	(870,143)
19.10.44	4669	(958,324)
28.2.46	4685	(1,048,781)
9.10.47	4690	(1,104,751)
15.3.49	4667	(1,175,302)
18.8.50	4682	(1,257,504)
11.1.52	4686	(1,335,152)
16.2.54	4679	(1,452,577)
11.10.56	8604	(1,564,734)
20.9.57	8614	(1,607,661)
2.10.59	..	(1,705,088)
6.12.61	8612	(1,794,324)
Final mileage:		1,830,386

Tenders:

First	2398
??	2401
17.7.30	2557
13.8.31	2388
26.9.33	2572
11.3.35	2612
11.9.36	2442
4.5.39	2728
21.1.43	2648
2.6.49	2715
1.8.52	2742
20.9.57	2564
2.10.59	2867
6.12.61	2685

........................ooo........................

6015 KING RICHARD III
To stock: June 1928

Summary of sheds:

15.6.28 Old Oak Common
4.6.62 Stafford Road
N.B: Alleged allocation to
Aylesbury in 5.47 taken
as erroneous (see text).

Engine history:

2.6.28	Swindon Factory *ATC fitted*
15.6.28	Old Oak Common
21.6.28	Swindon Factory **L**
7.7.28	Old Oak Common
13.8.28	Swindon Factory **L**
16.8.28	Old Oak Common
20.8.28	Old Oak Common Shops
21.8.28	Old Oak Common
17.9.28	Swindon Factory **L**
18.9.28	Old Oak Common
21.1.29	Swindon Factory **R**
25.3.29	Swindon Stock
27.3.29	Old Oak Common
22.6.29	Swindon Factory **R**
26.6.29	Swindon Stock
4.7.29	Old Oak Common
19.7.29	Swindon Factory **L**
27.7.29	Swindon Stock
3.8.29	Old Oak Common
19.8.29	Swindon Factory **L**
27.8.29	Swindon Stock
30.8.29	Old Oak Common
23.9.29	Old Oak Common Shps **R**
4.10.29	Old Oak Common
14.1.30	Swindon Factory **H**
28.3.30	Swindon Stock
3.4.30	Old Oak Common
11.4.30	Swindon Factory **R**
16.4.30	Swindon Stock
17.4.30	Old Oak Common
30.7.30	Old Oak Common Shps **L**
4.8.30	Swindon Stock
4.8.30	Old Oak Common
15.9.30	Swindon Factory **L**
11.10.30	Swindon Stock
16.10.30	Old Oak Common
1.12.30	Old Oak Common Shps **R**
16.12.30	Old Oak Common
21.2.31	Old Oak Common *(wait)*
28.2.31	Swindon Factory **G**
10.4.31	Swindon Stock
18.4.31	Old Oak Common
15.12.31	Old Oak Common *(wait)*
20.12.31	Swindon Stock **L**
14.1.32	Swindon Stock
16.1.32	Old Oak Common

14.9.32	Swindon Factory **G**	6.1.40	Old Oak Common	2.12.48	Old Oak Common Shps **R**	31.3.55	Old Oak Common
2.11.32	Swindon Stock	10.4.40	Swindon Factory **L**	31.12.48	Old Oak Common	20.4.55	Swindon Factory **U**
12.11.32	Old Oak Common	29.4.40	Swindon Stock	1.5.49	Old Oak Common Shps **U**	12.5.55	Old Oak Common
27.9.33	Swindon Factory **I**	3.5.40	Old Oak Common	26.5.49	Old Oak Common	22.6.55	Old Oak Common *(wait)*
9.11.33	Swindon Stock	1.2.41	Swindon Factory **I**	10.6.49	Taunton Shops **U**	28.6.55	Swindon Factor
11.33	Old Oak Common	29.3.41	Swindon Stock	18.7.49	Old Oak Common	8.9.55	Swindon Factory **U**
28.8.34	Swindon Factory **G**	4.4.41	Old Oak Common	25.7.49	Laira Shops **U**	24.1.56	Stafford Road **LC**
15.10.34	Swindon Stock	3.2.42	Old Oak Common Shps **L**	18.8.49	Old Oak Common	18.2.56	Old Oak Common
21.10.34	Old Oak Common	16.2.42	Old Oak Common	29.8.49	Westbury *(wait)*	9.8.56	Old Oak Common **U**
29.10.34	Stafford Road F'cty **R**	26.4.42	Old Oak Common *(wait)*	6.9.49	Swindon Factory **HG**	25.8.56	Old Oak Common
13.11.34	Old Oak Common	28.4.42	Swindon Factory **I**	14.10.49	Old Oak Common	19.10.56	Old Oak Common *(wait)*
30.7.35	Swindon Factory **L**	12.6.42	Swindon Stock	3.11.49	Taunton Shops **U**	24.10.56	Swindon Factory **HL**
31.7.35	Old Oak Common	16.6.42	Old Oak Common	23.11.49	Old Oak Common	6.12.56	Old Oak Common
2.10.35	Swindon Factory **L**	11.7.42	Old Oak Common Shps **L**	4.12.49	Old Oak Common Shps **U**	6.12.57	Old Oak Common Shps **U**
23.10.35	Swindon Stock	1.8.42	Old Oak Common	22.12.49	Old Oak Common	23.12.57	Old Oak Common
29.10.35	Old Oak Common	9.5.43	Old Oak Common Shps **R**	12.6.50	Westbury *(wait)*	22.3.58	Swindon Factory **HG**
1.1.36	Swindon Factory **I**	27.5.43	Old Oak Common	16.6.50	Swindon Factory **U**	2.5.58	Old Oak Common
19.2.36	Swindon Stock	28.6.43	Old Oak Common Shps **L**	30.6.50	Old Oak Common	19.5.58	Bath Road Shops *(wait)*
22.2.36	Old Oak Common	12.7.43	Old Oak Common	19.9.50	Old Oak Common Shps **U**	22.5.58	Swindon Factory **LC**
11.3.36	Swindon Factory **L**	4.8.43	Old Oak Common *(wait)*	19.10.50	Old Oak Common	12.6.58	Old Oak Common
25.3.36	Swindon Stock	30.8.43	Swindon Factory **G**	8.11.50	Laira Shops **U**	26.1.59	Old Oak Common Shps **U**
31.3.36	Old Oak Common	4.10.43	Swindon Stock	12.12.50	Old Oak Common	9.2.59	Old Oak Common
7.10.36	Swindon Factory **L**	16.10.43	Old Oak Common	10.1.51	Old Oak Common Shps **U**	29.5.59	Old Oak Common Shps **U**
6.11.36	Swindon Stock	21.8.44	Old Oak Common **R**	30.1.51	Old Oak Common	18.6.59	Old Oak Common
10.11.36	Old Oak Common	5.9.44	Old Oak Common	10.5.51	Swindon Factory **HG**	30.12.59	Old Oak Common *(wait)*
28.11.36	Swindon Factory **L**	23.3.45	Old Oak Common *(wait)*	14.6.51	Old Oak Common	2.1.60	Swindon Factory **HG**
6.1.37	Swindon Stock	29.3.45	Swindon Factory **I**	4.2.52	Old Oak Common *(wait)*	24.2.60	Old Oak Common
10.1.37	Old Oak Common	17.5.45	Old Oak Common	20.2.52	Swindon Factory **LC**	27.7.60	Old Oak Common Shps **U**
25.1.37	Old Oak Common *(wait)*	30.10.45	Laira Shops **R**	19.3.52	Old Oak Common	10.8.60	Old Oak Common
30.1.37	Swindon Factory **L**	8.11.45	Old Oak Common	24.8.52	Old Oak Common *(wait)*	23.2.61	Old Oak Common Shps **U**
19.2.37	Swindon Stock	27.5.46	Swindon Factory **R**	1.9.52	Swindon Factory **HG**	21.3.61	Old Oak Common
22.2.37	Old Oak Common	29.6.46	Old Oak Common	10.10.52	Old Oak Common	6.10.61	Old Oak Common *(wait)*
13.5.37	Swindon Factory **G**	24.11.46	Old Oak Common Shps **R**	3.1.53	Old Oak Common *(wait)*	18.10.61	Swindon Factory **LI**
3.7.37	Swindon Stock	13.12.46	Old Oak Common	16.1.53	Swindon Factory **LC**	11.12.61	Old Oak Common
16.7.37	Old Oak Common	5.47	Aylesbury (See text)	26.2.53	Old Oak Common	2.3.62	Old Oak Common
28.8.38	Old Oak Common *(wait)*	11.6.47	Old Oak Common **U**	31.7.53	Laira Shops **U**	22.3.62	Stafford Road F'cty **U**
31.8.38	Swindon Factory **I**	26.6.47	Old Oak Common	12.8.53	Old Oak Common	30.3.62	Old Oak Common
14.10.38	Swindon Stock	30.6.47	Old Oak Common **R**	5.10.53	Bath Road **U**	4.6.62	Stafford Road
23.10.38	Old Oak Common	7.8.47	Old Oak Common	29.10.53	Old Oak Common	**7.9.62**	Wthdrwn (alternatively stated to be 21.9.62)
17.3.39	Old Oak Common *(wait)*	2.10.47	Old Oak Common **R**	10.12.53	Old Oak Common *(wait)*	5.4.63	Sold as scrap to Cox & Danks of Langley Green.
21.3.39	Swindon Factory **L**	22.10.47	Old Oak Common	16.12.53	Swindon Factory **HI**		
5.4.39	Swindon Stock	9.11.47	Taunton Shops **R**	19.2.54	Old Oak Common		
7.4.39	Old Oak Common	9.12.47	Old Oak Common	9.4.54	Bath Road Shops **U**		
12.6.39	Swindon Factory **L**	5.1.48	Old Oak Common *(wait)*	28.4.54	Old Oak Common		
4.7.39	Swindon Stock	18.2.48	Swindon Factory **I**	6.10.54	Old Oak Common *(wait)*		
18.7.39	Old Oak Common	24.3.48	Old Oak Common	13.10.54	Swindon Factory **LC**		
31.10.39	Swindon Factory **I**	21.9.48	Bath Road Shops **R**	23.12.54	Old Oak Common		
22.12.39	Swindon Stock	1.11.48	Old Oak Common	23.2.55	Bath Road Shops **U**		

Boilers and mileages:

First	4676 *	
28.3.30	..	(93,308)
10.4.31	4675	(149,135)
2.11.32	4672	(252,249)
9.11.33	..	(326,991)
15.10.34	4666	(393,627)
19.2.36	..	(475,568)
3.7.37	4694	(546,469)
14.10.38	..	(655,486)
22.12.39	..	(727,312)
29.3.41	..	(807,681)
12.6.42	..	(891,483)
4.10.43	4691	(961,252)
17.5.45	..	(1,049,255)
29.6.46	4662	(1,124,746)
24.3.48	4676	(1,204,007)
14.10.49	4692	(1,273,601)
14.6.51	4673	(1,339,886)
10.10.52	8603 *	(1,412,058)
19.2.54	..	(1,471,133)
8.9.55	8609	(1,519,261)
6.12.56	..	(1,585,782)
2.5.58	8613	(1,673,305)
24.2.60	8606	(1,767,531)
11.12.61	..	(1,861,296)
Final mileage:		1,901,585

Tenders:

First	2399
25.3.29	2425
28.3.30	2395
11.10.30	2390
10.4.31	2395
14.1.32	2557
13.11.33	2402

Where else but Snow Hill? It's No.6015 KING RICHARD III during the last year of the Kings' activities - 1962. PHOTOGRAPH: MICHAEL MENSING

A splendid period picture - the year is 1935, and No.6016 KING EDWARD V approaches Iver with the 3.45pm Paddington-Torquay. PHOTOGRAPH: RAIL ARCHIVE STEPHENSON

6.2.37	2547	6.9.28	Laira
19.2.37	2550	22.10.28	Laira *(wait)*
21.10.38	2548	13.11.28	Swindon Factory **L**
22.12.39	2401	18.12.28	Laira
29.3.41	2665	16.3.29	Laira *(wait)*
25.4.42	2790	18.3.29	Swindon Factory **R**
12.6.42	2612	19.3.29	Swindon Stock
17.5.45	2815	22.3.29	Laira
10.10.52	2726	7.5.29	Swindon Factory **L**
19.2.54	2788	25.5.29	Swindon Stock
23.12.54	2759	6.6.29	Swindon Factory **R**
8.9.55	2922	13.6.29	Swindon Stock
3.11.56	2565	19.6.29	Laira
6.12.56	2878	9.8.29	Taunton Shops **L**
2.5.58	2629	16.8.29	Laira
21.2.59	2583	23.9.29	Laira *(wait)*
24.2.60	2846	1.10.29	Swindon Factory **H**
22.4.61	2875	26.11.29	Swindon Stock
11.12.61	2850	30.11.29	Laira

........................ooo........................

6016 KING EDWARD V
To stock: June 1928

Summary of sheds:

2.7.28	Laira
10.5.30	Newton Abbot
8.30	Laira
5.6.52	Stafford Road
9.12.54	Old Oak Common
2.12.58	Stafford Road
2.2.59	Laira
16.9.60	Old Oak Common
15.6.62	Stafford Road

Engine history:

16.6.28	Swindon Stock
2.7.28	Laira
28.8.28	Laira Shops **L**

12.2.30	Swindon Factory **L**
20.2.30	Laira
6.5.30	Laira Shops **L**
10.5.30	Newton Abbot
8.30	Laira
14.10.30	Swindon Factory **L**
13.11.30	Swindon Stock
15.11.30	Laira
9.2.31	Swindon Factory **L**
7.3.31	Swindon Stock
11.3.31	Laira
29.4.31	Laira *(wait)*
30.4.31	Swindon Factory **I**
24.6.31	Swindon Stock
1.7.31	Laira
4.1.32	Swindon Factory **L**
12.2.32	Swindon Stock
13.2.32	Laira
23.5.32	Laira Shops **R**
22.6.32	Laira
29.6.32	Swindon Factory **L**

7.7.32	Swindon Stock
18.7.32	Laira
6.10.32	Laira Shops **R**
22.10.32	Laira
1.11.32	Swindon Factory **G**
24.1.33	Laira
19.9.33	Swindon Factory **L**
17.10.33	Laira
25.1.34	Swindon Factory **I**
12.3.34	Swindon Stock
17.3.34	Laira
12.1.35	Laira Shops **R**
2.2.35	Laira
1.5.35	Swindon Factory **I**
21.6.35	Swindon Stock
9.7.35	Laira
12.8.36	Swindon Factory **G**
1.10.36	Swindon Stock
9.10.36	Laira
8.9.37	Swindon Factory **I**
20.10.37	Swindon Stock
28.10.37	Laira
2.3.38	Laira Shops **R**
24.3.38	Laira
20.6.38	Swindon Factory **L**
7.7.38	Swindon Stock
11.7.38	Laira
22.8.38	Swindon Factory **L**
3.10.38	Swindon Stock
8.10.38	Laira
1.1.39	Laira *(wait)*
2.1.39	Swindon Factory **I**
16.2.39	Swindon Stock
17.2.39	Laira
14.6.39	Swindon Factory **L**
4.7.39	Swindon Stock
10.7.39	Laira
30.8.39	Newton Abbot F'cty **R**
27.9.39	Laira
2.10.39	Swindon Factory

8.10.39	Leamington *(wait)*
9.10.39	Swindon Factory **L**
20.10.39	Swindon Stock
23.10.39	Laira
29.12.39	Laira Shops **R**
12.1.40	Laira
29.3.40	Swindon Factory **L**
9.5.40	Swindon Stock
15.5.40	Laira
12.7.40	Swindon Factory **G**
31.8.40	Swindon Stock
15.9.40	Laira
13.3.41	Laira Shops **R**
4.4.41	Laira
7.7.41	Laira Shops **R**
21.7.41	Laira
16.1.42	Swindon Factory **I**
6.3.42	Swindon Stock
12.3.42	Laira
17.9.42	Old Oak Common Shps **R**
7.10.42	Laira
8.11.42	Laira Shops **R**
25.11.42	Laira
14.12.42	Swindon Factory **R**
2.1.43	Laira
16.3.43	Laira *(wait)*
17.3.43	Swindon Factory **G**
22.6.43	Swindon Stock
25.6.43	Laira
27.10.43	Laira Shops **R**
24.11.43	Laira
16.2.44	Laira Shops **R**
6.3.44	Laira
18.3.44	Taunton Shops **R**
17.4.44	Laira
14.7.44	Laira *(wait)*
22.7.44	Swindon Factory **L**
23.8.44	Swindon Stock
23.8.44	Laira
27.10.44	Laira Shops **R**

13.11.44	Laira
15.12.44	Laira Shops **R**
25.12.44	Laira
19.1.45	Laira Shops **R**
11.2.45	Laira
17.2.45	Taunton *(wait)*
22.2.45	Swindon Factory **I**
7.4.45	Swindon Stock
19.4.45	Swindon Factory **R**
28.4.45	Laira
24.8.45	Laira *(wait)*
31.8.45	Swindon Factory **L**
2.10.45	Laira
5.2.46	Laira Shops **R**
25.2.46	Laira
23.4.46	Laira Shops *(wait)*
8.5.46	Swindon Factory **G**
11.6.46	Laira
23.10.46	Laira Shops **R**
7.11.46	Laira
6.12.46	Bath Road Shops **R**
22.1.47	Laira
17.2.47	Laira Shops **R**
22.3.47	Laira
30.4.47	Laira Shops **R**
17.6.47	Laira
1.7.47	Old Oak Common Shps **R**
22.7.47	Laira
6.8.47	Laira Shops **L**
11.9.47	Laira
26.9.47	Old Oak Common Shps **R**
17.10.47	Laira
8.12.47	Laira Shops **R**
6.1.48	Laira
19.1.48	Laira Shops **R**
3.3.48	Laira
5.3.48	Laira Shops **R**
22.3.48	Laira
10.5.48	Reading *(wait)*
1.6.48	Swindon Factory **I**
28.7.48	Laira
30.8.48	Laira Shops **R**
10.9.48	Laira
28.9.48	Laira Shops **R**
9.10.48	Laira
1.5.49	Old Oak Common Shps **U**
18.5.49	Laira
5.9.49	Laira Shops **U**
11.10.49	Laira
7.11.49	Old Oak Common *(wait)*
11.11.49	Swindon Factory **HG**
16.12.49	Laira
24.5.50	Laira Shops **U**
9.6.50	Laira
8.8.50	Old Oak Common Shps **U**
30.8.50	Laira
22.9.50	Swindon Factory **U**
11.10.50	Laira
24.10.50	Laira Shops **U**
8.11.50	Laira
14.1.51	Laira Shops **U**
2.2.51	Laira
14.2.51	Laira *(wait)*
2.3.51	Swindon Factory **HG**
10.4.51	Laira
12.6.51	Laira Shops **U**
23.6.51	Laira
8.8.51	Taunton **U**
28.9.51	Laira
15.10.51	Laira Shops **U**
31.10.51	Laira
25.4.52	Laira *(wait)*
7.5.52	Swindon Factory **LC**
5.6.52	Stafford Road
24.8.52	Old Oak Common **U**
11.9.52	Stafford Road
12.12.52	Swindon Factory **HG**
19.2.53	Stafford Road
1.5.53	Stafford Road *(wait)*
19.5.53	Swindon Factory **LC**
16.6.53	Stafford Road
14.7.53	Old Oak Common Shps **U**
31.7.53	Stafford Road
30.9.53	Old Oak Common *(wait)*
2.11.53	Swindon Factory **LC**
22.12.53	Stafford Road
27.4.54	Stafford Road *(wait)*
3.5.54	Swindon Factory **LC**
11.6.54	Stafford Road
27.7.54	Swindon Factory **HG**
9.12.54	Old Oak Common
27.5.55	Old Oak Common *(wait)*
30.5.55	Swindon Factory **LC**
29.6.55	Old Oak Common
26.7.55	Old Oak Common Shps **U**
19.8.55	Old Oak Common
29.12.55	Old Oak Common Shps **U**
27.1.56	Old Oak Common
30.1.56	Stafford Road F'cty **LC**
20.2.56	Old Oak Common
24.2.56	Old Oak Common Shps **U**
22.3.56	Old Oak Common
17.7.56	Old Oak Common *(wait)*
20.7.56	Swindon Factory **HI**
7.9.56	Old Oak Common
2.5.57	Old Oak Common **U**
17.5.57	Old Oak Common
10.9.57	Old Oak Common Shps **U**
25.9.57	Old Oak Common
9.11.57	Old Oak Common *(wait)*
27.11.57	Swindon Factory **HG**
14.1.58	Old Oak Common
18.1.58	Swindon Factory **LC**
3.2.58	Old Oak Common
17.2.58	Old Oak Common *(wait)*
21.2.58	Swindon Factory **LC**
13.3.58	Old Oak Common
2.12.58	Stafford Road
2.1.59	Stafford Road **U**
16.1.59	Stafford Road
2.2.59	Laira
27.2.59	Old Oak Common Shps **U**
14.3.59	Laira
5.8.59	Swindon Factory **HG**
3.11.59	Laira
14.3.60	Laira Shops **U**
29.3.60	Laira
24.8.60	Laira Shops **U**
16.9.60	Old Oak Common
20.9.60	Taunton Shops **U**
25.10.60	Old Oak Common
31.10.60	Taunton Shops **U**
23.11.60	Old Oak Common
8.12.60	Old Oak Common Shps **U**
22.12.60	Old Oak Common
4.1.61	Old Oak Common Shps **U**
27.1.61	Old Oak Common
19.5.61	Old Oak Common Shps **U**
14.6.61	Old Oak Common
12.9.61	Swindon Factory **LI**
9.11.61	Old Oak Common
15.6.62	Stafford Road
9.9.62	Withdrawn (alternatively stated to be 13.9.62)
14.11.63	Sold for scrap to Cox & Danks of Langley Green

Boilers and mileages:

First	4677 *	
26.11.29	..	(71,419)
24.6.31	..	(150,328)
24.1.33	4675	(219,787)
12.3.34	..	(283,855)
21.6.35	..	(360,390)
1.10.36	4688	(444,450)
20.10.37	..	(530,543)
16.2.39	..	(607,044)
31.8.40	4670	(697,722)
6.3.42	..	(794,881)
22.6.43	4693	(864,712)
7.4.45	..	(965,820)
11.6.46	4681	(1,038,013)
28.7.48	4662	(1,111,874)
16.12.49	4673	(1,190,541)
10.4.51	4677	(1,264,430)
19.2.53	8607 *	(1,355,861)
9.12.54	8618 *	(1,410,645)
7.9.56	..	(1,500,596)
14.1.58	8616	(1,582,269)
3.11.59	8622	(1,673,986)
9.11.61	..	(1,762,327)
Final mileage:		1,811,207

Tenders:

First	2400
25.5.29	2384
13.6.29	2402
26.11.29	2399
12.2.32	2551
1.10.36	2549
3.10.38	2552
6.3.42	2776
22.6.43	2665
23.8.44	2728
28.7.48	2710
16.12.49	2772
10.4.51	2710
11.6.54	2694
9.12.54	2931
.55	2808
7.9.56	2846
15.6.57	2544
14.1.58	2745
29.11.58	2771
3.11.59	2793
9.11.61	2815

.......................ooo.........................

6017 KING EDWARD IV
To stock: June 1928.

Summary of sheds:

2.7.28	Old Oak Common
20.9.28	Stafford Road
5.11.39	Bath Road
8.43	Laira
7.48	Old Oak Common
2.52	Newton Abbot (loan ?)
3.52	Laira
2.2.59	Stafford Road

Engine history:

23.6.28	Swindon Stock
2.7.28	Old Oak Common
16.7.28	Stafford Road
1.9.28	Swindon Factory **R**
20.9.28	Stafford Road
28.12.28	Stafford Road Shops
31.12.28	Stafford Road
1.5.29	Swindon Factory **L**
25.6.29	Swindon Stock
1.7.29	Stafford Road
18.11.29	Old Oak Common Shops
27.11.29	Stafford Road
12.4.30	Swindon Shed **L**
28.6.30	Swindon Stock
4.7.30	Swindon Shed **R**
10.7.30	Swindon Stock
11.7.30	Stafford Road
3.1.31	Swindon Factory **G**
14.2.31	Swindon Stock
19.2.31	Stafford Road
4.4.32	Stafford Road *(wait)*
11.4.32	Swindon Factory **G**
22.6.32	Swindon Stock
2.7.32	Stafford Road
8.2.33	Swindon Factory **L**
9.3.33	Stafford Road
5.6.33	Stafford Road Shops **L**
5.6.33	Stafford Road
8.9.33	Swindon Factory *Speedometer fitted*
20.9.33	Stafford Road
18.10.33	Stafford Road *(wait)*
30.10.33	Swindon Factory **I**
22.12.33	Swindon Stock
2.1.34	Stafford Road
26.2.34	Stafford Road *(wait)*
3.3.34	Swindon Factory **L**
5.3.34	Swindon Stock
6.3.34	Stafford Road
7.8.34	Stafford Road *(wait)*
14.8.34	Swindon Factory **L**
26.9.34	Swindon Stock
7.10.34	Stafford Road
7.1.35	Stafford Road F'cty **L**
14.1.35	Stafford Road
21.2.35	Swindon Factory **I**
13.4.35	Swindon Stock
17.4.35	Stafford Road
19.3.36	Swindon Factory **I**
6.5.36	Swindon Stock
17.5.36	Stafford Road
19.11.36	Stafford Road Shops **L**
12.12.36	Stafford Road
12.4.37	Stafford Road F'cty **L**
22.4.37	Stafford Road
4.5.37	Swindon Factory **G**
22.6.37	Swindon Stock
4.7.37	Stafford Road
26.9.38	Stafford Road *(wait)*
11.10.38	Swindon Factory **I**
23.11.38	Swindon Stock
29.11.38	Stafford Road
10.2.39	Stafford Road *(wait)*
18.2.39	Swindon Factory **L**
6.3.39	Swindon Stock
11.3.39	Stafford Road
11.7.39	Swindon Factory **L**
31.7.39	Swindon Stock
4.8.39	Stafford Road
12.10.39	Bath Road Shops **R**
5.11.39	Bath Road
22.1.40	Bath Road Shops **R**
9.2.40	Bath Road
22.2.40	Swindon Factory **G**
6.6.40	Swindon Stock
12.6.40	Bath Road
6.1.41	Bath Road Shops **R**
28.1.41	Bath Road
28.3.41	Swindon Factory **R**
15.4.41	Swindon Stock
21.4.41	Old Oak Common *(wait)*
12.5.41	Swindon Factory **L**
12.7.41	Swindon Stock
14.7.41	Bath Road
14.8.41	Bath Road *(wait)*
26.8.41	Swindon Factory **L**
3.9.41	Swindon Stock
4.9.41	Bath Road
20.1.42	Bath Road Shops **R**
3.2.42	Bath Road
10.4.42	Bath Road Shops **R**
25.4.42	Bath Road
5.5.42	Swindon Factory **I**
26.6.42	Bath Road
1.8.42	Bath Road *(wait)*
7.8.42	Swindon Factory **L**
1.9.42	Swindon Stock
1.9.42	Bath Road
24.9.42	Bath Road Shops **R**
10.10.42	Bath Road
5.6.43	Laira Shops **R**
21.7.43	Bath Road
8.43	Laira

No.6017 KING EDWARD IV sports the Coronation year 'Riviera' headboard as it heads west through Reading in 1953.
PHOTOGRAPH: NATIONAL RAILWAY MUSEUM

28.10.43	Swindon Factory **G**	16.3.49	Old Oak Common *(wait)*	24.2.55	Southall *(wait)*	30.1.60	Stafford Road **U**
8.12.43	Swindon Stock	23.3.49	Swindon Factory **HG**	1.3.55	Swindon Factory **LC**	26.2.60	Stafford Road
13.12.43	Laira	3.5.49	Old Oak Common	15.4.55	Laira	29.3.60	Stafford Road *(wait)*
6.8.44	Reading Shops **R**	6.8.49	Banbury Shops **U**	17.5.55	Newton Abbot F'cty **U**	14.4.60	Swindon Factory **LI**
2.9.44	Laira	27.8.49	Old Oak Common	23.5.55	Laira	15.6.60	Stafford Road
4.9.44	Laira Shops **R**	10.4.50	Old Oak Common *(wait)*	29.8.55	Laira Shops **U**	5.11.60	Stafford Road Shops **U**
26.9.44	Laira	18.4.50	Swindon Factory **LC**	14.9.55	Laira	3.12.60	Stafford Road
17.1.45	Reading *(wait)*	26.5.50	Old Oak Common	26.9.55	Swindon Factory **HG**	12.3.61	Stafford Road **U**
18.1.45	Swindon Factory **I**	23.7.50	Taunton Shops **U**	5.12.55	Laira	22.3.61	Stafford Road
16.3.45	Laira	18.9.50	Old Oak Common	27.1.56	Laira Shops **LC**	10.4.61	Stafford Road **U**
7.8.45	Laira Shops **R**	21.9.50	Bath Road Shops **U**	19.2.56	Laira	30.4.61	Stafford Road
17.9.45	Laira	21.10.50	Old Oak Common	13.6.56	Laira Shops **U**	21.6.61	Stafford Road **U**
16.2.46	Laira Shops **R**	7.12.50	Swindon Factory **HG**	27.6.56	Laira	10.7.61	Stafford Road
2.3.46	Laira	23.1.51	Old Oak Common	6.7.56	Bath Road Shops **U**	2.10.61	Stafford Road **U**
30.3.46	Swindon Factory **G**	12.8.51	Old Oak Common Shps **U**	23.7.56	Laira	24.11.61	Stafford Road
7.5.46	Laira	13.9.51	Old Oak Common	5.10.56	Laira Shops **U**	9.1.62	Stafford Road **U**
11.9.46	Laira Shops **R**	1.10.51	Old Oak Common **U**	10.10.56	Laira	24.1.62	Stafford Road
8.10.46	Laira	16.10.51	Old Oak Common	29.10.56	Laira Shops **U**	5.3.62	Old Oak Common Shps **U**
10.2.47	Laira Shops **R**	13.11.51	Stafford Road *(wait)*	6.11.56	Laira	2.4.62	Stafford Road
5.3.47	Laira	20.11.51	Swindon Factory **LC**	9.2.57	Laira Shops **U**	15.6.62	Stafford Road (In store)
9.6.47	Laira Shops **L**	3.1.52	Old Oak Common	27.2.57	Laira	**23.7.62**	Wthdawn (alternatively
9.6.47	Laira	2.52	Newton Abbot (loan ?)	29.4.57	Swindon Factory **HI**		stated to be 24.7.62)
30.6.47	Laira Shops **R**	3.52	Laira	18.6.57	Laira	24.4.63	Sold as scrap to Cox &
19.7.47	Laira	9.6.52	Swindon Factory **HG**	3.10.57	Laira Shops **U**		Danks of Langley Green
4.8.47	Laira Shops **R**	7.8.52	Laira	8.10.57	Laira		
27.8.47	Laira	2.10.52	Swindon Factory **U**	29.11.57	Laira *(wait)*	**Boilers and mileages:**	
26.9.47	Laira Shops **R**	20.10.52	Laira	3.12.57	Newton Abbot F'cty **LC**	First	4678 *
12.11.47	Laira	18.1.53	Laira Shops **U**	20.12.57	Laira	14.2.31	4662	(139,495)
14.11.47	Newton Abbot F'cty	1.2.53	Laira	16.4.58	Laira Shops **U**	22.6.32	4681	(211,053)
	Tender work only	6.3.53	Laira Shops **U**	26.4.58	Laira	22.12.33	..	(291,843)
21.11.47	Laira	13.3.53	Laira	8.7.58	Bath Road Shops **U**	26.9.34	4664	(331,785)
2.12.47	Laira Shops **R**	8.6.53	Laira Shops **U**	25.7.58	Laira	13.4.35	..	(358,209)
22.12.47	Laira	16.6.53	Laira	1.9.58	Laira Shops **U**	6.5.36	..	(423,673)
5.1.48	Laira *(wait)*	27.1.54	Swindon Factory **HI**	8.9.58	Laira	22.6.37	4674	(485,271)
16.1.48	Swindon Factory **I**	30.3.54	Laira	10.9.58	Swindon Factory **HG**	23.11.38	..	(567,137)
18.2.48	Laira	26.10.54	Taunton Shops **LC**	30.10.58	Laira	6.6.40	4667	(640,798)
7.48	Old Oak Common	17.11.54	Laira	2.2.59	Stafford Road	26.6.42	..	(736,644)
15.11.48	Old Oak Common Shps **L**	29.12.54	Laira Shops **U**	2.9.59	Stafford Road **U**	8.12.43	4668	(814,474)
10.12.48	Old Oak Common	10.1.55	Laira	24.9.59	Stafford Road	16.3.45	..	(896,435)

7.5.46	4664	
(966,225)		
18.2.48	4691	(1,058,314)
3.5.49	4679	(1,129,349)
23.1.51	4678	(1,210,999)
7.8.52	8602 *	(1,287,821)
30.3.54	..	(1,379,697)
5.12.55	8625 *	(1,477,610)
18.6.57	8621	(1,574,576)
30.10.58	8609	(1,667,558)
15.6.60	..	(1,751,360)
Final mileage:		1,853,262

Tenders:

First	2402
25.6.29	2413
10.7.30	2391
22.6.32	2389
23.11.38	2544
6.6.40	2612
26.6.42	2710
8.12.43	2733
16.3.45	2762
7.5.46	2642
14.5.47	2630
18.2.48	2707
23.1.51	2630
3.1.52	2707
15.4.55	2395
5.12.55	2715
18.6.57	2771
20.10.58	2436
24.1.62	2795

.........................ooo.........................

6018 KING HENRY VI
To stock: June 1928

Summary of sheds:

1.9.28	Laira
21.2.29	Newton Abbot
10.12.48	Bath Road
7.50	Old Oak Common
13.9.60	Canton
4.6.62	Old Oak Common

Engine history:

7.28	Swindon Factory *ATC fitted*
12.7.28	Swindon Stock
4.8.28	Swindon Factory L
1.9.28	Laira
28.12.28	Laira Shops
8.1.29	Laira
14.1.29	Swindon Factory L
16.2.29	Swindon Stock
21.2.29	Newton Abbot
8.4.29	Swindon Factory L
18.5.29	Swindon Stock
22.5.29	Swindon Factory L
10.6.29	Swindon Stock
15.6.29	Newton Abbot
29.8.29	Swindon Factory L
13.9.29	Swindon Stock
19.9.29	Newton Abbot
6.1.30	Newton Abbot Shops L
15.1.30	Newton Abbot
29.4.30	Swindon Factory H
5.7.30	Swindon Stock
14.7.30	Newton Abbot
23.5.31	Swindon Factory I
24.7.31	Swindon Stock
29.7.31	Newton Abbot
17.2.32	Newton Abbot Shops R
11.3.32	Newton Abbot
12.4.32	Swindon Factory G
5.7.32	Swindon Stock
19.7.32	Newton Abbot
11.10.32	Swindon Factory L
21.11.32	Swindon Stock
24.11.32	Newton Abbot
20.2.33	Swindon Factory L
23.3.33	Swindon Stock
3.33	Newton Abbot
20.7.33	Swindon Factory L
2.8.33	Newton Abbot
2.11.33	Swindon Factory I
4.1.34	Swindon Stock
11.1.34	Newton Abbot
27.11.34	Newton Abbot F'cty R
14.12.34	Newton Abbot
4.2.35	Swindon Factory G
12.4.35	Swindon Stock
25.4.35	Newton Abbot
4.10.35	Newton Abbot F'cty R
21.10.35	Newton Abbot
20.1.36	Newton Abbot F'cty R
4.2.36	Newton Abbot (wait)
6.2.36	Swindon Factory L
8.2.36	Swindon Stock
16.2.36	Newton Abbot
11.8.36	Swindon Factory I
26.9.36	Swindon Stock
7.10.36	Newton Abbot
28.7.37	Swindon Factory L
18.8.37	Swindon Stock
20.8.37	Newton Abbot
19.10.37	Swindon Factory L
4.11.37	Swindon Stock
22.11.37	Newton Abbot
7.1.38	Newton Abbot (wait)
25.1.38	Swindon Factory G
22.3.38	Swindon Stock
26.3.38	Newton Abbot
19.4.38	Taunton Shops R
17.5.38	Newton Abbot
13.8.38	Swindon Factory L
17.9.38	Swindon Stock
23.9.38	Newton Abbot
17.6.39	Swindon Factory L
7.7.39	Swindon Stock
14.7.39	Newton Abbot
15.2.40	Swindon Factory I
2.4.40	Swindon Stock
6.4.40	Newton Abbot
27.4.41	Newton Abbot R
14.5.41	Newton Abbot
18.7.41	Newton Abbot (wait)
11.8.41	Swindon Factory G
8.10.41	Swindon Stock
19.10.41	Newton Abbot
28.8.42	Newton Abbot R
11.9.42	Newton Abbot
20.12.42	Swindon Factory I
27.1.43	Swindon Stock
30.1.43	Newton Abbot
4.3.44	Newton Abbot R
22.3.44	Newton Abbot
24.5.44	Newton Abbot R
28.6.44	Newton Abbot
14.9.44	Swindon Factory G
2.11.44	Newton Abbot
25.3.45	Newton Abbot (wait)
6.4.45	Swindon Factory L
2.5.45	Newton Abbot
27.8.45	Newton Abbot R
10.9.45	Newton Abbot
27.2.46	Swindon Factory I
1.4.46	Newton Abbot
19.5.46	Newton Abbot R
4.6.46	Newton Abbot
19.8.46	Newton Abbot R
9.9.46	Newton Abbot
5.1.47	Newton Abbot R
11.1.47	Newton Abbot F'cty L
14.2.47	Newton Abbot
8.3.47	Newton Abbot R
27.3.47	Newton Abbot
20.5.47	Reading Shops R
1.7.47	Newton Abbot
22.9.47	Swindon Factory G
29.10.47	Newton Abbot
26.11.47	Taunton (wait)
8.12.47	Swindon Factory L
8.1.48	Newton Abbot
5.3.48	Swindon Shops
11.3.48	Newton Abbot
7.9.48	Swindon Shops
13.9.48	Newton Abbot
10.12.48	Bath Road (failed ?)
10.12.48	Swindon Factory U
22.12.48	Bath Road
28.4.49	Swindon Factory HG
27.5.49	Bath Road
12.2.50	Old Oak Comn Shps LC
8.3.50	Bath Road
7.50	Old Oak Common
3.10.50	Old Oak Common (wait)
17.10.50	Swindon Factory HG
4.12.50	Old Oak Common
25.7.51	Old Oak Common Shps U
24.8.51	Old Oak Common
4.12.51	Old Oak Common U
18.12.51	Old Oak Common
20.12.51	Taunton Shops U
4.2.52	Old Oak Common
12.3.52	Exeter (wait)
14.3.52	Swindon Factory HI
25.4.52	Old Oak Common
7.5.53	Old Oak Common Shps U
1.6.53	Old Oak Common
9.10.53	Old Oak Common (wait)
19.10.53	Swindon Factory HG
8.12.53	Old Oak Common
11.3.55	Swindon Factory HI
26.4.55	Old Oak Common
4.1.56	Laira (wait)
9.1.56	Swindon Factory LC
17.2.56	Old Oak Common
6.3.56	Old Oak Comn Shps LC
22.3.56	Old Oak Common
28.6.56	Laira (wait)
3.7.56	Swindon Factory HI
14.9.56	Old Oak Common
25.10.57	Old Oak Common Shps U
15.11.57	Old Oak Common
22.1.58	Swindon Factory HI
21.3.58	Old Oak Common
7.7.58	Old Oak Common Shps U
23.7.58	Old Oak Common
13.8.58	Taunton Shops U
10.9.58	Old Oak Common
30.3.59	Old Oak Common Shps U
22.4.59	Old Oak Common
1.9.59	Swindon Factory HG
11.11.59	Old Oak Common
30.4.60	Banbury Shops U
16.5.60	Old Oak Common
13.9.60	Canton
19.9.60	Old Oak Common Shps U
11.10.60	Canton
27.3.61	Canton Shops U
19.4.61	Canton
19.10.61	Canton Shops U
9.11.61	Canton
28.11.61	Canton (wait)
5.12.61	Swindon Factory HG
22.2.62	Canton
4.6.62	Old Oak Common
31.12.62	**Wthdrwn**
5.10.63	Cut up at Swindon

Boilers and mileages:

First	4679 *	
5.7.30	..	(89,548)
24.7.31	..	(141,170)
5.7.32	4663	(181,618)
4.1.34	..	(255,023)
12.4.35	4685	(325,593)
26.9.36	..	(404,001)
22.3.38	4679	(467,630)
2.4.40	..	(559,970)
8.10.41	4665	(646,946)
27.1.43	..	(729,632)
2.11.44	4690	(818,919)
1.4.46	4670	(882,849)
29.10.47	4677	(939,029)
27.5.49	4691	(1,018,549)
4.12.50	4689	(1,100,116)
25.4.52	..	(1,172,378)
8.12.53	8614 *	(1,263,193)
26.4.55	8605	(1,354,236)
14.9.56	8610	(1,420,986)
21.3.58	8606	(1,518,348)
11.11.59	8626	(1,612,955)
22.2.62	8618	(1,705,202)
Final mileage:		1,738,387

Tenders:

First	2403
18.5.29	2394
5.7.30	2403
24.7.31	2555
11.32	2553
21.11.32	2396
21.10.33	2441
29.6.35	2549
23.7.38	2648
17.9.38	2549
2.4.40	2694
2.11.44	2788
2.5.45	2715
27.5.49	2649
25.4.52	2775
26.4.55	2800
14.9.56	2544
15.6.57	2846
22.3.58	2841
11.11.59	2816
22.2.62	2619
19.3.63	2883

Loco already withdrawn; tender change presumably for book purposes

.........................ooo.........................

6019 KING HENRY V
To stock: July 1928

Summary of sheds:

1.8.28	Stafford Road
29.6.35	Laira
14.6.39	Newton Abbot (?)
7.39	Laira
1.1.49	Bath Road
7.49	Newton Abbot (loan?)
19.9.49	Bath Road
7.50	Old Oak Common
19.9.60	Canton
14.3.62	Old Oak Common

Engine history:

24.7.28	Swindon Stock
1.8.28	Stafford Road
26.9.28	Swindon Factory L
29.9.28	Stafford Road
5.10.28	Swindon Factory L
24.10.28	Stafford Road
22.11.28	Stafford Road F'cty
26.11.28	Stafford Road
1.3.29	Swindon Factory L
24.4.29	Swindon Stock
30.4.29	Stafford Road
22.6.29	Swindon Factory L

The very last King-hauled special (prior to the preservation era) was worked by No.6018 KING HENRY VI on 28 April 1963. It is seen at Southall. PHOTOGRAPH: R.C.RILEY

3.7.29	Stafford Road	24.8.38	Laira	13.11.45	Laira	21.2.52	Old Oak Common
16.11.29	Stafford Road *(wait)*	16.1.39	Swindon Factory **L**	2.2.46	Swindon Factory **I**	22.5.52	Old Oak Common Shps **U**
3.12.29	Swindon Factory **H**	1.2.39	Swindon Stock	12.3.46	Laira	10.6.52	Old Oak Common
2.4.30	Swindon Stock	3.2.39	Laira	13.5.46	Laira Shops **R**	7.10.52	Old Oak Common *(wait)*
9.4.30	Swindon (trials ?)	26.4.39	Swindon Factory **I**	30.5.46	Laira	21.10.52	Swindon Factory **HI**
12.4.30	Swindon Factory **L**	12.6.39	Swindon Stock	6.8.46	Laira Shops **R**	17.11.52	Old Oak Common
24.4.30	Stafford Road	14.6.39	Newton Abbot (loan?)	26.9.46	Laira	22.9.53	Old Oak Common Shps **U**
16.5.30	Swindon Factory **L**	7.39	Laira	27.11.46	Laira Shops **R**	27.10.53	Old Oak Common
5.6.30	Swindon Stock	13.11.39	Laira Shops **R**	22.12.46	Laira	1.2.54	Old Oak Common *(wait)*
7.6.30	Stafford Road	30.11.39	Laira	24.1.47	Westbury *(wait)*	8.2.54	Swindon Factory **HG**
21.4.31	Swindon Factory **I**	9.5.40	Swindon Factory **G**	24.1.47	Swindon Factory **L**	18.3.54	Old Oak Common
16.6.31	Swindon Stock	27.6.40	Swindon Stock	26.2.47	Laira	22.11.54	Bath Road Shops **U**
25.6.31	Stafford Road	2.7.40	Laira	15.8.47	Laira Shops **R**	31.12.54	Old Oak Common
31.3.32	Swindon Factory **G**	19.4.41	Laira Shops **R**	6.9.47	Laira	3.8.55	Swindon Factory **HI**
25.5.32	Swindon Stock	14.5.41	Laira	17.10.47	Laira Shops **R**	20.9.55	Old Oak Common
26.5.32	Stafford Road	19.8.41	Swindon Factory **I**	3.11.47	Laira	5.12.55	Old Oak Common Shps **U**
2.5.33	Stafford Road *(wait)*	15.10.41	Swindon Stock	8.12.47	Laira Shops **R**	16.12.55	Old Oak Common
3.5.33	Swindon Factory **I**	22.10.41	Laira	13.1.48	Laira	24.1.56	Old Oak Common *(wait)*
22.6.33	Stafford Road	7.4.42	Laira Shops **R**	2.3.48	Old Oak Common *(wait)*	31.1.56	Swindon Factory **LC**
7.3.34	Stafford Road *(wait)*	29.4.42	Laira	5.3.48	Swindon Factory **G**	2.3.56	Old Oak Common
16.3.34	Swindon Factory **G**	6.8.42	Laira Shops **R**	15.4.48	Laira	26.4.56	Taunton (wait)
3.5.34	Swindon Stock	20.8.42	Laira	12.7.48	Taunton Shops **R**	26.4.56	Swindon Factory **LC**
13.5.34	Stafford Road	1.12.42	Laira *(wait)*	4.8.48	Laira	5.6.56	Old Oak Common
30.4.35	Swindon Factory **I**	10.12.42	Swindon Factory **I**	8.9.48	Swindon Factory	18.2.57	Old Oak Common *(wait)*
18.6.35	Swindon Stock	14.1.43	Swindon Stock	22.9.48	Laira	22.2.57	Swindon Factory **HG**
29.6.35	Laira	19.1.43	Laira	7.12.48	Reading Shops **U**	24.4.57	Old Oak Common
25.11.35	Laira Shops **R**	5.7.43	Laira Shops **R**	1.1.49	Bath Road	1.8.58	Taunton Shops **U**
11.12.35	Laira	29.7.43	Laira	7.49	Newton Abbot (loan?)	15.8.58	Old Oak Common
7.5.36	Swindon Factory **L**	30.9.43	Swindon Factory **L**	16.7.49	Reading *(wait)*	27.8.58	Exeter Shops **U**
30.5.36	Swindon Stock	29.10.43	Swindon Stock	17.8.49	Swindon Factory **HG**	8.9.58	Old Oak Common
10.6.36	Laira	3.11.43	Swindon Factory **L**	19.9.49	Bath Road	3.10.58	Old Oak Common *(wait)*
8.10.36	Swindon Factory **G**	6.11.43	Swindon Stock	30.1.50	Bath Road *(wait)*	9.10.58	Swindon Factory **HI**
18.11.36	Swindon Stock	9.11.43	Laira	9.2.50	Swindon Factory **LC**	12.12.58	Old Oak Common
27.11.36	Laira	24.2.44	Laira Shops **R**	3.3.50	Bath Road	7.1.59	Stafford Road **U**
20.1.37	Swindon Factory *Tender work only*	14.3.44	Laira	9.3.50	Swindon Factory **U**	10.2.59	Old Oak Common
		24.5.44	Laira Shops **R**	28.3.50	Bath Road	21.6.60	Old Oak Common *(wait)*
21.1.37	Swindon Factory **I**	12.6.44	Laira	7.50	Old Oak Common	30.6.60	Swindon Factory **HG**
3.1.38	Swindon Factory **I**	30.8.44	Swindon Factory **G**	8.9.50	Taunton Shops **U**	19.9.60	Canton
22.2.38	Swindon Stock	26.10.44	Laira	18.10.50	Old Oak Common	14.8.61	Canton *(wait)*
1.3.38	Laira	20.3.45	Laira Shops **R**	29.12.50	Swindon Factory **HG**	30.8.61	Swindon Factory **HC**
20.4.38	Swindon Factory **L**	9.4.45	Laira	2.2.51	Old Oak Common	9.1.62	Canton
4.5.38	Swindon Stock	19.6.45	Laira Shops **R**	22.6.51	Old Oak Common *(wait)*	14.3.62	Old Oak Common
10.5.38	Laira	5.7.45	Laira	26.6.51	Swindon Factory **LC**	**7.9.62**	**Wthdrwn**
22.7.38	Laira *(wait)*	30.7.45	Swindon Factory **L**	19.7.51	Old Oak Common		Later sold as scrap to
28.7.38	Swindon Factory **L**	5.9.45	Laira	28.12.51	Old Oak Common *(wait)*		J.Cashmore of Newport
20.8.38	Swindon Stock	23.10.45	Laira Shops **R**	3.1.52	Swindon Factory **LC**		

Boilers and mileages:

First	4680 *	
2.4.30	4681	(77,003)
16.6.31	..	(135,150)
25.5.32	4680	(184,440)
22.6.33	..	(246,295)
3.5.34	4674	(293,354)
18.6.35	..	(361,651)
18.11.36	4675	(453,402)
22.2.38	..	(549,836)
12.6.39	..	(628,883)
27.6.40	4689	(698,385)
15.10.41	..	(782,989)
14.1.43	..	(864,969)
26.10.44	4670	(971,345)
12.3.46	4669	(1,058,579)
15.4.48	4675	(1,155,049)
19.9.49	4680	(1,215,159)
2.2.51	4690	(1,289,907)
17.11.52	4678	(1,384,512)
18.3.54	4694	(1,468,274)
20.9.55	4698	(1,557,963)
24.4.57	8612	(1,643,648)
12.12.58	..	(1,736,179)
19.9.60	8605	(1,817,502)
Final mileage:		1,912,309

Tenders:

First	2428
2.4.30	2425
21.4.31	2389
25.5.32	2391
15.11.37	2398
22.2.38	2694
1.2.39	2612
27.6.40	2762
14.1.43	2606
26.10.44	2694
5.9.45	2707
12.3.46	2695
19.7.51	2922
20.9.55	2398
5.6.56	2776
1.8.56	2398
3.11.56	2776
24.4.57	2815
8.57	2922
11.57	2775
12.12.58	2613
18.4.59	2786
19.6.60	2399
9.1.62	2558

......................ooo...........................

6020 KING HENRY IV
To stock: May 1930

Summary of sheds:

4.6.30	Newton Abbot
4.7.30	Laira
22.8.30	Old Oak Common
4.10.30	Laira
5.1.49	Stafford Road

Engine history:

4.6.30	Newton Abbot

7.6.30	Swindon Factory **L**
	ATC fitted
30.6.30	Swindon Stock
4.7.30	Laira
14.7.30	Swindon Factory **L**
9.8.30	Swindon Stock
22.8.30	Old Oak Comn (failed ?)
8.9.30	Swindon Factory **L**
20.9.30	Swindon Stock
25.9.30	Swindon Factory **R**
30.9.30	Swindon Stock
4.10.30	Laira
20.12.30	Swindon Factory **L**
21.1.31	Swindon Stock
26.1.31	Laira
27.4.31	Swindon Factory **L**
10.6.31	Swindon Stock
13.6.31	Laira
31.8.31	Laira Shops **R**
13.9.31	Laira
9.11.31	Swindon Factory **I**
15.12.31	Swindon Stock
19.12.31	Laira
3.1.32	Laira Shops **R**
20.1.32	Laira
24.7.32	Laira Shops **R**
13.8.32	Laira
26.9.32	Swindon Factory **L**
9.11.32	Swindon Stock
12.11.32	Laira
6.4.33	Laira Shops **R**
25.4.33	Laira
26.4.33	Swindon Factory **I**
7.7.33	Laira
12.1.34	Laira Shops **R**
26.1.34	Laira
27.3.34	Swindon Factory **L**
7.5.34	Swindon Stock
15.5.34	Laira
26.5.34	Swindon Factory **L**
21.6.34	Swindon Stock
26.6.34	Laira
3.7.34	Swindon Factory **L**
10.7.34	Swindon Stock
18.7.34	Laira
31.12.34	Swindon Factory **G**
28.2.35	Swindon Stock
7.3.35	Laira
4.10.35	Laira Shops **R**

23.10.35	Laira
5.2.36	Swindon Factory **I**
23.3.36	Swindon Stock
28.3.36	Laira
28.1.37	Laira Shops **R**
12.2.37	Laira
7.4.37	Swindon Factory **I**
24.5.37	Swindon Stock
3.6.37	Laira
5.10.37	Laira Shops **R**
22.10.37	Laira
29.11.37	Swindon Factory **L**
5.1.38	Swindon Stock
9.1.38	Laira
4.5.38	Swindon Factory **L**
7.6.38	Swindon Stock
14.6.38	Laira
7.9.38	Laira *(wait)*
8.9.38	Swindon Factory **G**
21.10.38	Swindon Stock
28.10.38	Laira
13.4.39	Laira *(wait)*
19.4.39	Swindon Factory **L**
5.5.39	Swindon Stock
10.5.39	Laira
27.12.39	Swindon Factory **I**
16.2.40	Swindon Stock
2.3.40	Laira
8.7.40	Newton Abbot F'cty **R**
26.7.40	Laira
21.12.40	Swindon Factory **L**
31.1.41	Swindon Stock
5.2.41	Laira
10.5.41	Swindon Factory **I**
8.7.41	Swindon Stock
12.7.41	Laira
8.10.41	Old Oak Common Shps **R**
19.10.41	Laira
23.12.41	Laira Shops **R**
7.1.42	Laira
9.4.42	Laira Shops **R**
9.5.42	Laira
7.7.42	Laira Shops **R**
29.7.42	Laira
7.8.42	Newton Abbot F'cty **R**
10.8.42	Laira
14.10.42	Swindon Factory **G**
28.11.42	Swindon Stock
1.12.42	Laira

12.2.43	Laira Shops **R**
28.2.43	Laira
4.6.43	Laira Shops **R**
25.6.43	Laira
28.8.43	Taunton Shops **R**
16.9.43	Laira
18.10.43	Laira Shops **R**
2.11.43	Laira
26.1.44	Laira *(wait)*
20.2.44	Swindon Factory **I**
3.4.44	Swindon Stock
6.4.44	Laira
7.6.44	Laira Shops **R**
26.6.44	Laira
10.11.44	Laira Shops **R**
28.11.44	Laira
4.5.45	Laira Shops **R**
6.6.45	Laira
10.7.45	Swindon Factory **I**
28.8.45	Laira
5.1.46	Laira Shops **R**
19.1.46	Laira
29.3.46	Laira Shops **R**
13.4.46	Laira
23.7.46	Laira Shops **R**
9.8.46	Laira
22.10.46	Swindon Factory **G**
10.12.46	Laira
15.2.47	Laira Shops **R**
26.2.47	Laira
27.8.47	Laira Shops **R**
19.9.47	Laira
3.1.48	Newton Abbot *(wait)*
9.2.48	Swindon Factory **I**
12.3.48	Laira
19.9.48	Laira Shops **R**
8.10.48	Laira
18.12.48	Stafford Road **U**
5.1.49	Stafford Road
28.5.49	Old Oak Common *(wait)*
8.6.49	Swindon Factory **HG**
28.7.49	Stafford Road
9.9.50	Stafford Road *(wait)*
21.9.50	Swindon Factory **HG**
25.10.50	Stafford Road
31.5.51	Stafford Road *(wait)*
13.6.51	Swindon Factory **LC**
9.7.51	Stafford Road
1.9.51	Old Oak Common *(wait)*

The up 'Inter-City' leaves the tunnel from Snow Hill, passing Moor Street station, on 23 April 1959. The engine is No.6019 KING HENRY V. PHOTOGRAPH: MICHAEL MENSING

The 7.30am Shrewsbury-Paddington, hauled by No.6020 KING HENRY IV, storms through West Bromwich station on 20 September 1958. PHOTOGRAPH: MICHAEL MENSING

13.9.51	Swindon Factory U
1.10.51	Stafford Road
1.1.52	Old Oak Common Shps U
29.1.52	Stafford Road
4.3.52	Swindon Factory HG
11.3.52	Stafford Road
13.6.52	Stafford Road (wait)
18.6.52	Swindon Factory U
3.7.52	Stafford Road
23.9.52	Stafford Road U
28.10.52	Stafford Road
19.11.52	Stafford Road F'cty U
19.12.52	Stafford Road
6.5.53	Swindon Factory HC
22.6.53	Stafford Road
24.12.53	Stafford Road (wait)
5.1.54	Swindon Factory HI
15.3.54	Stafford Road
18.10.54	Old Oak Common (wait)
27.10.54	Swindon Factory HC
10.12.54	Stafford Road
26.1.55	Stafford Road (wait)
2.2.55	Swindon Factory LC
28.3.55	Stafford Road
31.5.55	Stafford Road (wait)
16.6.55	Swindon Factory LC
5.8.55	Stafford Road
17.12.55	Stafford Road (wait)
22.12.55	Swindon Factory HG
28.2.56	Stafford Road
1.6.56	Stafford Road (wait)
7.6.56	Swindon Factory HC
15.8.56	Stafford Road
2.8.57	Stafford Road (wait)
13.8.57	Swindon Factory HG
4.10.57	Stafford Road
21.2.58	Stafford Road U
19.3.58	Stafford Road
24.9.58	Stafford Road U
7.10.58	Stafford Road
28.5.59	Stafford Road (wait)
9.6.59	Swindon Factory LI
19.8.59	Stafford Road
31.12.59	Stafford Road U

25.1.60	Stafford Road
4.4.60	Banbury Shops U
19.4.60	Stafford Road
9.6.60	Stafford Road F'cty LC
15.7.60	Stafford Road
19.8.60	Stafford Road U
12.9.60	Stafford Road
2.11.60	Stafford Road U
18.11.60	Stafford Road
15.2.61	Stafford Road U
6.3.61	Stafford Road
11.4.61	Leamington (wait)
18.4.61	Swindon Factory LI
20.6.61	Stafford Road
27.11.61	Tyseley Shops U
14.12.61	Stafford Road
2.5.62	Stafford Road U
29.5.62	Stafford Road
24.7.62	**Wthdrwn**
9.5.63	Sold as scrap to Cox & Danks of Langley Green

Boilers and mileages:

First	4683 *	
15.12.31	..	(63,297)
7.7.33	..	(134,424)
28.2.35	4687	(215,628)
23.3.36	..	(286,056)
24.5.37	..	(364,634)
21.10.38	4683	(456,906)
16.2.40	..	(541,849)
8.7.41	..	(631,572)
28.11.42	4672	(716,541)
3.4.44	..	(796,277)
28.8.45	..	(885,018)
10.12.46	4675	(969,531)
12.3.48	4684	
(1,045,276)		
28.7.49	4678	(1,114,800)
25.10.50	4667	(1,179,411)
18.4.52	8601 *	(1,244,400)
10.12.54	4697	(1,350,064)
28.2.56	8628 *	(1,390,550)
15.8.56	8603	(1,407,954)

4.10.57	4698	(1,460,824)
19.8.59	..	(1,544,375)
20.6.61	..	(1,621,858)
Final mileage:		1,686,568

Tenders:

First	2548
10.6.31	2396
15.12.31	2553
9.11.32	2403
23.7.35	2543
31.1.41	2715
28.11.42	2726
3.4.44	2710
28.8.45	2907
10.12.46	2776
12.3.48	2606
28.7.49	2922
9.7.51	2695
18.4.52	2649
15.3.54	2815
28.3.55	2707
28.2.56	2564
4.10.57	2815
19.8.59	2564
20.6.61	2749

.........................ooo.........................

6021 KING RICHARD II
To stock: June 1930

Summary of sheds:

12.6.30	Old Oak Common
9.56	Laira
11.12.59	Old Oak Common

Engine history:

12.6.30	Old Oak Common
20.6.30	Swindon Factory L
3.7.30	Swindon Stock
7.7.30	Old Oak Common
19.7.30	Old Oak Common Shps R
11.8.30	Old Oak Common

16.8.30	Swindon Factory L
1.9.30	Swindon Stock
11.9.30	Old Oak Common
16.7.31	Swindon Factory L
18.7.31	Old Oak Common
17.9.31	Old Oak Common Shps R
2.10.31	Old Oak Common
14.1.32	Swindon Factory I
24.3.32	Swindon Stock
30.3.32	Old Oak Common
31.8.32	Old Oak Common Shps R
7.9.32	Old Oak Common
12.10.32	Swindon Factory L
11.11.32	Swindon Stock
19.11.32	Old Oak Common
7.3.33	Swindon Factory L
7.4.33	Swindon Stock
4.33	Old Oak Common
5.10.33	Old Oak Common (wait)
10.10.33	Swindon Factory G
29.11.33	Swindon Stock
12.33	Old Oak Common
6.1.34	Swindon Factory L
11.1.34	Old Oak Common (wait)
15.1.34	Swindon Factory L
18.1.34	Swindon Stock
20.1.34	Old Oak Common
23.5.34	Old Oak Common Shps R
14.6.34	Old Oak Common
7.11.34	Old Oak Common (wait)
20.11.34	Swindon Factory I
17.1.35	Swindon Stock
22.1.35	Old Oak Common
2.4.35	Laira Shops R
18.4.35	Old Oak Common
14.9.35	Swindon Factory L
16.10.35	Swindon Stock
19.10.35	Old Oak Common
19.3.36	Old Oak Common Shps R
9.4.36	Old Oak Common
14.4.36	Old Oak Common Shps R
1.5.36	Old Oak Common
13.5.36	Old Oak Common (wait)
16.5.36	Swindon Factory G
3.7.36	Swindon Stock
10.7.36	Old Oak Common
7.12.36	Old Oak Common Shps R
21.12.36	Old Oak Common
5.5.37	Old Oak Common Shps R
1.6.37	Old Oak Common
14.6.37	Swindon Factory L
5.7.37	Swindon Stock
13.7.37	Old Oak Common
28.7.37	Swindon Factory L
10.8.37	Swindon Stock
15.8.37	Old Oak Common
6.9.37	Swindon Factory I
22.10.37	Swindon Stock
31.10.37	Old Oak Common
8.11.37	Swindon Factory L
23.11.37	Swindon Stock
28.11.37	Old Oak Common
16.3.38	Old Oak Common Shps R
30.3.38	Old Oak Common
6.8.38	Old Oak Common (wait)
10.8.38	Swindon Factory L
14.9.38	Swindon Stock
17.9.38	Old Oak Common
2.1.39	Swindon Factory G
9.2.39	Swindon Stock
17.2.39	Old Oak Common
22.1.40	Swindon Factory I
8.3.40	Swindon Stock
15.3.40	Old Oak Common
20.9.40	Old Oak Common (wait)
25.9.40	Swindon Factory L
31.10.40	Swindon Stock
4.11.40	Old Oak Common
13.2.41	Swindon Factory L

11.3.41	Swindon Stock	18.12.46	Reading *(wait)*
13.3.41	Old Oak Common	2.1.47	Reading Shops R
29.7.41	Old Oak Common *(wait)*	5.1.47	Old Oak Common
30.7.41	Swindon Factory I	16.2.47	Old Oak Common Shps R
23.9.41	Swindon Stock	13.3.47	Old Oak Common
26.9.41	Old Oak Common	30.4.47	Old Oak Common *(wait)*
5.1.42	Old Oak Common *(wait)*	6.5.47	Swindon Factory G
8.1.42	Swindon Factory L	16.6.47	Old Oak Common
25.2.42	Swindon Stock	28.6.47	Swindon Factory L
27.2.42	Old Oak Common	8.7.47	Old Oak Common
19.8.42	Old Oak Common Shps R	28.7.47	Old Oak Common *(wait)*
2.9.42	Old Oak Common	30.7.47	Swindon Factory L
18.12.42	Old Oak Common *(wait)*	12.8.47	Old Oak Common
30.12.42	Swindon Factory G	6.4.48	Old Oak Common *(wait)*
12.2.43	Swindon Stock	16.4.48	Swindon Factory L
18.2.43	Old Oak Common	19.5.48	Old Oak Common
19.5.43	Old Oak Common Shps R	5.10.48	Old Oak Common *(wait)*
6.6.43	Old Oak Common	9.11.48	Swindon Factory I
8.9.43	Old Oak Common R	20.12.48	Old Oak Common
29.9.43	Old Oak Common	15.4.49	Exeter Shops U
8.3.44	Newton Abbot *(wait)*	5.5.49	Old Oak Common
14.3.44	Swindon Factory L	30.9.49	Old Oak Common Shps U
27.4.44	Swindon Stock	20.10.49	Old Oak Common
5.5.44	Old Oak Common	23.1.50	Bath Road Shops U
5.6.44	Old Oak Common Shps L	24.2.50	Old Oak Common
24.7.44	Old Oak Common	27.3.50	Old Oak Common *(wait)*
12.8.44	Old Oak Common Shps R	4.4.50	Old Oak Common HG
1.9.44	Old Oak Common	10.5.50	Old Oak Common
9.11.44	Old Oak Common *(wait)*	16.5.50	Swindon Factory U
22.11.44	Swindon Factory I	23.5.50	Old Oak Common
10.1.45	Old Oak Common	12.9.50	Old Oak Comn Shps LC
2.5.45	Laira Shops L	9.10.50	Old Oak Common
14.6.45	Old Oak Common	23.1.51	Taunton Shops U
27.7.45	Old Oak Common R	7.2.51	Old Oak Common
14.8.45	Old Oak Common	12.4.51	Old Oak Common *(wait)*
8.11.45	Old Oak Common Shps L	17.4.51	Swindon Factory HC
26.1.46	Old Oak Common	25.5.51	Old Oak Common
17.4.46	Old Oak Common *(wait)*	1.9.51	Swindon Factory U
29.4.46	Swindon Factory I	1.10.51	Old Oak Common
24.5.46	Old Oak Common	15.10.51	Reading *(wait)*
26.9.46	Old Oak Common Shps L	19.10.51	Swindon Factory HI
16.10.46	Old Oak Common	26.11.51	Old Oak Common

18.9.52	Old Oak Common U
3.10.52	Old Oak Common
29.10.52	Laira Shops U
10.12.52	Old Oak Common
9.2.53	Taunton Shops U
26.2.53	Swindon Factory U
17.3.53	Old Oak Common
17.4.53	Swindon Factory HG
28.5.53	Old Oak Common
21.9.53	Bath Road Shops U
14.10.53	Old Oak Common
29.12.53	Old Oak Common Shps U
19.1.54	Old Oak Common
25.5.54	Old Oak Common Shps U
14.6.54	Old Oak Common
13.9.54	Old Oak Common *(wait)*
20.9.54	Swindon Factory HI
26.10.54	Old Oak Common
28.2.55	Old Oak Common Shps U
24.3.55	Old Oak Common
9.8.55	Old Oak Common Shps U
7.9.55	Old Oak Common
12.10.55	Old Oak Common Shps U
8.11.55	Old Oak Common
9.1.56	Swindon Factory HG
2.3.56	Old Oak Common
9.56	Laira
25.9.56	Laira *(wait)*
20.11.56	Swindon Factory HC
4.3.57	Laira
26.4.57	Taunton Shops U
5.6.57	Laira
31.10.57	Laira Shops U
15.11.57	Laira
6.1.58	Swindon Factory HI
28.2.58	Laira
12.6.58	Taunton Shops U
26.6.58	Laira
11.8.58	Taunton Shops U
27.8.58	Laira
15.1.59	Newton Abbot F'cty U
30.1.59	Laira
22.9.59	Old Oak Common *(wait)*
6.10.59	Swindon Factory HI
11.12.59	Old Oak Common
19.12.60	Leamington Shops U
9.1.61	Old Oak Common
16.2.61	Old Oak Common Shps U
13.3.61	Old Oak Common
5.5.61	Old Oak Common U
25.5.61	Old Oak Common
22.7.61	Swindon Factory HG
7.9.62	Wthdrwn (alternatively stated to be 21.9.62)
14.11.62	Sold as scrap to J.Cashmore of Newport.

Boilers and mileages:

First	4684 *	
24.3.32	..	(87,140)
29.11.33	4670	(179,060)
17.1.35	..	(244,108)
3.7.36	4692	(332,473)
22.10.37	..	(418,234)
9.2.39	4690	(502,604)
8.3.40	..	(575,622)
23.9.41	..	(673,294)
12.2.43	4681	(755,146)
10.1.45	..	(850,583)
24.5.46	4677	(914,104)
16.6.47	4668	(976,614)
20.12.48	4672	(1,058,473)
10.5.50	4664	(1,131,620)
25.5.51	4665	(1,186,136)
26.11.51	..	(1,211,453)
28.5.53	4672	(1,295,882)
26.10.54	..	(1,385,001)
2.3.56	8602	(1,446,856)

28.2.58	..	(1,549,090)
11.12.59	8617	(1,657,589)
26.9.61	8604	(1,741,591)
Final mileage:		1,793,439

Tenders:

First	2549
7.4.33	2552
14.9.38	2648
9.2.39	2441
8.3.40	2759
31.10.40	2556
23.9.41	2800
10.1.45	2808
1.10.51	2694
26.11.51	2742
9.8.52	2715
28.5.53	2630
1.6.54	2428
19.6.54	2759
26.10.54	2694
26.3.55	2648
5.11.55	2583
2.3.56	2762
3.11.56	2666
4.3.57	2695
28.2.58	2899
11.12.59	2740
3.12.60	2865
26.9.61	2696

........................ooo........................

No 6022 KING EDWARD III
To stock: June 1930

Summary of sheds:

5.7.30	Laira
27.9.48	Newton Abbot
24.4.49	Old Oak Common
24.10.55	Old Oak Common
18.6.59	Stafford Road

Engine history:

4.7.30	Swindon Factory
	ATC fitted
5.7.30	Laira
5.1.31	Swindon Factory L
29.1.31	Laira
15.10.31	Swindon Factory L
16.11.31	Swindon Stock
24.11.31	Laira
26.1.32	Swindon Factory I
4.3.32	Swindon Stock
12.3.32	Laira
2.6.32	Swindon Factory L
6.6.32	Swindon Stock
8.6.32	Laira
11.7.32	Laira Shops R
27.7.32	Laira
14.11.32	Swindon Factory L
9.12.32	Swindon Stock
15.12.32	Laira
20.2.33	Swindon Factory L
17.3.33	Laira
10.11.33	Laira Shops R
27.11.33	Laira
10.1.34	Swindon Factory I
23.2.34	Swindon Stock
5.3.34	Laira
31.7.34	Stafford Road F'cty
17.8.34	Laira
15.1.35	Swindon Factory G
27.3.35	Swindon Stock
2.4.35	Laira
22.11.35	Swindon Factory L
14.1.36	Swindon Stock

Cowley Bridge Junction, to the north of Exeter, was where the Paddington-West of England main line met the SR line to Okehampton, North Devon and Cornwall. No.6021 KING RICHARD II heads a down excursion on the WR line on 14 June 1959. PHOTOGRAPH: MICHAEL MENSING

23.1.36	Laira	
7.2.36	Swindon Factory	L
22.2.36	Swindon Stock	
2.3.36	Laira	
15.4.36	Swindon Factory	I
22.5.36	Swindon Stock	
3.6.36	Laira	
27.4.37	Swindon Factory	I
12.6.37	Swindon Stock	
20.6.37	Laira	
25.10.37	Laira Shops	R
10.11.37	Laira	
27.12.37	Laira Shops	R
14.1.38	Laira	
26.5.38	Swindon Factory	G
6.8.38	Swindon Stock	
17.8.38	Laira	
19.9.38	Swindon Factory	L
29.9.38	Swindon Stock	
7.10.38	Laira	
11.1.39	Bath Road Shops	L
7.2.39	Laira	
23.3.39	Laira (wait)	
30.3.39	Swindon Factory	L
5.4.39	Swindon Stock	
6.4.39	Laira	
16.8.39	Swindon Factory	L
6.9.39	Swindon Stock	
17.9.39	Laira	
15.12.39	Swindon Factory	I
30.1.40	Swindon Stock	
10.2.40	Laira	
16.3.40	Swindon Factory	L
9.4.40	Swindon Stock	
14.4.40	Laira	
1.10.40	Laira (wait)	
26.10.40	Swindon Factory	L
15.11.40	Swindon Stock	
11.40	Laira	
4.2.41	Swindon Factory	L
22.2.41	Swindon Stock	
23.2.41	Laira	
2.5.41	Laira Shops	R
24.5.41	Laira	
19.6.41	Laira (wait)	
23.6.41	Swindon Factory	I
27.8.41	Swindon Stock	
31.8.41	Laira	
24.9.41	Swindon Factory	L
29.10.41	Swindon Stock	
31.10.41	Laira	
26.11.41	Swindon Factory	L
10.12.41	Swindon Stock	
17.12.41	Laira	
4.5.42	Laira Shops	R
27.5.42	Laira	
24.6.42	Newton Abbot F'cty	L
9.7.42	Laira	
23.9.42	Laira Shops	R
8.10.42	Laira	
23.2.43	Swindon Factory	G
30.4.43	Swindon Stock	
4.5.43	Laira	
11.2.44	Laira Shops	R
6.3.44	Laira	
18.7.44	Laira Shops	R
4.8.44	Laira	
7.9.44	Swindon Factory	I
24.10.44	Laira	
2.3.45	Taunton Shops	R
28.3.45	Laira	
30.4.45	Laira Shops	R
18.5.45	Laira	
7.8.45	Laira Shops	L
2.10.45	Laira	
29.10.45	Laira Shops	R
9.11.45	Laira	
19.11.45	Laira Shops	R
8.12.45	Laira	
29.1.46	Swindon Factory	I
1.3.46	Laira	
25.4.46	Laira Shops	R
17.5.46	Laira	
15.7.46	Laira Shops	R
3.8.46	Laira	
9.10.46	Laira Shops	R
9.11.46	Laira	
1.1.47	Old Oak Common Shps	R
3.2.47	Laira	
4.2.47	Swindon Factory	L
8.3.47	Laira	
15.5.47	Laira Shops	R
21.5.47	Laira	
8.11.47	Laira Shops	R
5.12.47	Laira	
22.12.47	Laira (wait)	
9.1.48	Swindon Factory	G
5.3.48	Laira	
10.3.48	Swindon Factory *Test plant*	
23.4.48	Laira	
4.5.48	Old Oak Common (wait)	
7.5.48	Swindon Factory	R
27.5.48	Laira	
4.6.48	Swindon Factory	L
1.7.48	Laira	
11.8.48	Laira (wait)	
20.8.48	Swindon Factory	L
27.9.48	Newton Abbot	
11.4.49	Laira Shops	U
24.4.49	Laira	
23.8.49	Laira Shops	U
6.9.49	Laira	
31.10.49	Swindon Factory	HI
12.12.49	Laira	
18.12.49	Old Oak Common (wait)	
30.12.49	Swindon Factory	LC
26.1.50	Laira	
27.4.50	Laira Shops	U
11.5.50	Laira	
19.5.50	Exeter Shops	U
5.6.50	Laira	
27.6.50	Laira Shops	U
14.7.50	Laira	
30.8.50	Swindon Factory	LC
26.9.50	Laira	
15.11.50	Laira Shops	U
6.12.50	Laira	
22.1.51	Old Oak Common Shps	U
7.2.51	Laira	
15.5.51	Swindon Factory	HG
21.6.51	Laira	
19.9.51	Taunton Shops	U
8.11.51	Laira	
28.12.51	Old Oak Common	U
16.1.52	Laira	
28.3.52	Laira Shops	U
16.4.52	Laira	
14.5.52	Laira (wait)	
22.5.52	Swindon Factory	LC
17.6.52	Laira	
25.8.52	Taunton Shops	U
21.9.52	Laira	
25.9.52	Laira Shops	U
7.10.52	Laira	
11.11.52	Old Oak Common (wait)	
19.11.52	Swindon Factory	LC
16.1.53	Laira	
12.2.53	Laira Shops	U
6.3.53	Laira	
29.4.53	Swindon Factory	HI
16.6.53	Laira	
1.12.53	Laira (wait)	
6.1.54	Swindon Factory	LC
10.2.54	Laira	
16.4.54	Laira Shops	U
27.4.54	Laira	
17.5.54	Old Oak Common Shps	U
1.6.54	Laira	
20.7.54	Laira (wait)	
26.7.54	Swindon Factory	HG
1.11.54	Laira	
3.11.54	Swindon Factory	U
9.11.54	Laira	
13.11.54	Taunton Shops	U
10.12.54	Laira	
23.2.55	Laira Shops	U
27.2.55	Laira	
18.5.55	Laira Shops	U
6.6.55	Laira	
20.9.55	Taunton (wait)	
24.9.55	Swindon Factory	LC
24.10.55	Old Oak Common	
28.1.56	Laira Shops	LC
21.2.56	Old Oak Common	
12.4.56	Swindon Factory	HI
31.5.56	Old Oak Common	
6.6.56	Swindon Factory	U
21.6.56	Old Oak Common	
9.3.57	Swindon Factory	U
23.4.57	Old Oak Common	
24.9.57	Old Oak Common (wait)	
1.10.57	Swindon Factory	HI
15.11.57	Old Oak Common	
16.4.58	Laira Shops	U
25.4.58	Old Oak Common	
5.6.58	Exeter (wait)	
12.6.58	Swindon Factory	LC
22.7.58	Old Oak Common	
6.3.59	Swindon Factory	HG
18.6.59	Stafford Road	
13.11.59	Stafford Road	U
8.12.59	Stafford Road	
10.2.60	Old Oak Common Shps	U
3.3.60	Stafford Road	
21.8.60	Stafford Road	U
23.9.60	Stafford Road	
22.11.60	Stafford Road (wait)	
29.11.60	Swindon Factory	LI
9.2.61	Stafford Road	
30.8.61	Stafford Road	U
11.10.61	Stafford Road	
30.3.62	Stafford Road	U
19.4.62	Stafford Road	
30.3.62	Stafford Road	U
23.4.62	Stafford Road	
28.6.62	Oxley Shops	U
20.7.62	Stafford Road	
7.9.62	Wthdrwn (Alternatively stated to be 21.9.62)	
5.6.63	Sold as scrap to Cox & Danks of Langley Green	

Boilers and mileages:

First	4685 *	
4.3.32	..	(91,289)
23.2.34	..	(199,363)
27.3.35	4683	(261,556)
22.5.36	..	(329,508)
12.6.37	..	(413,097)
6.8.38	4685	(493,414)
30.1.40	..	(587,341)
27.8.41	..	(670,792)
30.4.43	4683	(755,282)
24.10.44	..	(855,342)
1.3.46	4684	(928,866)
5.3.48	4670	(1,025,375)
12.12.49	..	(1,096,713)
21.6.51	4695 *	(1,171,458)
16.6.53	..	(1,255,402)
1.11.54	8617 *	(1,320,524)
31.5.56	..	(1,406,598)
15.11.57	8603	(1,490,382)
18.6.59	8625	(1,572,653)
9.2.61	..	(1,650,274)
Final mileage:		1,733,189

Tenders:

First	2550
4.3.32	2554
30.1.40	2556
15.11.40	2642
27.8.41	2743
24.10.44	2759
3.11.45	2695
1.3.46	2707
5.3.48	2776
1.7.48	2716
17.5.49	2763
21.6.51	2743
17.6.52	2788
10.2.54	2849
22.5.54	2759
4.6.54	2648
1.11.54	2788
31.5.56	2775
15.11.57	2598
22.7.58	2565
18.6.59	2438

.........................ooo........................

6023 KING EDWARD II
To stock: June 1930

Summary of sheds:

19.7.30	Newton Abbot
23.11.36	Laira
12.36	Newton Abbot
2.2.49	Laira
30.8.56	Old Oak Common
13.9.60	Canton

Engine history:

6.30	Swindon Factory *ATC fitted*	
5.7.30	Swindon Stock	
9.7.30	Swindon Factory	L
19.7.30	Newton Abbot	
13.1.31	Newton Abbot F'cty	R
19.1.31	Newton Abbot	
2.2.31	Newton Abbot F'cty	R
16.2.31	Newton Abbot	
28.10.31	Swindon Factory	L
3.11.31	Swindon Stock	
7.11.31	Newton Abbot	
16.11.31	Swindon Factory	L
17.11.31	Swindon Stock	
21.11.31	Newton Abbot	
14.12.31	Swindon Factory	R
19.12.31	Newton Abbot	
2.2.32	Swindon Factory	I
7.4.32	Swindon Stock	
13.4.32	Newton Abbot	
4.7.32	Newton Abbot F'cty	R
23.7.32	Newton Abbot	
19.10.32	Swindon Factory	L
7.11.32	Swindon Stock	
10.11.32	Newton Abbot	
30.1.33	Swindon Factory	G
7.4.33	Swindon Stock	
4.33	Newton Abbot	
25.8.33	Swindon Factory *Speedometer fitted*	
30.8.33	Newton Abbot	
24.4.34	Swindon Factory	I
19.6.34	Swindon Stock	
24.6.34	Newton Abbot	
11.2.35	Newton Abbot F'cty	R
26.2.35	Newton Abbot	
8.4.35	Swindon Factory	
10.4.35	Newton Abbot	
25.5.35	Swindon Factory	L
10.7.35	Swindon Stock	
20.7.35	Newton Abbot	

The down 'Riviera' leaves Newton Abbot on Sunday 13 March 1955, No.6022 KING EDWARD III in charge. PHOTOGRAPH: PETER GRAY

11.10.35	Swindon Factory	**L**
18.10.35	Swindon Stock	
25.10.35	Newton Abbot	
28.1.36	Swindon Factory	**G**
9.3.36	Swindon Stock	
16.3.36	Newton Abbot	
15.4.36	Swindon Factory	**L**
24.4.36	Swindon Stock	
29.4.36	Newton Abbot	
11.5.36	Swindon Factory	
	Tender work only	
12.5.36	Swindon Stock	
13.5.36	Newton Abbot	
11.36	Laira	
12.36	Newton Abbot	
11.1.37	Swindon Factory	**L**
3.2.37	Swindon Stock	
5.2.37	Newton Abbot	
15.6.37	Swindon Factory	**L**
9.7.37	Swindon Stock	
12.7.37	Newton Abbot	
14.12.37	Swindon Factory	**I**
4.2.38	Swindon Stock	
8.2.38	Newton Abbot	
14.12.38	Newton Abbot	*(wait)*
29.12.38	Swindon Factory	**G**
10.2.39	Swindon Stock	
15.2.39	Newton Abbot	
29.2.40	Swindon Factory	**I**
13.4.40	Swindon Stock	
20.4.40	Newton Abbot	
21.10.40	Newton Abbot Shops	**R**
5.11.40	Newton Abbot	
27.8.41	Swindon Factory	**I**
21.10.41	Swindon Stock	
24.10.41	Newton Abbot	
8.4.42	Newton Abbot Shops	**L**
9.4.42	Newton Abbot	
5.8.42	Newton Abbot Shops	**R**
21.8.42	Newton Abbot	
12.10.42	Swindon Factory	**L**
19.11.42	Swindon Stock	
20.11.42	Newton Abbot	
18.1.43	Newton Abbot F'cty	**R**
27.1.43	Newton Abbot	

20.4.43	Swindon Factory	**I**
5.6.43	Newton Abbot	
5.8.43	Old Oak Common	*(wait)*
16.8.43	Swindon Factory	**L**
21.9.43	Swindon Stock	
26.9.43	Newton Abbot	
23.2.44	Newton Abbot	**R**
8.3.44	Newton Abbot	
1.6.44	Newton Abbot	*(wait)*
26.6.44	Swindon Factory	**L**
27.7.44	Swindon Stock	
2.8.44	Newton Abbot	
25.2.45	Newton Abbot	*(wait)*
3.3.45	Swindon Factory	**G**
21.4.45	Newton Abbot	
19.10.45	Newton Abbot Shops	**R**
4.11.45	Newton Abbot	
8.2.46	Swindon Factory	**R**
25.2.46	Newton Abbot	
14.3.46	Laira Shops	**R**
16.4.46	Newton Abbot	
1.5.46	Swindon Factory	**L**
5.6.46	Newton Abbot	
2.10.46	Exeter Shops	**R**
22.10.46	Newton Abbot	*(wait)*
6.11.46	Newton Abbot F'cty	**R**
12.11.46	Newton Abbot	
25.1.47	Newton Abbot	**L**
13.3.47	Newton Abbot	
9.4.47	Swindon Factory	**I**
16.5.47	Newton Abbot	
20.5.47	Swindon Factory	**L**
30.5.47	Newton Abbot	
16.9.47	Newton Abbot	**L**
1.10.47	Newton Abbot	
31.1.48	Exeter Shops	**L**
16.2.48	Newton Abbot	
25.2.48	Old Oak Common Shps	**R**
22.3.48	Newton Abbot	
13.10.48	Exeter	*(wait)*
1.12.48	Swindon Factory	**HG**
11.1.49	Newton Abbot	
18.1.49	Swindon Factory	**HG**
2.2.49	Laira	
20.5.49	Laira Shops	**U**

12.6.49	Laira	
3.8.49	Laira Shops	**U**
17.8.49	Laira	
6.9.49	Laira Shops	**U**
28.9.49	Laira	
10.10.49	Laira Shops	**U**
27.10.49	Laira	
3.12.49	Laira	*(wait)*
30.12.49	Swindon Factory	**LC**
19.1.50	Laira	
8.6.50	Swindon Factory	**HG**
1.8.50	Laira	
23.10.50	Laira Shops	**U**
8.11.50	Laira	
10.1.51	Laira Shops	**U**
26.1.51	Laira	
13.4.51	Laira Shops	**U**
24.4.51	Laira	
28.4.51	Taunton Shops	**U**
12.6.51	Laira	
26.6.51	Newton Abbot F'cty	**LC**
14.7.51	Laira	
3.8.51	Laira	*(wait)*
22.8.51	Swindon Factory	**LC**
18.9.51	Laira	
20.11.51	Swindon Factory	**U**
30.11.51	Laira	
21.1.52	Laira	*(wait)*
29.1.52	Swindon Factory	**HG**
7.3.52	Laira	
19.6.52	Laira Shops	**U**
3.7.52	Laira	
3.9.52	Laira Shops	**U**
24.9.52	Laira	
3.11.52	Laira	*(wait)*
14.11.52	Swindon Factory	**LC**
14.1.53	Laira	
10.4.53	Laira Shops	**U**
14.5.53	Laira	
30.5.53	Swindon Factory	**HI**
17.8.53	Laira	
26.12.53	Laira Shops	**U**
28.12.53	Laira	
29.3.54	Laira Shops	**U**
20.4.54	Laira	

20.8.54	Laira Shops	**U**
4.9.54	Laira	
18.9.54	Taunton Shops	**U**
15.10.54	Laira	
3.1.55	Swindon Factory	**HG**
8.2.55	Laira	
28.5.55	Reading Shops	**U**
5.8.55	Laira	
5.9.55	Laira Shops	**U**
10.10.55	Laira	
9.11.55	Taunton Shops	**U**
30.11.55	Laira	
3.1.56	Taunton Shops	**U**
27.2.56	Laira	
23.3.56	Laira Shops	**U**
27.3.56	Laira	
18.4.56	Bath Road Shops	**U**
18.5.56	Laira	
9.6.56	Westbury	*(wait)*
12.6.56	Swindon Factory	**LC**
30.8.56	Old Oak Common	
25.12.56	Taunton Shops	**U**
9.4.57	Old Oak Common	*(wait)*
13.4.57	Swindon Factory	**HI**
4.6.57	Old Oak Common	
25.7.57	Swindon Factory	**LC**
13.8.57	Old Oak Common	
27.2.58	Stafford Road F'cty	**U**
14.3.58	Old Oak Common	
24.7.58	Old Oak Common	*(wait)*
6.10.58	Old Oak Common	
23.6.59	Stafford Road	**U**
23.8.59	Old Oak Common	
21.3.60	Old Oak Common	*(wait)*
31.3.60	Swindon Factory	**HG**
27.6.60	Old Oak Common	
13.9.60	Canton	
13.11.60	Canton Shops	**U**
2.12.60	Canton	
9.1.61	Ebbw Jctn	*(wait)*
23.1.61	Swindon Factory	**LC**
9.3.61	Canton	
23.5.61	Canton Shops	**U**
8.6.61	Canton	
14.9.61	Canton Shops	**U**

Low afternoon sunshine at Paddington, sometime in 1955. The engine is No.6023 KING EDWARD II. PHOTOGRAPH: NATIONAL RAILWAY MUSEUM

11.10.61	Canton
20.11.61	Canton Shops **U**
7.12.61	Canton
19.2.62	Old Oak Common Shps **U**
12.3.62	Canton
19.6.62	**Wthdrwn**
10.10.62	Sold as scrap to T.W.Ward Ltd of Briton Ferry
26.11.62	Re-sold to Woodham Bros of Barry
12.62	Purchased by Messrs Harveys of Bristol and taken to Temple Meads pending restoration
3.90	Transferred to GWR Society at Didcot for completion of restoration

Boilers and mileages:

First	4686 *	
4.7.32	..	(87,948)
7.4.33	4677	(130,971)
19.6.34	..	(196,034)
9.3.36	4669	(289,452)
4.2.38	..	(374,751)
10.2.39	4687	(427,909)
13.4.40	..	(496,014)
21.10.41	..	(587,165)
19.11.42	4666	(647,759)
5.6.43	..	(675,049)
21.4.45	4671	(766,707)
16.5.47	..	(845,835)
11.4.49	4688	(916,200)
1.8.50	4683	(985,969)
7.3.52	4670	(1,064,561)
17.8.53	..	(1,126,074)
8.2.55	8621 *	(1,221,295)
4.6.57	8600	(1,315,191)
6.10.58	8624	(1,388,709)
27.6.60	8619	(1,464,528)
Final mileage:		1,554,201

Tenders:

First	2551
3.11.31	2399
17.11.31	2396
7.11.32	2553
10.7.35	2441
10.2.39	2694

13.4.40	2549
21.10.41	2606
19.11.42	2715
5.6.43	2763
21.9.43	2715
21.4.45	2772
16.5.47	2694
18.9.51	2648
7.3.52	2905
17.8.53	2762
1.1.55	2742
3.12.55	2717
30.8.56	2913
26.1.57	2805
4.6.57	2752
6.10.58	2771
29.11.58	2745
10.59	2427
27.6.60	2668

.........................ooo.........................

6024 KING EDWARD I
To stock: June 1930

Summary of sheds:

10.7.30	Laira
1.34	Newton Abbot
1.49	Laira
10.8.54	Old Oak Common
11.9.61	Canton

Engine history:

6.30	Swindon Stock
	ATC fitted
5.7.30	Swindon Stock
10.7.30	Laira
9.2.31	Newton Abbot F'cty
18.2.31	Laira
12.1.32	Swindon Factory **I**
26.2.32	Swindon Stock
5.3.32	Laira
24.5.32	Swindon Factory **L**
27.5.32	Swindon Stock
28.5.32	Laira
15.8.31	Swindon Factory **L**
24.8.32	Swindon Stock
31.8.32	Laira
30.11.32	Swindon Factory **L**
15.12.32	Swindon Stock

1.1.33	Laira
27.3.33	Swindon Factory **L**
7.4.33	Swindon Stock
4.33	Laira
8.5.33	Swindon Factory **I**
5.7.33	Swindon Stock
7.33	Laira
1.34	Newton Abbot
10.4.34	Swindon Factory **L**
25.5.34	Swindon Stock
6.6.34	Newton Abbot
28.8.34	Swindon Factory **L**
30.8.34	Swindon Stock
31.8.34	Newton Abbot
9.11.34	Swindon Factory **G**
24.1.35	Swindon Stock
31.1.35	Newton Abbot
8.10.35	Swindon Factory **L**
6.11.35	Swindon Stock
9.11.35	Newton Abbot
17.3.36	Swindon Factory **L**
4.4.36	Swindon Stock
7.4.36	Newton Abbot
21.4.36	Swindon Factory **I**
29.5.36	Swindon Stock
6.6.36	Newton Abbot
11.5.37	Swindon Factory **L**
22.6.37	Swindon Stock
26.6.37	Newton Abbot
26.1.38	Newton Abbot *(wait)*
15.2.38	Swindon Factory **G**
14.4.38	Swindon Stock
3.5.28	Newton Abbot
26.4.39	Newton Abbot *(wait)*
2.5.39	Swindon Factory **I**
23.6.39	Swindon Stock
5.7.39	Newton Abbot
6.3.40	Newton Abbot F'cty **R**
20.3.40	Newton Abbot
8.10.40	Swindon Factory **I**
3.12.40	Swindon Stock
8.12.40	Newton Abbot
28.4.41	Newton Abbot **R**
15.5.41	Newton Abbot
14.7.41	Newton Abbot F'cty **R**
30.7.41	Newton Abbot
3.2.42	Swindon Factory **I**
14.3.42	Swindon Stock
18.3.42	Newton Abbot
19.8.42	Newton Abbot F'cty **R**

3.9.42	Newton Abbot
20.1.43	Newton Abbot *(wait)*
28.1.43	Swindon Factory **L**
4.6.43	Swindon Stock
8.6.43	Newton Abbot
27.8.43	Laira Shops **R**
14.9.43	Newton Abbot
9.1.44	Newton Abbot **R**
23.1.44	Newton Abbot
16.2.44	Newton Abbot Shops **L**
2.3.44	Newton Abbot
27.3.44	Newton Abbot **R**
16.4.44	Newton Abbot
25.7.44	Swindon Factory **G**
4.10.44	Newton Abbot
24.9.45	Reading *(wait)*
10.10.45	Swindon Factory **L**
12.11.45	Newton Abbot
6.4.46	Swindon Factory **I**
14.5.46	Newton Abbot
16.1.47	Newton Abbot **R**
1.2.47	Newton Abbot
28.2.47	Newton Abbot Shops **R**
8.4.47	Newton Abbot
16.7.47	Newton Abbot *(wait)*
2.8.47	Swindon Factory **G**
11.9.47	Newton Abbot
4.3.48	Newton Abbot Shops **L**
	Tender work only
8.3.48	Newton Abbot
1.49	Laira
8.1.49	Laira Shops **U**
28.1.49	Laira
9.2.49	Laira Shops **U**
24.2.49	Laira
2.3.49	Swindon Factory **HG**
6.4.49	Laira
9.7.49	Laira Shops **U**
28.7.49	Laira
22.8.49	Laira Shops **U**
6.9.49	Laira
12.10.49	Old Oak Common *(wait)*
21.10.49	Swindon Factory **LC**
17.11.49	Laira
28.1.50	Laira *(wait)*
9.2.50	Swindon Factory **LC**
9.3.50	Laira
10.5.50	Laira *(wait)*
15.5.50	Swindon Factory **LC**
20.6.50	Laira

27.9.50	Old Oak Common (wait)	16.6.55	Old Oak Common	13.7.62	Swindon Factory	14.5.46 2733
2.10.50	Swindon Factory **HG**	30.8.55	Old Oak Common (wait)		Sold as scrap to Woodham	22.3.47 2905
7.11.50	Laira	6.9.55	Swindon Factory **LC**		Bros of Barry	11.9.47 2762
22.2.51	Laira Shops **U**	20.10.55	Old Oak Common	3.73	Arrived at	11.9.53 2905
7.3.51	Laira	30.12.55	Laira Shops **U**		Buckinghamshire Railway	9.10.54 2710
16.5.51	Laira Shops **U**	2.1.56	Old Oak Common		Society for preservation.	26.3.55 2694
4.7.51	Laira	25.1.56	Old Oak Comn Shps **LC**	10.89	Moved to Tyseley	16.6.55 2763
20.9.51	Laira Shops **U**	21.2.56	Old Oak Common	5.90	Moved to Didcot	20.3.57 2531
26.10.51	Laira	26.4.56	Bath Road Shops **U**			19.4.58 2393
24.11.51	Laira (wait)	4.6.56	Old Oak Common			18.9.53 2625
3.12.51	Swindon Factory **HI**	19.6.56	Southall Shops **U**	**Boilers and mileages:**		16.5.59 2846
23.1.52	Laira	11.7.56	Old Oak Common	First 4687 *		13.4.60 2839
29.1.52	Laira (wait)	12.9.56	Newton Abbot **U**	26.2.32	.. (96,552)	
6.2.52	Swindon Factory **LC**	12.10.56	Old Oak Common	5.7.33	.. (162,665)	
22.2.52	Laira	16.1.57	Old Oak Common (wait)	24.1.35	4672 (237,871)	
27.4.52	Laira Shops **U**	24.1.57	Swindon Factory **HG**	29.5.36	.. (312,278)	....................ooo....................
14.5.52	Laira	20.3.57	Old Oak Common	14.4.38	4668 (411,054)	
29.6.52	Laira Shops **U**	18.4.57	Laira Shops **U**	23.6.39	.. (472,231)	
20.7.52	Laira	21.4.57	Old Oak Common	3.12.40	.. (554,714)	**6025 KING HENRY III**
29.8.52	Laira Shops **U**	28.8.57	Old Oak Common Shps **U**	14.3.42	.. (637,629)	**To stock: July 1930**
12.9.52	Laira	11.9.57	Old Oak Common	4.6.43	4690 (689,241)	
26.9.52	Laira (wait)	11.2.58	Taunton Shops **U**	4.10.44	4677 (735,643)	**Summary of sheds:**
16.10.52	Newton Abbot F'cty **LC**	26.2.58	Old Oak Common	14.5.46	4663 (805,304)	24.7.30 Old Oak Common
30.10.52	Laira	22.7.58	Swindon Factory **HI**	11.9.47	4679 (864,212)	7.48 Laira
5.1.53	Laira (wait)	18.9.58	Old Oak Common	6.4.49	4690 (941,557)	15.7.59 Old Oak Common
15.1.53	Swindon Factory **LC**	22.10.58	Old Oak Common (wait)	7.11.50	4694 (1,015,772)	
24.2.53	Laira	28.10.58	Swindon Factory **HI**	23.1.52	4684 (1,074,755)	**Engine history:**
8.6.53	Laira (wait)	4.12.58	Old Oak Common	11.9.53	8611 * (1,144,028)	24.7.30 Old Oak Common
17.6.53	Swindon Factory **HG**	25.1.60	Old Oak Common (wait)	16.6.55	.. (1,236,039)	? Swindon Factory
11.9.53	Laira	29.1.60	Swindon Factory **HI**	20.3.57	8605 (1,320,206)	*ATC fitted*
26.12.53	Laira Shops **U**	13.4.60	Old Oak Common	18.9.58	.. (1,408,510)	2.8.30 Swindon Stock
3.1.54	Laira	22.2.61	Stafford Road **U**	13.4.60	8610 (1,475,631)	8.30 Old Oak Common
8.5.54	Laira Shops **U**	21.3.61	Old Oak Common	Final mileage:	1,570,015	10.9.30 Exeter Shops **R**
30.5.54	Laira	24.4.61	Old Oak Common Shps **U**			27.9.30 Old Oak Common
12.6.54	Old Oak Common (wait)	16.5.61	Old Oak Common	**Tenders:**		7.10.30 Old Oak Common (wait)
16.6.54	Swindon Factory **LC**	11.9.61	Canton	First 2552		10.10.30 Swindon Factory **L**
10.8.54	Old Oak Common	10.10.61	Canton Shops **U**	7.4.33	2549	22.11.30 Swindon Stock
29.9.54	Old Oak Comn Shps **LC**	27.10.61	Canton	29.6.35	2553	24.11.30 Swindon Factory **R**
5.11.54	Old Oak Common	10.4.62	In store (Canton)	3.12.40	2763	2.12.30 Swindon Stock
4.4.55	Old Oak Common (wait)	**19.6.62**	Wthdrwn (Alternatively	4.6.43	2643	5.12.30 Old Oak Common
11.4.55	Swindon Factory **HI**		stated to be 25.6.62)	18.7.44	2649	3.10.31 Old Oak Common (wait)
				4.10.44	2790	26.10.31 Swindon Factory **I**

No.6024 KING EDWARD I, sporting the slotted bogie, passes Hatton station with the 9.10am Paddington-Birkenhead in September 1957. PHOTOGRAPH: MICHAEL MENSING

The up 'Inter-City', with No.6025 KING HENRY III in charge, speeds through Acocks Green station on 23 March 1961.
PHOTOGRAPH: MICHAEL MENSING

22.12.31 Swindon Stock	19.3.39 Old Oak Common	7.11.45 Old Oak Common Shps **R**	15.2.51 Laira Shops **U**
30.12.31 Old Oak Common	12.5.39 Swindon Factory **I**	24.11.45 Old Oak Common	27.2.51 Laira
18.10.32 Old Oak Common (wait)	24.6.39 Swindon Stock	25.1.46 Old Oak Common Shps **R**	5.3.51 Laira Shops **U**
24.10.32 Swindon Factory **L**	4.7.39 Old Oak Common	15.2.46 Old Oak Common	25.3.51 Laira Shops
25.11.32 Swindon Stock	1.3.40 Old Oak Common Shps **R**	1.3.46 Old Oak Common (wait)	6.4.51 Laira (wait)
1.12.32 Old Oak Common	16.3.40 Old Oak Common	11.3.46 Swindon Factory **I**	17.4.51 Swindon Factory **LC**
12.6.33 Swindon Factory **G**	21.5.40 Swindon Factory **I**	15.4.46 Old Oak Common	8.5.51 Laira
1.8.33 Swindon Stock	21.6.40 Swindon Stock	24.10.46 Old Oak Common Shps **L**	29.6.51 Laira Shops **U**
8.33 Old Oak Common	28.6.40 Old Oak Common	10.12.46 Old Oak Common	3.8.51 Laira
25.11.33 Swindon Factory **L**	20.1.41 Old Oak Common Shps **R**	9.4.47 Old Oak Common (wait)	31.1.52S windon Factory **HG**
19.12.33 Old Oak Common	15.3.41 Old Oak Common	17.4.47 Swindon Factory **G**	14.3.52 Laira
5.2.34 Old Oak Common Shps **R**	23.5.41 Old Oak Common Shps **R**	22.5.47 Old Oak Common	24.7.52 Laira Shops **U**
19.2.34 Old Oak Common	26.6.41 Old Oak Common	21.11.47 Old Oak Common Shps **R**	20.8.52 Laira
12.7.34 Old Oak Common (wait)	8.9.41 Old Oak Common Shps **R**	12.12.47 Old Oak Common	26.1.53 Laira (wait)
17.7.34 Swindon Factory **I**	11.10.41 Old Oak Common	29.12.47 Old Oak Common Shps **R**	18.2.53 Swindon Factory **LC**
17.9.34 Swindon Stock	17.11.41 Old Oak Common (wait)	13.1.48 Old Oak Common	20.3.53 Laira
21.9.34 Old Oak Common	19.11.41 Swindon Factory **I**	5.2.48 Old Oak Common (wait)	15.7.53 Taunton Shops **U**
21.2.35 Old Oak Common Shps **R**	3.1.42 Swindon Stock	11.2.48 Swindon Factory **L**	31.7.53 Laira
11.3.35 Old Oak Common	9.1.42 Old Oak Common	16.3.48 Old Oak Common	23.9.53 Laira Shops **U**
15.10.35 Swindon Factory **I**	21.7.42 Old Oak Common Shps **R**	30.4.48 Old Oak Common (wait)	25.10.53 Laira
28.11.35 Swindon Stock	8.8.42 Old Oak Common	6.5.48 Swindon Factory **L**	25.11.53 Swindon Factory **HI**
6.12.35 Old Oak Common	3.2.43 Swindon Factory **G**	30.6.48 Old Oak Common	15.1.54 Laira
14.4.36 Old Oak Common Shps **R**	26.3.43 Swindon Stock	7.48 Laira	15.4.54 Laira Shops **U**
1.5.36 Old Oak Common	1.4.43 Old Oak Common	12.10.48 Old Oak Common Shps **R**	6.5.54 Laira
15.6.36 Old Oak Common Shps **R**	14.5.43 Laira Shops **R**	19.11.48 Laira	9.8.54 Laira Shops **U**
3.7.36 Old Oak Common	3.6.43 Old Oak Common	10.2.49 Laira Shops **U**	22.8.54 Laira
29.9.36 Old Oak Common Shps **L**	20.8.43 Old Oak Common Shps **L**	24.2.49 Laira	22.9.54 Taunton Shops **U**
20.11.36 Old Oak Common	7.9.43 Old Oak Common	18.3.49 Swindon Factory **HI**	6.10.54 Laira
22.2.37 Swindon Factory **G**	30.4.44 Old Oak Common Shps **L**	27.4.49 Laira	19.11.54 Laira (wait)
19.4.37 Swindon Stock	10.6.44 Old Oak Common	1.9.49 Laira Shops **U**	13.12.54 Swindon Factory **LC**
25.4.37 Old Oak Common	22.6.44 Old Oak Common Shps **R**	23.9.49 Laira	3.2.55 Laira
2.4.38 Swindon Factory **I**	3.8.44 Old Oak Common	21.11.49 Laira (wait)	2.5.55 Laira (wait)
20.5.38 Swindon Stock	30.11.44 Old Oak Common **R**	4.12.49 Swindon Factory **LC**	10.5.55 Swindon Factory **HG**
22.5.38 Old Oak Common	30.12.44 Old Oak Common	4.1.50 Laira	5.7.55 Laira
20.12.38 Taunton Shops **R**	11.1.45 Old Oak Common (wait)	29.3.50 Laira Shops **U**	8.11.55 Reading (wait)
7.2.39 Old Oak Common	5.2.45 Swindon Factory **I**	12.4.50 Laira	10.11.55 Swindon Factory **LC**
22.2.39 Old Oak Common (wait)	16.3.45 Old Oak Common	10.7.50 Old Oak Common (wait)	28.11.55 Laira
27.2.39 Swindon Factory **L**	21.3.45 Bath Road (wait)	13.7.50 Swindon Factory **HG**	23.1.56 Old Oak Comn Shps **LC**
14.3.39 Swindon Stock	6.4.45 Old Oak Common	25.8.50 Laira	13.2.56 Laira

10.3.56	Laira Shops **U**
13.4.56	Laira
15.5.56	Laira Shops **U**
30.5.56	Laira
20.6.56	Taunton Shops **U**
19.7.56	Laira
4.12.56	Swindon Factory **HI**
22.3.57	Laira
24.4.57	Bath Road Shops **U**
14.5.57	Laira
9.10.57	Newton Abbot F'cty **LC**
12.10.57	Laira
7.11.57	Laira Shops **U**
27.11.57	Laira
14.2.58	Laira Shops **U**
13.3.58	Laira
20.5.58	Swindon Factory **HI**
27.8.58	Laira
15.7.59	Old Oak Common
12.2.60	Old Oak Common *(wait)*
19.2.60	Swindon Factory **HI**
12.5.60	Old Oak Common
26.8.60	Swindon Factory **U**
14.9.60	Old Oak Common
20.1.61	Old Oak Common Shps **U**
3.2.61	Old Oak Common
9.11.61	Old Oak Common *(wait)*
24.11.61	Swindon Factory **HG**
9.2.62	Old Oak Common
3.8.62	In store
19.11.62	Old Oak Common
8.12.62	Wthdrwn (alternatively stated to be 21.12.62)
31.12.62	Swindon Factory
16.5.64	Cut up at Swindon

Boilers and mileages:

First	4688 *	
22.12.31	..	(80,851)
1.8.33	4665	
(174,916)		
17.9.34	..	
(242,864)		
28.11.35	..	
(330,623)		
19.4.37	4693	
(412,300)		
20.5.38	..	
(499,338)		
24.6.39	..	
(572,162)		
21.6.40	..	
(643,403)		
3.1.42	..	
(734,088)		
26.3.43	4687	
(805,600)		
16.3.45	..	
(902,323)		
15.4.46	4690	
(968.689)		
22.5.47	4686	(1,029,137)
30.6.48	4694	(1,078,309)
27.4.49	..	(1,115,692)
25.8.50	4666	(1,192,837)
14.3.52	4699 *	(1,280,457)
15.1.54	..	(1,383,049)
5.7.55	8601	(1,465,519)
22.3.57	..	(1,549,030)
27.8.58	..	(1,631,951)
12.5.60	4696	(1,727,935)
9.2.62	8617	(1,810,247)
Final Mileage:		1,836,713

Tenders:

First	2553
22.12.31	2428
22.10.32	2395

14.3.39	2440
24.6.39	2730
21.6.41	2406
3.1.42	2775
16.3.45	2733
15.4.46	2694
22.5.47	2772
30.6.48	2875
3.2.55	2763
5.7.55	2544
28.12.55	2905
3.11.56	2762
22.3.57	2776
19.4.58	2681
27.8.58	2817
14.11.59	2667
28.11.59	2745
12.5.60	2725
9.2.62	2835

.........................ooo.........................

6026 KING JOHN
To stock: July 1930

Summary of sheds:

26.7.30	Old Oak Common
30.3.35	Stafford Road
20.10.39	Bath Road
18.2.43	Laira
18.11.59	Old Oak Common

Engine history:

26.7.30	Old Oak Common
2.8.30	Swindon Factory *ATC fitted*
3.8.30	Old Oak Common
29.8.30	Reading Shops **R**
12.9.30	Old Oak Common
20.9.30	Swindon Factory **L**
9.10.30	Swindon Stock
11.10.30	Old Oak Common
25.10.30	Swindon Factory **L**
19.11.30	Swindon Stock
22.11.30	Old Oak Common
13.2.31	Swindon Factory **L**
21.2.31	Swindon Stock
26.2.31	Old Oak Common
13.7.31	Swindon Factory **L**
24.7.31	Swindon Stock
28.7.31	Old Oak Common
7.1.32	Swindon Factory **I**
15.3.32	Swindon Stock
19.3.32	Old Oak Common
15.11.32	Old Oak Common Shps **R**
29.11.32	Old Oak Common
27.12.32	Swindon Factory **L**
27.1.33	Swindon Stock
1.33	Old Oak Common
19.4.33	Swindon Factory **L**
23.6.33	Swindon Stock
6.33	Old Oak Common
24.10.33	Swindon Factory **G**
10.1.34	Swindon Stock
14.1.34	Old Oak Common
8.1.35	Swindon Factory **I**
19.3.35	Swindon Stock
30.3.35	Stafford Road
13.3.36	Swindon Factory **G**
4.5.36	Swindon Stock
12.5.36	Stafford Road
11.8.37	Swindon Factory **I**
28.9.37	Swindon Stock
3.10.37	Stafford Road
24.12.37	Swindon Factory **L**
10.1.38	Swindon Stock
16.1.38	Stafford Road
12.3.38	Swindon Factory **L**
25.3.38	Swindon Stock
29.3.38	Stafford Road

10.8.38	Swindon Factory **L**
19.9.38	Swindon Stock
28.9.38	Stafford Road
12.12.38	Swindon Factory **G**
3.2.39	Swindon Stock
12.2.39	Stafford Road
27.3.39	Stafford Road F'cty **L**
5.4.39	Stafford Road
6.10.39	Bath Road Shops **R**
20.10.39	Bath Road
13.11.39	Bath Road Shops **R**
4.12.39	Bath Road
14.12.39	Bath Road Shops **R**
6.1.40	Bath Road
20.4.40	Swindon Factory **L**
30.5.40	Swindon Stock
5.6.40	Bath Road
3.9.40	Bath Road Shops
26.9.40	Bath Road
12.11.40	Swindon Factory **I**
16.1.41	Swindon Stock
23.1.41	Bath Road
7.4.41	Swindon Factory **R**
26.5.41	Swindon Stock
27.5.41	Bath Road
13.6.41	Old Oak Common Shps **R**
12.7.41	Bath Road
31.7.41	Bath Road Shops **R**
23.8.41	Bath Road
18.11.41	Bath Road Shops **R**
6.12.41	Bath Road
8.7.42	Bath Road Shops **R**
25.7.42	Bath Road
29.9.42	Swindon Factory **I**
16.11.42	Swindon Stock
18.11.42	Bath Road
8.1.43	Laira Shops **R**
18.2.43	Laira
20.3.43	Taunton Shops **R**
13.4.43	Laira
12.6.43	Laira Shops Shops **R**
5.7.43	Laira
26.8.43	Old Oak Common Shps **R**
17.9.43	Laira
27.9.43	Swindon Factory **L**
18.11.43	Swindon Stock
26.11.43	Laira
20.1.44	Laira Shops **R**
29.1.44	Laira
23.3.44	Laira Shops **R**
6.4.44	Laira
26.6.44	Newton Abbot F'cty **R**
11.7.44	Laira
13.7.44	Taunton Shops **R**
5.9.44	Laira
20.9.44	Laira Shops **R**
24.10.44	Laira
16.12.44	Laira Shops **R**
18.1.45	Laira
10.3.45	Swindon Factory **I**
30.4.45	Laira
28.5.45	Swindon Factory **R**
21.6.45	Laira
18.10.45	Laira Shops **R**
1.11.45	Laira
20.12.45	Reading *(wait)*
8.1.46	Swindon Factory **L**
16.2.46	Laira
27.3.46	Laira Shops **L**
18.5.46	Laira
18.5.46	Swindon Factory **G**
20.6.46	Laira
7.10.46	Westbury *(wait)*
11.10.46	Swindon Factory **L**
8.11.46	Laira
17.3.47	Laira Shops **R**
2.4.47	Laira
9.4.47	Laira Shops **R**
25.4.47	Laira

16.5.47	Reading
3.7.47	Laira
16.7.47	Old Oak Common Shps **R**
31.7.47	Laira
22.10.47	Old Oak Common Shps **L**
11.11.47	Laira
2.12.47	Laira Shops **R**
16.12.47	Laira
23.12.47	Newton Abbot *Tender work only*
23.12.47	Laira
29.1.48	Laira Shops **L**
5.3.48	Laira
1.4.48	Swindon Factory **I**
1.6.48	Laira
24.2.49	Laira Shops **U**
27.3.49	Laira
7.6.49	Swindon Factory **U**
24.6.49	Laira
8.8.49	Laira Shops **U**
19.8.49	Laira
24.8.49	Reading Shops **U**
23.9.49	Laira
4.10.49	Swindon Factory **HG**
11.11.49	Laira
15.5.50	Laira Shops **U**
25.5.50	Laira
11.9.50	Old Oak Common Shps **U**
3.10.50	Laira
8.1.51	Laira Shops **U**
31.1.51	Laira
1.2.51	Swindon Factory **HI**
9.3.51	Laira
26.3.51	Bath Road Shops **U**
1.5.51	Laira
12.7.51	Laira Shops **U**
3.8.51	Laira
4.9.51	Taunton Shops **U**
4.10.51	Laira
17.12.51	Laira Shops **U**
17.1.52	Laira
19.2.52	Taunton Shops **U**
13.3.52	Laira
20.3.52	Taunton Shops **U**
25.4.52	Laira
28.4.52	Swindon Factory **HG**
6.6.52	Laira
22.12.52	Swindon Factory **LC**
29.1.53	Laira
27.4.53	Exeter Shops **U**
12.5.53	Laira
18.6.53	Swindon Factory **HI**
28.9.53	Laira
1.10.53	Swindon Factory
10.53	Laira
31.3.54	Laira Shops **LC**
26.4.54	Laira
17.5.54	Laira Shops **U**
26.5.54	Laira
21.6.54	Laira Shops **U**
18.7.54	Laira
2.10.54	Laira Shops **U**
27.10.54	Laira
23.12.54	Bath Road Shops **U**
31.1.55	Laira
2.2.55	Swindon Factory **HI**
21.3.55	Laira
13.5.55	Swindon Factory **LC**
20.6.55	Laira
8.10.55	Laira Shops **U**
24.10.55	Laira
14.1.56	Taunton Shops **LC**
27.2.56	Laira
30.8.56	Swindon Factory **HG**
17.10.56	Laira
25.10.56	Swindon Factory **LC**
29.10.56	Laira
25.4.57	Laira Shops **U**
13.5.57	Laira

Newton Abbot, 3 July 1957; No.6026 KING JOHN with an up express. PHOTOGRAPH: R.C.RILEY

12.11.57	Taunton Shops **U**	
25.11.57	Laira	
3.1.58	Swindon Factory **HI**	
6.3.58	Laira	
9.4.58	Swindon Factory **U**	
24.4.58	Laira	
29.7.58	Laira Shops **U**	
22.8.58	Laira	
14.11.58	Laira Shops **U**	
3.12.58	Laira	
9.4.59	Newton Abbot F'cty **U**	
23.4.59	Laira	
23.9.59	Swindon Factory **HI**	
18.11.59	Old Oak Common	
15.6.60	Old Oak Common *(wait)*	
13.7.60	Swindon Factory **LC**	
19.8.60	Old Oak Common	
21.9.60	Old Oak Comn Shps **LC**	
4.11.60	Old Oak Common	
6.1.61	Old Oak Common Shps **U**	
10.2.61	Old Oak Common	
26.4.61	Old Oak Common Shps **U**	
19.5.61	Old Oak Common	
27.8.61	Swindon Factory **HG**	
3.1.62	Old Oak Common	
16.5.62	Old Oak Common Shps **U**	
30.5.62	Old Oak Common	
30.6.62	Southall Shops **U**	
19.7.62	Old Oak Common	
7.9.62	Wthdrwn (Alternatively stated to be 12.9.62) 28.12.62 Cut up at Swindon Both nameplates reserved (for separate buyers)	

Boilers and mileages:

First	4689 *	
15.3.32	..	(89,560)
10.1.34	4692	(192,102)
19.3.55	..	(270,834)
4.5.36	4691	(339,384)
28.9.37	..	(423,539)
3.2.39	4677	(487,816)
16.1.41	..	(567,265)
16.11.42	..	(654,988)
18.11.43	4662	(694,127)
30.4.45	..	(757,558)
20.6.46	4673	(815,897)
1.6.48	4693	(894,641)
11.11.49	4663	(960,569)
9.3.51	4680	(1,042,398)
6.6.52	4666	(1,097,364)
28.9.53	..	(1,163,975)
21.3.55	4684	(1,248,665)
17.10.56	8620	(1,336,473)
6.3.58	..	(1,417,752)
18.11.59	8618	(1,511,455)
3.1.62	8623	(1,588,879)
Final mileage:		1,622,350

Tenders:

First	2554
24.7.31	2557
15.3.32	2395
22.10.32	2428
26.7.34	2548
3.2.39	2648
16.11.42	2772
30.4.45	2612
1.6.48	2788

6.6.52	2772
17.10.56	2881
6.3.58	2730
18.11.59	2820
19.8.60	2779
3.1.63	4013
	Changed after withdrawal, presumably for book urposes

...........................ooo........................

6027 KING RICHARD I
To stock: July 1930

Summary of sheds:

9.8.30	Old Oak Common
2.4.44	Newton Abbot
12.48	Laira
4.11.59	Old Oak Common
6.1.60	Stafford Road
9.6.60	Old Oak Common
11.12.61	Stafford Road (loan)
19.12.61	Old Oak Common

Engine history:

2.8.30	Swindon Factory *ATC fitted*
9.8.30	Old Oak Common
17.6.31	Swindon Factory **L**
14.7.31	Swindon Stock
17.7.31	Old Oak Common
30.12.31	Swindon Factory **L**
18.1.32	Swindon Stock

19.1.32	Old Oak Common
5.4.32	Swindon Factory **I**
31.5.32	Swindon Stock
4.6.32	Old Oak Common
23.2.33	Old Oak Common *(wait)*
1.3.33	Swindon Factory **G**
24.5.33	Swindon Stock
5.33	Old Oak Common
29.6.33	Swindon Factory **L**
7.7.33	Old Oak Common
22.5.34	Swindon Factory **I**
10.7.34	Swindon Stock
31.7.34	Old Oak Common
23.1.35	Swindon Factory **L**
8.2.35	Swindon Stock
9.2.35	Old Oak Common
4.4.35	Old Oak Common *(wait)*
8.4.35	Swindon Factory **L**
15.4.35	Swindon Stock
16.4.35	Old Oak Common
27.5.35	Swindon Factory **G**
12.7.35	Swindon Stock
21.7.35	Old Oak Common
6.9.35	Swindon Factory **L**
10.9.35	Swindon Stock
11.9.35	Old Oak Common
25.8.36	Swindon Factory **I**
6.10.36	Swindon Stock
11.10.36	Old Oak Common
9.1.37	Newton Abbot Shops
10.1.37	Old Oak Common
4.10.37	Swindon Factory **G**
19.11.37	Swindon Stock
1.12.37	Old Oak Common
2.8.38	Old Oak Common Shps **L**

15.8.38	Old Oak Common	15.2.44	Old Oak Common (wait)	10.2.48	Exeter Shops **R**	7.12.51	Laira
23.9.38	Old Oak Common (wait)	25.2.44	Swindon Factory **L**	25.2.48	Newton Abbot	15.4.52	Laira Shops **U**
27.9.38	Swindon Factory **I**	28.3.44	Swindon Stock	17.9.48	Newton Abbot (wait)	29.4.52	Laira
8.11.38	Swindon Stock	2.4.44	Newton Abbot	29.9.48	Swindon Factory **G**	4.8.52	Laira Shops **U**
13.11.38	Old Oak Common	10.5.44	Newton Abbot **R**	10.11.48	Newton Abbot	5.9.52	Laira
14.12.38	Old Oak Common	25.5.44	Newton Abbot	12.48	Laira	12.1.53	Exeter Shops **U**
	Tender work only	3.8.44	Newton Abbot (wait)	24.3.49	Laira Shops **U**	30.1.53	Laira
31.12.38	Old Oak Common	23.8.44	Swindon Factory **L**	7.4.49	Laira	20.2.53	Laira Shops **U**
6.3.39	Taunton Shops **R**	28.9.44	Newton Abbot	14.6.49	Laira Shops **U**	18.3.53	Laira
20.3.39	Old Oak Common	24.3.45	Newton Abbot (wait)	8.7.49	Laira	26.3.53	Swindon Factory **HG**
1.5.39	Old Oak Common Shps **L**	13.4.45	Swindon Factory **L**	16.9.49	Swindon Factory **LC**	9.6.53	Laira
13.5.39	Old Oak Common	25.5.45	Newton Abbot	7.10.49	Laira	4.9.53	Laira (wait)
19.6.39	Old Oak Common Shps **R**	30.7.45	Newton Abbot **R**	3.11.49	Laira Shops **U**	22.9.53	Swindon Factory **LC**
7.7.39	Old Oak Common	13.8.45	Newton Abbot	10.11.49	Laira	27.10.53	Laira
17.10.39	Swindon Factory **I**	5.9.45	Bath Road Shops **L**	1.12.49	Taunton Shops **LC**	19.11.53	Laira Shops **U**
25.11.39	Swindon Stock	27.10.45	Newton Abbot	30.12.49	Laira	16.12.53	Laira
29.11.39	Old Oak Common	18.2.46	Swindon Factory **G**	27.3.50	Laira (wait)	1.2.54	Laira (wait)
8.10.40	Old Oak Common (wait)	27.3.46	Newton Abbot	5.4.50	Swindon Factory **HG**	23.2.54	Swindon Factory **LC**
18.10.40	Swindon Factory **G**	29.7.46	Newton Abbot **R**	12.5.50	Laira	30.3.54	Laira
20.12.40	Swindon Stock	11.8.46	Newton Abbot	16.10.50	Taunton Shops **U**	7.10.54	Taunton Shops **U**
11.1.41	Old Oak Common	2.12.46	Newton Abbot **R**	31.10.50	Laira	24.10.54	Laira
21.3.41	Swindon Factory **L**	18.12.46	Newton Abbot	1.12.50	Exeter (wait)	12.11.54	Laira (wait)
25.4.51	Swindon Stock	12.3.47	Swindon Factory **I**	12.12.50	Swindon Factory **LC**	24.11.54	Swindon Factory **HI**
30.4.41	Old Oak Common	21.4.47	Newton Abbot	16.1.51	Laira	17.1.55	Laira
4.12.41	Old Oak Common Shps **R**	12.6.47	Swindon Factory **L**	17.2.51	Swindon (In store)	21.1.55	Swindon Factory **U**
24.12.41	Old Oak Common	20.6.47	Newton Abbot	16.3.51	Laira	8.2.55	Laira
4.7.42	Swindon Factory **I**	29.9.47	Newton Abbot Shops **R**	18.4.51	Laira Shops **U**	15.2.55	Laira Shops **U**
20.8.42	Swindon Stock	16.10.47	Newton Abbot	2.5.51	Laira	1.3.55	Laira
28.8.42	Old Oak Common	21.10.47	Bath Road (wait)	6.6.51	Laira Shops **U**	1.9.55	Taunton Shops **U**
9.11.43	Old Oak Common (wait)	5.11.47	Swindon Factory **L**	26.6.51	Laira	6.10.55	Laira
9.11.43	Swindon Factory **I**	1.12.47	Newton Abbot	25.9.51	Old Oak Common Shps **U**	6.1.56	Laira Shops **LC**
17.12.43	Swindon Stock	16.12.47	Reading Shops **R**	30.10.51	Laira	23.2.56	Laira
23.12.43	Old Oak Common	30.1.48	Newton Abbot	2.11.51	Swindon Factory **HI**	19.5.56	Swindon Factory **HI**

No.6027 KING RICHARD I passes through Lapworth station. The year is 1960. PHOTOGRAPH: MICHAEL MENSING

No.6028 KING GEORGE VI passes through Solihull. 1962. PHOTOGRAPH: MICHAEL MENSING

31.8.56	Laira	22.9.61	Old Oak Common	31.8.56	8613	(1,505,800)	**6028 KING HENRY II**
14.3.57	Laira Shops **U**	11.12.61	Stafford Road (on loan)	13.3.58	8618	(1,610,775)	**(r/n KING GEORGE VI)**
26.3.57	Laira	19.12.61	Old Oak Common	25.9.59	4697	(1,706,396)	**To stock: July 1930**
16.10.57	Laira Shops **U**	20.6.62	Old Oak Common Shps **U**	21.3.61	..	(1,779,233)	
30.10.57	Laira	4.7.62	Old Oak Common	Final mileage:		1,836,535	**Summary of sheds:**
28.12.57	Swindon Factory **HG**	**21.9.62**	**Wthdrwn**				31.7.30 Old Oak Common
13.3.58	Laira	16.7.63	Sold as scrap to Cox &	**Tenders:**			27.4.44 Newton Abbot
17.5.58	Laira Shops **U**		Danks of Langley Green	First	2555		12.48 Old Oak Common
19.5.58	Laira			14.7.31	2547		13.9.60 Canton
16.7.58	Taunton Shops **U**	**Boilers and mileages:**		31.5.32	2556		15.6.62 Old Oak Common
31.7.58	Laira	First	4690 *	24.5.33	2547		
24.3.59	Laira Shops **U**	31.5.32	..	(117,618)	15.12.34	2442	**Engine history:**
10.4.59	Laira	24.5.33	4686	(180,609)	22.8.36	2612	31.7.30 Old Oak Common
24.3.59	Laira Shops **U**	10.7.34	..	(259,430)	7.1.39	2402	1.8.30 Swindon Factory
10.4.59	Laira	12.7.35	4673	(321,972)	25.11.39	2742	*ATC fitted*
31.7.59	Swindon Factory **HG**	6.10.36	..	(412,200)	20.12.40	2733	2.8.30 Swindon Stock
25.9.59	Laira	19.11.37	4665	(499,557)	17.12.43	2710	5.8.30 Old Oak Common Shps **L**
1.10.59	Swindon Factory **U**	8.11.38	..	(567,090)	28.3.44	2815	16.9.30 Old Oak Common
15.10.59	Laira	17.10.39	..	(633,082)	25.5.45	2726	29.10.30 Swindon Factory **L**
4.11.59	Old Oak Common	20.12.40	4673	(702,997)	10.11.48	2759	17.12.30 Swindon Stock
6.1.60	Stafford Road	20.8.42	..	(813,348)	16.1.51	2707	18.12.30 Old Oak Common
12.5.60	Stafford Road **U**	17.12.43	..	(906,385)	7.12.51	2630	14.1.32 Old Oak Common *(wait)*
3.6.60	Stafford Road	27.3.46	4683	(1,003,776)	9.6.53	2715	19.1.32 Swindon Factory **I**
9.6.60	Old Oak Common	21.4.47	4682	(1,064,354)	17.1.55	2875	24.3.32 Swindon Stock
9.11.60	Old Oak Common Shps **U**	10.11.48	4686	(1,127,797)	31.8.56	2800	2.4.32 Old Oak Common
6.12.60	Old Oak Common	12.5.50	4684	(1,211,576)	13.3.58	2792	2.2.33 Swindon Factory **L**
27.1.61	Swindon Factory **HI**	16.3.51	..	(1,256,044)	25.9.59	2815	15.3.33 Swindon Stock
21.3.61	Old Oak Common	7.12.51	4661	(1,278,987)	21.3.61	2431	3.33 Old Oak Common
12.5.61	Old Oak Common *(wait)*	9.6.53	8610 *	(1,350,740)	22.9.61	2861	28.3.33 Swindon Factory **L**
27.5.61	Swindon Factory **LC**	17.1.55	..	(1,433,809)	...................ooo....................		

7.4.33	Swindon Stock	9.3.43	Swindon Factory **L**
4.33	Old Oak Common	30.3.43	Swindon Stock
11.9.33	Old Oak Common *(wait)*	3.4.43	Old Oak Common
20.9.33	Swindon Factory **G**	1.5.43	Swindon Factory **L**
3.11.33	Swindon Stock	26.5.43	Swindon Stock
11.33	Old Oak Common	30.5.43	Old Oak Common Shps **L**
23.1.34	Old Oak Common *(wait)*	5.1.44	Old Oak Common Shps **L**
27.2.34	Swindon Factory **L**	14.1.44	Old Oak Common
14.3.34	Swindon Stock	11.4.44	Newton Abbot **R**
18.3.34	Old Oak Common	27.4.44	Newton Abbot
14.8.34	Swindon Factory **L**	8.8.44	Newton Abbot ? *(wait)*
14.9.34	Swindon Stock	18.8.44	Swindon Factory **G**
27.9.34	Old Oak Common	10.10.44	Newton Abbot
11.10.34	Old Oak Common Shps **R**	26.10.45	Newton Abbot **R**
16.11.34	Old Oak Common	12.11.45	Newton Abbot
31.1.35	Swindon Factory **I**	25.3.46	Swindon Factory **I**
4.4.35	Swindon Stock	1.5.56	Newton Abbot
8.4.35	Old Oak Common	9.7.46	Taunton *(wait)*
2.7.35	Swindon Factory **L**	24.7.46	Swindon Factory **L**
9.7.35	Swindon Stock	22.8.46	Newton Abbot
17.7.35	Old Oak Common	22.7.47	Newton Abbot *(wait)*
20.12.35	Swindon Factory **L**	30.7.47	Swindon Factory **G**
23.1.36	Swindon Stock	15.9.47	Newton Abbot
26.1.36	Old Oak Common	30.9.47	Newton Abbot F'cty **L**
21.5.36	Old Oak Common *(wait)*	30.9.47	Newton Abbot
3.6.36	Swindon Factory **G**	9.4.48	Laira Shops **R**
7.8.36	Swindon Stock	21.4.48	Newton Abbot
13.8.36	Old Oak Common	12.48	Old Oak Common
24.4.37	Taunton Shops **R**	30.12.48	Old Oak Common Shops
4.5.37	Old Oak Common		*Tender work only*
7.5.37	Swindon Factory **L**	7.1.49	Old Oak Common
19.5.37	Swindon Stock	25.2.49	Swindon Factory **HG**
23.5.37	Old Oak Common	28.3.49	Old Oak Common
2.6.37	Old Oak Common **R**	18.4.49	Laira *(wait)*
18.6.37	Old Oak Common	27.4.49	Swindon Factory **LC**
15.11.37	Swindon Factory **I**	12.5.49	Old Oak Common
3.1.38	Swindon Factory	17.11.49	Old Oak Common Shps **U**
16.1.38	Old Oak Common	10.12.49	Old Oak Common
22.4.38	Old Oak Common Shps **R**	19.4.50	Old Oak Common Shps **U**
25.5.38	Old Oak Common	10.5.50	Old Oak Common
19.9.38	Old Oak Common Shps **R**	22.6.50	Bath Road Shops **U**
8.10.38	Old Oak Common	21.7.50	Old Oak Common
8.12.38	Reading *(wait)*	27.9.50	Westbury *(wait)*
13.12.38	Swindon Factory **L**	10.10.50	Swindon Factory **HI**
23.12.38	Swindon Stock	23.11.50	Old Oak Common
1.1.39	Old Oak Common	16.7.51	Old Oak Common *(wait)*
20.2.39	Old Oak Common *(wait)*	29.7.51	Swindon Factory **LC**
21.2.39	Swindon Factory **G**	24.8.51	Old Oak Common
4.4.39	Swindon Stock	10.9.51	Taunton Shops **U**
9.4.39	Old Oak Common	1.10.51	Old Oak Common
19.7.39	Swindon Factory **L**	28.11.51	Taunton Shops **U**
26.7.39	Old Oak Common	23.12.51	Old Oak Common
1.4.40	Swindon Factory **I**	3.1.52	Old Oak Common *(wait)*
21.5.40	Old Oak Common	18.1.52	Swindon Factory **HG**
3.12.40	Swindon Factory **I**	13.3.52	Old Oak Common
	Accident repair	7.8.52	Old Oak Common *(wait)*
13.2.41	Swindon Stock	26.8.52	Swindon Factory **LC**
21.2.41	Old Oak Common	18.9.52	Old Oak Common
1.9.41	Old Oak Common Shps **R**	13.10.52	Laira Shops **U**
27.9.41	Old Oak Common	17.11.52	Old Oak Common
10.10.41	Old Oak Common *(wait)*	6.1.53	Old Oak Common Shps **U**
13.10.41	Swindon Factory **L**	3.2.53	Old Oak Common
1.12.41	Swindon Stock	27.3.53	Old Oak Common *(wait)*
2.12.41	Old Oak Common	9.4.53	Swindon Factory **LC**
27.2.42	Old Oak Common *(wait)*	20.5.53	Old Oak Common
3.3.42	Swindon Factory **L**	4.8.53	Old Oak Common Shps **U**
4.5.42	Swindon Stock	1.9.53	Old Oak Common
7.5.42	Old Oak Common	8.9.53	Old Oak Common *(wait)*
4.7.42	Old Oak Common Shps **R**	16.9.53	Swindon Factory **HI**
18.7.42	Old Oak Common	17.11.53	Old Oak Common
7.8.42	Old Oak Common *(wait)*	3.9.54	Old Oak Common Shps **U**
10.8.42	Swindon Factory **L**	23.9.54	Old Oak Common
31.8.42	Swindon Stock	1.11.54	Old Oak Common Shps **U**
2.9.42	Old Oak Common	10.12.54	Old Oak Common
2.10.42	Swindon Factory **L**	5.1.55	Old Oak Common Shps **U**
22.10.42	Swindon Stock	7.2.55	Old Oak Common
11.42	Old Oak Common	17.3.55	Old Oak Common *(wait)*
15.12.42	Swindon Factory **I**	19.3.55	Swindon Factory **HI**
29.1.43	Swindon Stock	3.5.55	Old Oak Common

Manoeuvring at Lapworth - due to permanent way works on the up track beyond the end of the station (yes, it WAS a Sunday!), No.6029 KING EDWARD VIII backs the 4.30pm Wolverhampton-Paddington from the up to the down track on 8 October 1961. PHOTOGRAPH: MICHAEL MENSING

18.5.55	Old Oak Common *(wait)*	12.11.56	Swindon Factory **HG**
19.5.55	Swindon Factory **U**	31.1.57	Old Oak Common
27.6.55	Old Oak Common	16.10.57	Old Oak Common Shps **U**
11.7.55	Banbury *(wait)*	6.11.57	Old Oak Common
19.7.55	Swindon Factory **U**	1.1.58	Old Oak Common *(wait)*
8.8.55	Old Oak Common	2.1.58	Swindon Factory **LC**
12.9.55	Old Oak Common Shps **U**	12.2.58	Old Oak Common
14.10.55	Old Oak Common	18.6.58	Old Oak Common *(wait)*
24.10.55	Old Oak Common Shps **U**	24.6.58	Swindon Factory **HI**
2.12.55	Old Oak Common	4.9.58	Old Oak Common
25.1.56	Old Oak Comn Shps **LC**	18.9.59	Old Oak Common Shps **U**
24.2.56	Old Oak Common	9.10.59	Old Oak Common
23.7.56	Laira Shops **U**	12.11.59	Old Oak Common Shps **U**
12.9.56	Old Oak Common	27.11.59	Old Oak Common
8.11.56	Laira Shops **U**	20.3.60	Swindon Factory **HI**

9.6.60	Old Oak Common	**20.11.62** Wthdrwn	29.1.43	..	(743,510)	**Tenders:**
13.9.60	Canton	3.6.64 Sold as scrap to Messrs	10.10.44	4663	(819,392)	First 2556
2.3.61	Canton Shops **U**	Birds of Risca	1.5.46	4687	(892,916)	30.6.31 2388
21.3.61	Canton		15.9.47	4683	(949,628)	24.3.32 2548
5.5.61	Canton Shops **U**		28.3.49	4671	(1,036,412)	3.11.33 2557
20.5.61	Canton	**Boilers and mileages:**	23.11.50	..	(1,125,284)	19.5.37 2724
24.8.61	Canton Shops **U**	First 4691 *	13.3.52	4698 *	(1,187,003)	15.11.37 ?
4.10.61	Canton	24.3.32 .. (89,536)	17.11.53	..	(1,253,058)	23.12.38 2609
18.11.61	Swindon Factory **HG**	3.11.33 4688 (187,149)	3.5.55	8612	(1,327,735)	4.4.39 2726
4.1.62	Swindon Stock	4.4.35 .. (263,129)	31.1.57	8628	(1,388,243)	21.5.40 2695
5.1.62	Canton	7.8.36 4689 (349,702)	4.9.58	..	(1,471,209)	13.2.41 2543
16.4.62	Swindon Factory **U**	3.1.38 .. (450,783)	9.6.60	8613	(1,555,344)	1.12.41 2772
10.5.62	Canton	4.4.39 4671 (529,725)	4.1.62	8620	(1,634,195)	22.10.42 2648
15.6.62	Old Oak Common	21.5.40 .. (608,725)	Final mileage:		1,663,271	29.1.43 2643
3.8.62	In store (Old Oak)	13.2.41 .. (645,334)				30.3.43 2763

26.5.43	2790
10.10.44	2606
1.5.46	2762
15.9.47	2905
13.3.52	2648
27.2.54	2800
27.6.55	2694
31.1.57	2620
30.11.57	2565
4.9.58	2427
10.59	2745
11.59	2667
9.6.60	2695
5.1.62	2544

........................ooo........................

6029 KING STEPHEN
(r/n KING EDWARD VIII)
To stock: August 1930

Summary of sheds:
8.9.30 Old Oak Common
10.39 Laira
21.5.59 Old Oak Common

Engine history:
29.8.30 Swindon Factory *ATC fitted*
3.9.30 Swindon Stock
8.9.30 Old Oak Common
10.9.30 On loan for Liverpool & Manchester centenary exhibition
7.10.30 Old Oak Common
30.10.31 Old Oak Common Shps **R**
19.11.31 Old Oak Common
8.2.32 Swindon Factory **I**
14.4.32 Swindon Stock
4.32 Old Oak Common
11.1.33 Old Oak Common Shps **R**
28.1.33 Old Oak Common
6.2.33 Swindon Factory **L**
10.3.33 Swindon Stock
3.33 Swindon Stock
14.10.33 Swindon Factory
1.12.33 Swindon Stock
2.4.34 Old Oak Common *(wait)*
9.4.34 Swindon Factory **L**
17.5.34 Swindon Stock
22.5.34 Old Oak Common
20.11.34 Swindon Factory **I**
22.1.35 Swindon Stock
29.1.35 Old Oak Common
28.6.35 Swindon Factory **L**
11.7.35 Swindon Stock
17.7.35 Old Oak Common
5.12.35 Swindon Factory **L**
14.12.35 Swindon Stock
17.12.35 Old Oak Common
12.2.36 Swindon Factory **G**
25.4.36 Swindon Stock
29.4.36 Old Oak Common
14.5.36 Swindon Factory
15.5.36 Old Oak Common
24.11.36 Swindon Factory **L**
9.12.36 Swindon Stock
15.12.36 Old Oak Common
10.5.37 Swindon Factory **I**
23.6.37 Swindon Stock
27.6.37 Old Oak Common
15.11.37 Exeter Shops **R**
1.12.37 Old Oak Common
2.3.38 Old Oak Common Shps **R**
23.3.38 Old Oak Common
6.6.38 Old Oak Common *(wait)*
7.6.38 Swindon Factory **G**

4.8.38 Swindon Stock
10.8.38 Old Oak Common
26.4.39 Old Oak Common Shps **L**
12.5.39 Old Oak Common
15.5.39 Swindon Factory **I**
30.6.39 Swindon Stock
9.7.39 Old Oak Common
10.39 Laira
23.5.40 Swindon Factory **I**
27.6.40 Swindon Stock
2.7.40 Laira
22.5.41 Laira Shops **R**
18.6.41 Laira
6.9.41 Swindon Factory **G**
10.11.41 Swindon Stock
17.11.41 Laira
16.1.42 Laira Shops **R**
31.1.42 Laira
13.3.42 Swindon Factory **L**
11.4.42 Swindon Stock
12.4.42 Laira
9.9.42 Laira Shops **R**
24.9.42 Laira
26.3.43 Swindon Factory **I**
17.5.43 Laira
28.9.43 Laira Shops **R**
21.10.43 Laira
28.12.43 Laira Shops **R**
21.1.44 Laira
23.3.44 Laira Shops **R**
6.4.44 Laira
27.5.44 Old Oak Common *(wait)*
30.6.44 Swindon Factory **L**
16.8.44 Laira
5.12.44 Laira Shops **R**
21.12.44 Laira
4.2.45 Laira Shops **R**
28.2.45 Laira
25.6.45 Laira Shops **R**
20.7.45 Laira
27.7.45 Old Oak Common Shps **R**
10.8.45 Laira
27.8.45 Laira *(wait)*
28.8.45 Swindon Factory **G**
10.10.45 Laira
14.2.46 Laira Shops **R**
2.3.46 Laira
8.7.46 Laira Shops **R**
3.8.46 Laira
30.8.46 Taunton Shops **L**
18.10.46 Laira
28.10.46 Laira Shops **R**
11.11.46 Laira
29.11.46 Swindon Factory **I**
8.1.47 Laira
30.1.47 Swindon Factory **L**
6.2.47 Laira
15.5.47 Exeter *(wait)*
26.5.47 Laira Shops **R**
    Engine only
2.6.47 Newton Abbot F'cty **L**
    Tender only
3.7.47 Laira
15.7.47 Laira Shops **R**
30.7.47 Laira
8.8.47 Laira Shops **R**
16.8.47 Laira
8.10.47 Laira Shops **R**
29.10.47 Laira
8.12.47 Swindon Factory **L**
23.12.47 Laira
30.12.47 Laira Shops **R**
13.1.48 Laira
28.2.48 Laira Shops **R**
14.3.48 Laira
27.4.48 Old Oak Common *(wait)*
20.5.48 Swindon Factory **L**
17.6.48 Laira
18.10.48 Laira Shops **R**

5.11.48 Laira
24.1.49 Laira *(wait)*
26.1.49 Swindon Factory **HG**
28.2.49 Laira
27.6.49 Laira Shops **U**
23.7.49 Laira
25.10.49 Laira Shops **U**
9.11.49 Laira
4.12.49 Laira Shops **U**
26.1.50 Laira
29.1.50 Old Oak Common Shps **U**
17.2.50 Laira
7.3.50 Old Oak Common Shps **U**
30.3.50 Laira
28.4.50 Laira Shops **U**
17.5.50 Laira
22.5.50 Laira *(wait)*
2.6.50 Swindon Factory **LC**
29.6.50 Laira
7.9.50 Exeter *(wait)*
10.9.50 Laira Shops **U**
10.10.50 Laira
10.11.50 Swindon Factory **HG**
22.12.50 Laira
4.6.51 Laira Shops **U**
19.6.51 Laira
16.10.51 Swindon Factory **U**
29.10.51 Laira
23.12.51 Laira Shops **U**
7.1.52 Laira
5.3.52 Laira Shops **U**
23.3.52 Laira
31.3.52 Swindon Factory **HI**
19.5.52 Laira
5.11.52 Laira Shops **U**
26.11.52 Laira
12.1.53 Laira *(wait)*
23.1.53 Swindon Factory **LC**
5.3.53 Laira
6.7.53 Laira Shops **U**
18.7.53 Laira
5.8.53 Swindon Factory **HG**
6.10.53 Laira
1.1.54 Taunton Shops **U**
27.1.54 Laira
12.5.54 Laira *(wait)*
17.5.54 Newton Abbot Shops **LC**
21.5.54 Laira
26.6.54 Taunton Shops **U**
15.7.54 Laira
23.7.54 Reading Shops **U**
6.8.54 Laira
19.8.54 Bath Road Shops **LC**
28.9.54 Laira
12.10.54 Old Oak Common Shps **U**
12.11.54 Laira
26.11.54 Laira Shops **U**
6.12.54 Laira
23.2.55 Laira Shops **U**
3.3.55 Laira
20.4.55 Swindon Factory **HI**
27.5.55 Laira
31.10.55 Laira Shops **U**
16.11.55 Laira
27.1.56 Bath Road Shops **LC**
11.2.56 Laira
8.3.56 Laira Shops **U**
22.3.56 Laira
6.4.56 Bath Road Shops **U**
25.4.56 Laira
19.5.56 Laira Shops **U**
21.5.56 Laira
13.8.56 Westbury *(wait)*
16.8.56 Swindon Factory **HI**
1.10.56 Laira
21.3.57 Bath Road Shops **U**
15.4.57 Laira
12.6.57 Laira Shops **U**
2.11.57 Laira *(wait)*

8.11.57 Swindon Factory **HG**
18.12.57 Laira
3.2.58 Newton Abbot Shops **LC**
14.2.58 Laira
9.7.58 Laira Shops **U**
22.7.58 Laira
3.10.58 Laira Shops **U**
11.10.58 Laira
26.11.58 Newton Abbot F'cty **U**
12.12.58 Laira
6.2.59 Swindon Factory **HI**
21.5.59 Old Oak Common
7.12.59 Exeter *(wait)*
30.12.59 Newton Abbot F'cty **U**
30.12.59 Old Oak Common
13.5.60 Old Oak Common Shps **U**
14.6.60 Old Oak Common
14.10.60 Old Oak Common Shps **U**
1.11.60 Old Oak Common
14.1.61 Swindon Factory **HG**
29.3.61 Old Oak Common
16.4.62 Old Oak Common Shps **U**
2.5.62 Old Oak Common
24.7.62 Wthdrwn (Alternatively stated to be 23.7.62)
14.11.62 Sold as scrap to J.Cashmore of Newport

Boilers and mileages:

First	4692 *	
14.4.32	..	(97,026)
1.12.33	4691	(199,738)
22.1.35	..	(268,559)
25.4.36	4677	(346,427)
23.6.37	..	(427,954)
4.8.38	4672	(504,968)
30.6.39	..	(566,617)
27.6.40	..	(639,108)
10.11.41	4686	(732,110)
8.5.43	..	(823,725)
10.10.45	4666	(952,568)
8.1.47	4665	(1,017,522)
28.2.49	4668	(1,115,790)
10.11.50	4675	(1,200,487)
19.5.52	4667	(1,277,155)
6.10.53	8613 *	(1,353,813)
27.5.55	4696	(1,449,091)
1.10.56	..	(1,537,135)
18.12.57	8604	(1,624,250)
21.5.59	..	(1,708,338)
29.3.61	8611	(1,789,263)
Final mileage:		1,859,278

Tenders:

First	2413
29.7.33	2388
1.12.33	2392
30.6.39	2606
10.11.41	2716
17.6.48	2776
27.5.55	2723
1.10.56	2772
9.1.59	2904
21.5.59	2865
3.12.60	2740
29.3.61	2580

NOTES ON LOCOMOTIVE NAMES

KING GEORGE V (6000): Reigned 1910-1936. Second son of Edward VII and Queen Alexandra, but became heir to the throne after his elder brother's death in 1892. Joined the Navy as a cadet in 1877 and retained a keen interest in maritime matters, hence his nickname the 'Sailor King'. In 1932, he instigated the Christmas Day royal broadcast.

KING EDWARD VII (6001): Reigned 1901-1910. Eldest son of Queen Victoria. Enjoyed what can only be described as an active social life, which endeared him to the people after the somewhat dull years of the late Victoria period.

KING WILLIAM IV (6002): Reigned 1830-1837. The third son of King George III, he succeeded his brother George IV after the latter's death. He was another maritime monarch; having been sent to sea at the age of 13 he was also known as the 'Sailor King'. In public, he spoke forcefully against adultery, but privately enjoyed frequent *liaisons*.

KING GEORGE IV (6003): Reigned 1820-1830. Styled 'the first gentleman of Europe', he had a keen interest in art and architecture. He seemed to have been less interested in keeping the subjects happy, and his active social life was often regarded with distaste during a time of distress and of demand for social reform. He nevertheless gained a degree of popularity in Ireland, becoming the first reigning monarch to visit there for 430 years (albeit mainly for the purpose of staying with his mistress). His marriage to Queen Caroline wasn't one of his wiser decisions - he forbade her to attend his Coronation and, shortly afterwards, tried to divorce her. In his less lucid moments, he used to hallucinate that he had led troops into battle.

KING GEORGE III (6004): Reigned 1760-1820. Well intentioned but a political disaster, his statesmanship was not helped by intermittent mental illnesses. During his reign, Britain lost the American colonies, saw prolonged French wars, and was was questioned for its for power in India.

KING GEORGE II (6005): Reigned 1727-1760. Operated within the limits of his powers and capacity, and survived a second Jacobite uprising. He was the last British King to lead his troops into battle - at the Battle of Dettingen in 1743, when he was 58 years old.

KING GEORGE I (6006): Reigned 1714-1727. Claimed the throne under the terms of the Act of Settlement, his claim going back to his maternal grandmother, Elizabeth, daughter of King James I. Usually described as dull or undistinguished, his poor command of the English language didn't help his popularity. The public nevertheless enjoyed poking fun at his two mistresses, one being nicknamed the 'Maypole' and the other the 'Elephant'.

KING WILLIAM III (6007): Reigned 1689-1702. As William of Orange, he was married to Mary, the daughter of the Duke of York (later James II). After her father's abdication, Mary (as Queen Mary II) and William became joint monarchs. In this country, he failed to gain the popularity to which he had been accustomed in Holland. He died after being thrown from his horse which had, allegedly, stumbled on a molehill - hence the Catholic toast to the 'little man in the black velvet jacket'.

KING JAMES II (6008): Reigned 1685-1688. Was also King James VI of Scotland. Political and diplomatic understanding were not his best traits, and in 1688 he was forced to flee the country. He died in France in 1701, but his grave in Paris was destroyed during the French Revolution; the whereabouts of his body are now unknown. He would have been King James VII of Scotland, had the title been.

KING CHARLES II (6009): Reigned 1660-1685. Returning from France after the Civil War, he succeeded to the throne and became a popular monarch (particularly in the eyes of a certain Nell Gwynn), his generally outgoing but realistic nature being seen as a welcome change after the Spartan times of the Cromwell era.

KING CHARLES I (6010): Reigned 1625-1649. Politically naive, his public image was not helped by his unpopular marriage to the French princess Henrietta Maria. He tried to rule without Parliament, but this resulted in the Civil War in which he came second to Oliver Cromwell. The price of Charles's defeat was his head, which was removed in 1649.

KING JAMES I (6011): Reigned 1603-1625. Also King James VI of Scotland. His spendthrift ways didn't endear him to the public, and during his reign there was increasing criticism of the established church. His academic prowess gave rise to him being described as the 'wisest fool in Christendom'. Early on in his reign - in 1605 - the attempt by Guy Fawkes to blow him up was foiled.

KING EDWARD VI (6012): Reigned 1547-1553. The son of Henry VIII and Jane Seymour, Edward succeeded to the throne when only nine years old. Although a studious lad, during his reign the country was effectively administered by senior politicians. He died of tuberculosis in 1553 and was succeeded by Lady Jane Grey, whom he had been forced to name as his successor.

KING HENRY VIII (6013): Reigned 1509-1547. Famous for having six wives and beheading two of them. When denied a divorce by the church he rejected papal supremacy and dissolved the monasteries, acquiring considerable property and wealth in the process. These days, might be described by some as a 'lovable rogue' or a 'bit of a lad', though feminists might disagree.

KING HENRY VII (6014): Reigned 1485-1509. Took the throne after defeating Richard III at the Battle of Bosworth. As the first Tudor king of England, he was firm and shrewd, but was respected as a fair monarch. He finally put an end to the War of the Roses by marrying Elizabeth of York, thus robbing the Yorkists of their figurehead. Founded the Royal Navy.

KING RICHARD III (6015): Reigned 1483-1485. Alleged to have murdered his two nephews in the Tower, but there are suspicions that the story was a smear campaign. Last of the Plantagenets

KING EDWARD V (6016): Reigned 1483. He succeeded his late father when only twelve years old, and became a pawn in family feuds. He was never crowned, and along with his younger brother was imprisoned in the Tower of London and was never seen again.

KING EDWARD IV (6017): Reigned 1461-1470 and 1471-1483 (in exile 1470-71). An able but quarrelsome monarch, his reign was turbulent. He died at the age of just 41.

KING HENRY VI (6018): Reigned 1422-1461 and briefly in 1470/71. Was still a baby when he came to the throne. He was a gentle and retiring king, but suffered attacks of paralysis and insanity. His reign was plagued by quarrels amongst the noblemen and the on-going wars with France. The last of the Lancastrian kings, he was deposed in 1461 by Richard, Duke of York, and held prisoner in the Tower until murdered in 1471.

KING HENRY V (6019): Reigned 1413-1422. Gained fame for his success at the Battle of Agincourt. France reaped a form of revenge in 1422 when he contracted a fatal dose of dysentery at Meaux.

KING HENRY IV (6020): Reigned 1399-1413. A solid and practical monarch, the government was consolidated during his reign.

KING RICHARD II (6021): Reigned 1377-1399. Another child king, he was ten years old when he succeeded to the throne. Described as erratic and egocentric - he was only fourteen when he personally quelled the Peasants' Revolt, albeit with untenable promises - he became increasingly bitter and arbitrary after the death of his wife, Queen Anne of Bohemia, in 1394. He was deposed in 1399 and was imprisoned at Pontefract Castle, where he was starved to death. He is the first English king to have been immortalised in a painting, earlier kings having had to make do with statues or carvings. He is said to be the 'inventor' of the pocket handkerchief.

KING EDWARD III (6022): Reigned 1327-1377. Ambitious for military glory, he waged war with Scotland and started the Hundred Years War with France. In his last years, he became senile. Several centuries later, a GWR locomotive was named after his wife, Queen Phillipa, and it claimed the glory of notching up more miles than any other GWR engine - 2,429,722.

KING EDWARD II (6023): Reigned 1307-1327. Although a competent soldier, as a monarch he can best be described, as inept. He continued the seemingly obligatory wars with France, Scotland, and his wife (losing to the Scots at the famous Battle of Bannockburn) and was ultimately usurped. He was murdered at Berkeley Castle, though some believe that he escaped to Europe, to eke out an existence as a nomadic peasant.

KING EDWARD I (6024): Reigned 1272-1307. An able and energetic, if ruthless, monarch, he conquered Wales but could not maintain a hold over Scotland. He erected several crosses in memory of his first wife, among them Charing Cross in London (the present cross is a replica) and Banbury Cross in Oxfordshire.

KING HENRY III (6025): Reigned 1216-1272. Came to the throne when only nine years old, but nevertheless enjoyed a lengthy reign. He was devout and well-educated but a poor military leader, and his reign was punctuated by baronial opposition.

KING JOHN (6026): Reigned 1199-1216. His wars with France were funded by high taxes and, somewhat inevitably, powerful barons soon started to grumble. The outcome was that, in 1215, the king was forced to sign the Magna Carta, which was an undertaking to rule in a just and fair manner. Magna Carta or not, the manner of his ruling subsequently changed very little. Also famous for managing to lose the Crown Jewels in the Wash. Allegedly fond of lampreys.

KING RICHARD I (6027): Reigned 1189-1199. Richard the Lionheart, as he is popularly remembered, spent much of his time participating in the Crusades, much to the financial detriment of his long-suffering English subjects. He survived against Saladin's forces, but fared less well against the French, being killed during a war with France in 1199. Legend has it he could speak only French.

KING HENRY II (6028): Reigned 1154-1189. The first of the Plantagenet kings, he was a strong ruler who established the basis of many laws and administrative practices to which we adhere today. However, his conflict with the church resulted in the murder of Thomas Becket.

KING STEPHEN (6029): Reigned 1135-1154. Wrested the crown from Henry I's daughter, Mathilda, and survived civil wars to retain it until his death. Tenure of the crown was perhaps fortunate, as he was a rather weak monarch.

KING GEORGE VI (6028): (Locomotive renamed 12 January 1937). Reigned 1936-1952. Came to the throne after the controversial abdication of his elder brother, Edward VIII. Was, arguably, ill-prepared for his accession, but went on to gain tremendous respect, especially for his strength of character during the war.

KING EDWARD VIII (6029): (Locomotive renamed 14 May 1936). Reigned 1936. The monarch-in-waiting was seemingly more concerned with his love life than the GWR's time and trouble in fabricating the new nameplates for No.6029 and, when it became apparent that the public would not accept their king

marrying a twice-divorced American woman, he abdicated on 10 December without having been crowned. He was subsequently created Duke of Windsor.

RENAMING OF 'STAR' CLASS 4-6-0s

To avoid even the vaguest duplication of names, ten Stars had their names changed when the Kings were introduced in 1927. The discarded nameplates, incidentally, were offered for sale at 17/6d each, which included free delivery to any GWR station; those which still exist in private collections are now valued at around £4,000 each. As can be seen from the following list, the new names were not intended to relate to the original ones:

No.	Old name	New name
4021	KING EDWARD	THE BRITISH MONARCH
4022	KING WILLIAM	THE BELGIAN MONARCH
4023	KING GEORGE	THE DANISH MONARCH
4024	KING JAMES	THE DUTCH MONARCH
4025	KING CHARLES	ITALIAN MONARCH
4026	KING RICHARD	THE JAPANESE MONARCH
4027	KING HENRY	THE NORWEGIAN MONARCH
4028	KING JOHN	THE ROUMANIAN MONARCH
4029	KING STEPHEN	THE SPANISH MONARCH
4030	KING HAROLD	THE SWEDISH MONARCH

As mentioned in the text, Duke class 4-4-0 No.3257 KING ARTHUR and Bulldog 4-4-0 No.3361 EDWARD VII also had their nameplates removed.

An official list of livery changes does not exist. The dates quoted above have been deduced by cross-referencing reports (usually of 'first locos to be repainted') in the contemporary railway press with officially documented dates of works visits. Consequently, there may be very slight inaccuracies in one or two cases. If any reader has different (and substantiated) information, we would be very interested to know.

KING SUMMARY

6000-6019=Lot 243; 6020-6029=Lot 267; 6007 (rebuild)=Lot 309

No.	NAME	BUILT	BR BLUE first	BR BLUE second	BR GREEN	WB BOILER	DOUBLE CHIMNEY	W'DWN
6000	KING GEORGE V	6/27	-	6/49	4/52	4/52	12/56	12/62
6001	KING EDWARD VII	7/27	6/48	12/49	1/53	3/53	2/56	9/62
6002	KING WILLIAM IV	7/27	-	10/49	3/52	10/52	3/56	9/62
6003	KING GEORGE IV	7/27	-	4/50	10/52	10/52	4/57	6/62
6004	KING GEORGE III	7/27	-	9/50	9/53	9/53	11/56	6/62
6005	KING GEORGE II	7/27	-	2/50	1/53	1/53	7/56	11/62
6006	KING GEORGE I	2/28	-	3/50	4/53	4/53	6/56	2/62
6007	KING WILLIAM III	3/28	-	1/50	10/52	6/55	9/56	9/62
6008	KING JAMES II	3/28	-	11/49	1/53	12/55	7/57	6/62
6009	KING CHARLES II	3/28	5/28	11/49	3/53	7/54	5/56	9/62
6010	KING CHARLES I	3/28	-	6/50	2/53	10/51	3/56	6/62
6011	KING JAMES I	4/28	-	7/49	12/52	12/52	3/56	12/62
6012	KING EDWARD VI	4/28	-	5/50	4/53	10/54	2/58	9/62
6013	KING HENRY VIII	4/28	-	6/50	3/53	10/51	6/56	6/62
6014	KING HENRY VII	5/28	-	8/50	2/54	10/56	9/57	9/62
6015	KING RICHARD III	6/28	-	10/49	10/52	10/52	9/55	9/62
6016	KING EDWARD V	6/28	-	12/49	2/53	2/53	1/58	9/62
6017	KING EDWARD IV	6/28	-	5/50	8/52	8/52	12/55	7/62
6018	KING HENRY VI	6/28	-	12/50	4/52	12/53	3/58	9/62
6019	KING HENRY V	7/28	-	9/49	11/52	9/55	4/57	9/62
6020	KING HENRY IV	5/30	-	7/49	3/52	4/52	8/56	7/62
6021	KING RICHARD II	6/30	-	11/51	5/53	3/56	3/57	9/62
6022	KING EDWARD III	6/30	-	12/49	6/53	6/51	5/56	9/62
6023	KING EDWARD II	6/30	-	8/50	3/52	2/55	6/57	6/62
6024	KING EDWARD I	6/30	-	11/50	9/53	9/53	3/57	6/62
6025	KING HENRY III	7/30	6/48	8/50	1/54	3/52	3/57	12/62
6026	KING JOHN	7/30	6/48	11/49	6/52	10/56	3/58	9/62
6027	KING RICHARD I	7/30	-	5/50	6/53	6/53	8/56	9/62
6028	KING HENRY II*	7/30	-	11/50	11/53	3/52	1/57	11/62
6029	KING STEPHEN*	8/30	-	6/50	5/52	10/53	12/57	7/62

*6028 renamed KING GEORGE VI 12 January 1937

*6029 renamed KING EDWARD VIII 14 may 1936